About the Author

Born in 1898, Paul Brunton travelled extensively in the East and published thirteen books between 1935 and 1952. He is generally recognized as having introduced yoga and meditation to the West, and for presenting their philosophical background in non-technical language. He died in Switzerland (where he lived for 20 years) in 1981.

The Quest of the Overself

PAUL BRUNTON

RIDER
LONDON SYDNEY AUCKLAND JOHANNESBURG

1 3 5 7 9 10 8 6 4 2

First published in Great Britain by Rider in 1970
This edition first published in 1996
Rider is an imprint of Ebury Press,
Random House, 20 Vauxhall Bridge Road,
London SW1V 2SA

Random House Australia (Pty) Limited
20 Alfred Street, Milsons Point, Sydney,
New South Wales 2061, Australia

Random House New Zealand Limited
18 Poland Road, Glenfield,
Auckland 10, New Zealand

Random House South Africa (Pty) Limited
PO Box 337, Bergvlei 2012, South Africa

Random House UK Limited Reg. No. 954009

Papers used by Rider Books are natural, recyclable products made
from wood grown in sustainable forests. In addition, the paper in this
book is recycled

Typeset by SX Composing DTP, Rayleigh, Essex
Printed by Guernsey Press Ltd

A CIP catalogue record for this book is available from the British
Library

ISBN 0-7126-7217-6

Your Highness,

When, wearied by tropical heat and debilitated by South India's mounting temperature, I was faced with the formidable task of writing the bulk of this book, Your Highness most kindly placed at my disposal an isolated summer retreat on the summit of Kemmangandi Mount, in the Baba Budan Hills, thus rendering It possible for me to carry on my task in a cooler air and with a stronger body.

Here, amid tranquil and solitary surroundings, I was able to devote myself unhindered to the difficult task of building a bridge between the ancient methods of mind-mastery as practised in Your Highness's land and the modern psychological needs of my Western people. Here, too, the superb charm and opulent grandeur of Nature brought a generous inspiration to the help of this work. Those who have formed their notions of India from the dull monotonous plains must ever keep as a fixed memory, if they are fortunate enough to make the visit, the panorama of Mysore's green and brown forest-wrapped hills, thickly grown jungles, leaping waterfalls and lovely valleys, no less than its sunset skies flaked with delicate mauve and fiery gold or weirdly attractive with phosphorescent silver clouds.

I found it pleasant to remember that Kemmangandi has been sanctified by the neighbourhood of the Cave of Baba Budan, where centuries ago the God-realized Mystic Dattatreya made his final meditation and then disappeared completely from the face of the earth – to return only, he predicted, when the misery and materialism of the world called for a divine Avatar to help mankind. Certainly he has left his seraphic impress in that underground crypt for almost as soon as I sat down on its rough-hewn floor my mind slipped away into vision and then into untellable peace.

He who puts a roof over my head shelters my body from the elements, yet does nothing for my soul. Your Highness, however, has done both. For it was through your indirect instrumentality that I was initiated into the study of the higher intellectual wisdom of India.

Meanwhile Your Highness illustrates in your own person that lofty character, comprehensive wisdom and practical enterprise which have made the State of Mysore famous throughout India as one of the best-governed and most progressive of all. Your Highness's mind is directed not only to philosophy but also to science, and you have sought to make available for the prosperity of your people those technical applications of science which are changing the world's face. Did I not view at Bhadravati the great Mysore Iron Works, second

largest charcoal-burning pig-iron plant in the British Empire? You have rescued
philosophy from those who would make it a mere refuge from disappointment, and converted it into a dynamic inspiration to higher action for service.

If the world's rulers would emulate Your Highness and bestow but a fragment of their time on pure philosophy, the illumination thereby gained would immensely profit them in wiser policies and their peoples in happier lives: peace would then become a reality and not the phantom that it is today. Your Highness provides an exemplification for all men by showing that it is possible to attain a lofty spirituality and yet attend to one's immediate duties as effectively as the most materialistic person, and indeed infinitely better.

The clear Hellenic mind of Plato foresaw that, "the world can only be saved if the kings become philosophers or if the philosophers become kings." The love which everyone in the State bears for you reveals how true are those words. In dedicating these pages to Your Highness with the deepest respect, 1 but make articulate sincere, widely held and strongly felt sentiments.

PAUL BRUNTON.

Note: Three years after accepting this Dedication the Maharajah of Mysore left his earthly body, its cremation being attended by the author.

CONTENTS

PART I

THE ANALYSES

1

PREFATORY: A WRITER ON HIS WRITINGS

A man who undertakes the task of communicating his deeper thoughts to a number of readers and especially of leading them into realms of knowledge, forms of experience and phases of consciousness that surpass what is usual, must always do so in a spirit of devotion to his task if he would reach their hearts and not merely cover the white sheets with cold words. It was because I fully realized this truism some years ago that I refrained from writing my first book of teachings, *The Secret Path*, until an inner compulsion came to me which I could not, and would not, disobey. Many people had requested me, either by letter or in person, to write a book of definite instruction upon the art of spiritual meditation. For they knew that I had learned a little of this art both by dint of many years' hard effort and also by spending, during my wanderings in the East, intermittent periods as the pupil of some Wise Men of the Orient who are admittedly adepts in this domain of knowledge. Again and again, I refused to accede to their request for such a book, and the more they pressed me, the more adamant, the more obstinate I became in the negative course which I had chosen. The reasons for this refusal were purely personal ones, the chief among them being a cynical dislike, amounting at times almost to a horror, of being classed as a spiritual teacher, prophet or messenger. If I yielded eventually and was induced to uncap my fountain-pen and write the book, it was, as I have said, at the bidding of a force which I could not disobey, and which I heed more than my personal preference. But, once embarked upon my task, I deliberately put aside those personal disinclinations which had hitherto held me back and tried by an act of will to fulfil in a spirit of service the task which had been set me.

My position was simply this: "Here is a part of an exotic technique which has helped me; I offer it to others because it might help them too, but I have no desire to propagate it in any way. If there exist some persons who can appreciate this method I shall be content, but if there are none I shall not be discontented either. The laurels of successful advocacy of a spiritual message, so far as they include publicity and followers and correspondence and visitors, are equally as distasteful to me as are the thorns of martyrdom. If I do not desire these laurels of the evangelistic faith-founder, neither do I care for the crown of thorns that is also the lot of the heretical pioneer. I ask nothing more of the world than that it leave me to my wandering and scribbling and contemplating."

It is a threadbare truism that a prophet is without honour in his own country and, one ought also to add, in his own time, but because I am one who takes the whole world for his country I cannot complain of such treatment as that which I have so far received, for I have been fortunate enough to receive a little notice during my own lifetime, despite an inherent dislike of personal publicity.

My position before writing *The Secret Path* is mentioned here because it was curiously similar to my position before writing the present work. People who had read, and apparently profited by, that little book, began to ask me for a further development of the teaching contained therein, for a volume which would treat the same subject but in greater detail. Again and again I was asked one question after another which had arisen during the course of the reader's efforts to understand and practise the teaching of *The Secret Path*. I discovered, moreover, that different readers repeatedly asked the same questions and seemed to encounter the same problems, and this to such an extent that I soon began to realize that there certainly was a very real need for a larger work giving a more exhaustive treatment of the subject. After all, I had not intended *The Secret Path* to be anything more than a mere sketchily formulated introduction to this obscure and not easily comprehended subject of meditation, and to be an outline of the way to unfold potential forms of consciousness of the highest worth to the human kingdom. Quite a number of points in the practice had been deliberately omitted in order that beginners should not be confused as to the main issues, just as quite a number of points in the theory had likewise been omitted in order that people might go direct to the heart of the subject.

I had regarded such a preliminary simplification of the subject as essential because my experience had shown that the greatest confusion and misapprehension existed even among people who were already interested and studying the subject. How much greater, then, would be this confusion and misunderstanding among those who were coming upon it for the first time, as something entirely new?

All this, then, was responsible for my presenting at the outset an outline only, the first aim of which was to clarify the essentials of meditation, but now the necessity has arisen for a fuller work which shall, as it were, not only put the flesh upon the skeleton-like construction of *The Secret Path* and give a detailed analysis of every step of the way for the benefit of those who wish to tread this path with success, but also show how the divine inside of one's material self works. The need of a book of this character was constantly brought home to me by the flood of letters received from readers of my other books, who wished for further explanations of points raised therein, or who met with difficulties in their efforts to practise meditation and sought to have their problems solved. *The Secret Path* was admittedly a literary bow drawn at a venture, as I announced in the Preface, but the arrow hit the mark, and its success might have caused any other writer to expand on such a theme. I again hesitated to write, however, for I not only feared but definitely knew this time, that a further work would set me up still more firmly in the popular mind as a spiritual teacher, a label which would probably stick to me for ever, and which I disliked to wear so much that a chill would creep over me at the thought. So once again I resisted my readers' demands and my friends' adjurations and obstinately maintained my previously adopted attitude of non-action.

I refused to be put on a little pedestal and called a spiritual teacher – a designation which I knew well enough would immediately cause people to associate me with a certain type. I continued to refute the term "spiritual teacher" when it was applied to me, because I realized that acceptance of this designation classed me at once among the abhorrent category of cult-founders. I wished to be known only for what I am – as nothing more than a normal man, with a few abnormal interests, but living a normal life and laying no claims to superiority.

I wished to emphasize what I had already stated elsewhere – that I did not seek to *teach* people, but rather to show them how to direct their thinking inwards, and in so doing, build up an inner life which would enable them to live in constant communication with the spiritual realm whilst pursuing their normal activity in the market-places and on the busy thoroughfares of the external world. I did not desire disciples, because I wished rather to lead men to the discovery of the Teacher and Guide within themselves, the all-powerful Overself, and so make them the disciples, not of any person or object outside, but of the True Supernal Spirit which resides in their own hearts.

Anyhow, it may now be confessed that I liked my work on *The Secret Path* because I hoped the book would help people, although its basic message was an invitation to investigate themselves. I foresaw that it would assist them to find some inner peace and control of mind amid the world turmoil of today: it would encourage and inspire them. The message of hope in that little work has gone all over the world and found its way into the most incongruous classes of society. Many declared that the reading of it became a turning-point in their lives and enabled them to face existence with better courage and brighter understanding. I tried to strip the whole subject of meditation – and yoga, its Indian equivalent – from the mystery-mongering, the theological obscurities and the unnecessary complications with which I found it covered. So in the end it gave me much pleasure to remember that I had been obedient enough to write the book.

The title has come under some criticism, as being sensational and incorrect. My reply is that I have described a certain path of spiritual attainment which has been mostly lost to the modern world and which in the ancient world was taught only in secret and personally, by word of mouth and to accepted disciples only. In proof of this I give a few quotations from the writing of those who followed this same Path, or a variation of it.

The first comes from Tibet and is more than seven hundred years old. "If ye tread *the Secret Path,* ye shall find the shortest way," says the "Hymn of Yogic Precepts", contained in the "Jetsun Kahbum" or Biographical History of Milarepa, the most famed of medieval Tibetan yogis.

The second is taken from an untranslated Tamil volume, *The Tamil Sacred Scriptures,* and is written by Tirumoolar, a seer who flourished many hundred years ago. It runs: "Those who study this *Secret Path* realize that the individual soul is the Divine Self and nothing else."

The third also comes from South India and belongs to our own era. In a work, entitled *The Catechism of Enquiry,* whose English translation has not yet been published, the famous Maharishee of Arunachala Hill, writes: "This method of realizing the Absolute is *known as the Secret Path of the Heart.* What more is there to say? One should experience it intuitionally."

I have thus endeavoured to make clear some of the peculiar circumstances attending the publication of *The Secret Path* and my personal attitude thereto; the time is therefore opportune to turn toward my other books and put them on review, making them march again in retrospect as I refer briefly to their genesis, object and results. Such a reference is now necessary because they stand independently, in a class apart, and because colossal misunderstandings of their nature and frequent criticisms of their author are also rife.

§

First in order stands *A Search in Secret India.* I was glad to have had the opportunity therein to show that there is something worth while in India – a country which deserves far better treatment than it usually receives in contemporary Western conversation and writing – beyond the vision of some recent writers on India.

We Westerners are rightly proud of our achievements in "facelifting" this world of ours, but we get a little disturbed sometimes when we hear of a half-naked fakir performing a feat which we can neither match nor understand. The thing keeps on occurring sufficiently often to remind us that there are ancient secrets and hoary wisdom in the lands which lie East of Suez, and that the inhabitants of those colourful countries are not all the benighted heathens some of us think they are. We picture these yogis as dreaming enthusiasts who desert the normal ways of mankind to go off into strange hiding-places, into gloomy caves, lonely mountains and secluded forests. But they go off with a clear objective, setting themselves no less a task than the acquisition of a perfect and incredible control over the frail tenement of flesh. To attain this end they practise the hard and exacting discipline laid down in their traditions. That nowadays the public comes into contact mainly with vagabonds, impostors and idle tramps, who delude others, or themselves, into the belief that they are yogis, does not invalidate the truth of the tradition nor the genuineness of its best exponents.

When Macaulay came out to India to take his seat in its Government and prepare a plan for some system of education, he flung all its ancient lore on the scrap-heap, remarking with disgust that it was a miserable collection of crude puerilities and fantastic superstitions. Was he altogether right? Anyway, I doubted his judgment and went out to explore things for myself.

I hope that Truth is lord of my horoscope, for at her bidding I took ship across far seas and at her voice I threw away the tempting fruits of many years' ambitious work. I travelled at high pressure, concentrating on my quest of worth-while yogis, and making an intensive research into their practices. I did not spare a moment for the starched and stiff etiquette of European social life in India. I could not dance and drink the hours away. The thirst to pry beneath the surface of Indian existence for its strange secrets pursued me like a demon.

My path in this alien land seemed to be smoothed by the favours of a strange Providence, and I met all kinds of queer men and queer adventures. There were all the wandering votaries of yoga – faqueers who looked like galvanized mummies, thought-haunted philosophers who contemplated themselves into a coma, strolling parasites on society and sanctimonious tramps, half-maniacs with long unkempt hair and ash-bedaubed bodies, who gazed frighteningly into my eyes, but also world-scorning, women-shy and wine-aloof saints who sincerely devoted themselves to finding the Great Spirit, all as mixed a crew of human beings as I had ever seen – and lastly, here and there a rare, real, normal-living Sage, who greeted me with folded hands and benignant words, according me a confidence which is not easily won by white strangers in the Orient, and who made me the momentary heir to ultimate truths too subtle to be put into the pages of a popular book.

I lived a life of strange switchback vicissitudes, dining with the Prime Minister of a Maharajah's state one week and consorting with penniless and homeless holy men the next. Each day I began to expect the unexpected, or to walk around the corner of a village street into new bewilderment.

It might be well to answer an oft-asked question and confess that I did not see the famous Rope Trick, although I wandered vainly throughout the length and breadth of India and found no faqueer able or willing to work this seeming miracle. I am convinced that the mass of testimony as to its former and recent existence is too overwhelming, too authentic, not to be accepted by those who have open minds. But if I cannot recount this feat, I can recount its explanation as derived from one of my teachers, who saw a similar marvel in his youth. He definitely states that – where it is not a mere piece of conjuring and jugglery – it is a feat of hypnotism, an operation practised by a more powerful mind upon a crowd of weaker ones. The fact that when a photograph was taken no boy could be seen climbing the rope in the picture, is one proof of this statement. The objection that five hundred people in a crowd could not be mass hypnotised is overruled by him on the principle that five hundred weaker minds will always yield to a single stronger one, or in arithmetical terms, 500 multiplied by 0 still equals 0.

By dint of digging hard for that which I sought I learnt much, and despite the days when thermometers mounted mercilessly and one's mutinous muscles could not be induced to fulfil their normal functions, I sifted science from superstition, wisdom from nonsense and truth from fiction. Now, I perceive that if we would regard India's knowledge not as contradictory to Western science and religion, but as ancillary to both, we might be all the better and wiser for the addition.

A chance-met Muhammadan faqueer who dreamily predicted, as he sat with crossed feet and clasped hands on his mat: *"Thou shalt make long writings of thy experiences among my class and put them into printed books for the Western people to read. Thou shalt tell the sahibs of thy life with those whom they hold in contempt and thy words shall cause their minds to wonder,"* was the real originator of *A Search in Secret India,* because he put into my head the idea of passing on to others what I had hitherto regarded as a purely private concern. Thenceforward I took notes more carefully.

It might be added here that there were many men about whom I had not the space or inclination to write. I endeavoured in the book to tell the story of a quest and to refer only to certain episodes and persons possessed of some importance in connection with this quest.

I returned from the East with a new sight. My mystic experiences had performed the operation for cataract upon my soul, and much disease was gone from my eyes. I saw the society of this modern world no longer as a glorious civilization, but as an unhappy catacomb of *dormant souls*. Let me not be misunderstood. I am not propagating yoga or any other Eastern "ism" or cult, but I am trying to call attention to a few worth-while ideas which can be picked up from the East. Neither am I of those who praise the so-called spirituality of the East in order to deride Western materialism. All such comparisons are foolish and incorrect. Sacredness is in ourselves, not in any spot on this planet. Nevertheless, the fact remains that Asia and Africa, on account of their age and their more leisurely existence, have had time to discover some profound secrets, of a spiritual, mental and material nature, as well as a wisdom which seems to me to have some value for us. Those secrets and this philosophy are now to be traced out with the greatest difficulty, because time has narrowed their ownership down to a reclusive few, yet they do exist, and may be found.

India holds an ancient heritage of spiritual thought from its past that stands unparalleled for profundity and unmatched for width. Young Indians, therefore, should claim this birthright, finding what is worthy and applicable to present needs. They should neither be awed by Western scepticism, nor corrupted by modern materialism, nor stupefied by religious wrangling, but go to their best thinkers for guidance.

Mysticism, too, has its representation in India and in the mysterious personality of the Maharishee I found its highest embodiment. Unlike that of religious medieval Europe, his mysticism took a thoroughly rational turn. His was, indeed, the outstanding figure in my book, and it was but fitting that I should have devoted so much of its space to a portrayal of him and his environment. The latter, however, has greatly changed since my first visit many years ago and lost its former peaceful character; it no longer attracts me, for I prefer honest worldliness to pious materialism.

A Search in Secret India has been very widely read. As the novelist, John Knittel, generously wrote in the Foreword to the German edition: "In this book a bridge will be built." Europeans and Americans may now appraise India a little more highly, I hope, and bestow a little more respect upon her.

I must now touch on a matter about which I have long lain silent. The extraordinary nature of the contents of my book brought several criticisms which either scouted their possibility or sneered at my veracity. Being, somewhat selfishly perhaps, more interested by habit in my private quest of truth than in public controversies about it, I complacently ignored my critics. And even when an Indian gentleman of good standing and governmental associations wrote and accused me of having written a romance or semi-novel, adding that he was quite sure that the Maharishee did not exist outside my imagination, and my publishers passed the letter to me for comment, I thrust it aside in proud silence, too hurt to make a reply. If I say something on the matter now, it is because my books of the past have now provided a foundation for my message of the present. If the foundation is not acceptable, then the superstructure will be still less so. I am compelled therefore to put in a few paragraphs to defend myself in this opportune place.

First of all, it is surely needless to remark that Sir Francis Younghusband – so distinguished as an authority on India – would not have lent his name, as writer of the Foreword to my book, if he thought I had composed an imaginary account. Even if he had nothing more, he had ample proofs in the large number of still unpublished photographs which he examined in London one afternoon at the Travellers' Club. But I am glad to feel that I enjoy his confidence on other and *deeper* grounds.

Secondly, the pictorial impressionist style of the book created the false impression among other critics that I had embroidered the stuff of truth with the coloured wool of fiction. They were wholly wrong. I have every right, if I choose to do so, to break away from the manner of conventional travel books in order to present my material as interestingly as possible. The fact that I try to report unusual incidents and scenes, to interview unusual men and to record my own unusual experiences, does not make me less a reporter for that, because I have to present them to the popular mind. In that sense, my book is but glorified journalese. I claim, therefore, the right of every reporter to make the most of his materials and work them up into effective journalistic results. I do not see why I should render these reports in the dullest, most colourless and bloodless style I can find; I do not see why I should refuse to make my experiences as living to the reader as they were to me. And even if I were to claim, which I do not, that my book is a piece of literature, I would surely have the privilege of the artist consciously to select and reshape his material rather than present it causally and syllogistically as the professor. And it must likewise be remembered that I tried to come down in my conversations with these yogis to the quintessence of things, to get at the final meaning which these men had for me, and then for the reader's sake I distilled our talks into still more concentrated forms.

The book is a faithful and honest narrative, written to record truth without its dullness. Indeed, when I re-visited Dayalbagh, near Agra, last year in the company of my friend, Major Francis Yeats-Brown, His Holiness the late Sir Sahabji Maharaj was kind enough to remark, when all three of us were at lunch, that my published account of interviews with him had evinced an amazingly accurate memory.

Finally, it is amusing to me to remember that when I first

made tentative enquiries about the Maharishee in the city of Madras several years ago, no one had even heard of his existence, and I could discover nothing at all about him prior to making my visit. Today, one may ask almost anyone in the same city about the Mystic of Arunachala and a great deal of information will quickly be forthcoming. It was left for me, an infidel foreigner, to make the Maharishee famous in his own country.

If any other doubts exist, let me add that this "romantic creation" of mine, this "imaginary literary figure", was recently granted a special and unique exemption by the Government of Madras from attending to give evidence in a law-court. This was in connection with a civil suit about the ownership of the land upon which his new ashram (monastic building) had been erected. It is unlikely, I think, that the Government would have granted such an exemption to a person who did not exist!

§

The book which had the most meteoric success was *A Search in Secret Egypt*. Despite its high price – due to the number of costly illustrations – it was instantaneously appreciated by the public as achieving for the sun-burned land of the Nile what had never previously been attempted. Nevertheless, I know that much comment, controversy and criticism was occasioned amongst those who read it. The time has come to criticize my critics. I shall be perfectly frank at the outset and admit that I went to Egypt not only in search of wisdom, but also of wonders. I regret, in this incredulous age, to state that I found them. The narrative of my experience during the night spent in the Great Pyramid and the revelations which came to me therein were, as I fully expected, too much for many people to believe, so much so, that some even doubted whether I had ever spent the night there at all, whilst others thought I was merely seeking for cheap publicity. That a man could have a genuinely serious purpose in undertaking such an unusual enterprise did not occur to quite a number of people. Meanwhile six "confirmations" of the more extraordinary statements made in my book have come to hand since its publication, whilst if the history of recent world diplomacy is also included, that counts as a seventh because the Adept Ra-Mak-Hotep's prophecy of international treacheries has been sadly fulfilled.

The first confirmation concerns the gigantic figure of the Sphinx, before whose origin and purpose the world had remained baffled right up to our own time. On page 29 of my book I formulated the following precise solution:

"The purpose of the Sphinx had now become a little plainer. The Egyptian Atlanteans had built it as their grandest statue, their sublimest figure of remembrance, and they had dedicated it to their Light-God, the sun. . . . The Sphinx was the revered emblem in stone of a race which looked upon Light as the nearest thing to God in this dense material world. . . . Ra, the sun-god, was first, the father and creator of all other gods, the Maker of all things, the one, the self-born."

Within a year of writing those words, i.e. in October, 1936, the following despatch was circulated by Reuter's News Agency from Cairo and printed in the world's leading newspapers:

NEW LIGHT ON THE SPHINX
MONUMENT TO RA, THE SUN-GOD

"Important discoveries just made throw new light on the mystery of the great Sphinx of Gizeh, the enormous stone figure with the head of a man and the body of a lion, which gazes across the Valley of the Nile.

After intensive excavation work Professor Selim Hassan of Cairo University has unearthed a granite stela – a tablet – evidently of the 18th Dynasty, bearing an inscription which furnishes an additional link in the story of the great monument.

For years past, Professor Hassan has been engaged in an attempt to solve the problem of the Sphinx – who carved it out of the solid limestone rock, and whom it was intended to represent.

The inscription on the tablet which he has just discovered refers to the Sphinx as being a monument to Ra, the Sun-God.

It confirms, and possibly completes, the inscription on a previously discovered tablet, part of which had been flaked off."

Thus, that which came to me by interior revelation during a night spent in absorbed meditation at the Sphinx's feet, was later proved correct by a chance archaeological discovery!

Secondly, I was glad to read in a Cairo newspaper called *The Sphinx* the following lines in a review of my book:

"I went to no little trouble to make personal enquiries and investigations about some of the remarkable statements in this book. In reference to the author's weird experience during the night he spent in the Great Pyramid, the local police commandant who was in charge of Mr. Brunton assured me that he himself would not have emulated the author for all the wealth of Egypt; this was from an officer whose courage has often been convincingly demonstrated. Mr. Brunton's book will appeal because of the presentation of proven facts about which the oldest residents among us have been quite unaware."

Let those critics, who are so brave in their denunciations with pen and paper and tongue, pass a similar night in total darkness inside this haunted pyramid; and then only, if they still retain their sanity and scepticism, they may have something interesting to report to the world.

Thirdly, the apparition of the spirit of an old Egyptian priest who instructed me about the existence of a hidden pyramid chamber containing immensely ancient sacred records, and who even conducted my own freed spirit into a slanting passageway leading thereto – this raised, as I fully expected, sarcastic and severe criticisms, even from those who regarded my other revelations as acceptable. This book is not the place to undertake the much-needed task of exposing the real truth about the after-world and its inhabitants, as distinct from the pitiful illusions and gross fantasies which are current about it in both materialistic and spiritualistic circles, but suffice to say that the dream-world is not much different from the spirit world; that whereas at its lowest and therefore most frequently contacted fringes, it merely returns to us a subdued consciousness of ordinary material-life experiences and of bodily processes, at its highest frontiers it rises into revelatory mingling with the world of disembodied spirits. A mingling of this kind is uncommon, but not so rare that it does not happen to almost everyone at least once in his lifetime.

By the merest chance I lately happened upon a record of an experience not too dissimilar from that of mine in the pyramid. Herein a University professor was visited in dream by the spirit of a Babylonian priest, who gave him precise details concerning the correct decipherment of two inscribed agates. This interpretation was later fully proved to be authentic.

Here is the condensed record for the curious and for comparison with my own. This case was recorded by Professor W. Romaine Newbold of the University of

Pennsylvania, in a paper entitled "Subconscious Reasoning", in the "Proceedings: Society for Psychical Research," Vol. XII, pp. 11-20. I give the following extracts:

"For this case I am indebted to another friend and colleague, Dr. Herman V. Hilprecht, Professor of Assyrian in the University of Pennsylvania. I was told of the experience shortly after it happened, and here translate an account written in German by Professor Hilprecht, 8th August, 1893, before the more complete confirmation was received:

One Saturday evening, about the middle of March, 1893, I had been wearying myself, as I had done so often in the weeks preceding, in the vain attempt to decipher two small fragments of agate which were supposed to belong to the finger-rings of some Babylonian. The labour was much increased by the fact that the fragments presented remnants only of characters and lines, that dozens of similar small fragments had been found in the ruins of the temple of Bel at Nippur with which nothing could be done, that in this case, furthermore, I had never had the originals before me, but only a hasty sketch made by one of the members of the expedition sent by the University of Pennsylvania to Babylonia. I could not say more than that the fragments, taking into consideration the place in which they were found and the peculiar characteristics of the cuneiform characters preserved upon them, sprang from the Cassite period of Babylonian history (1700-1440 B.C.); moreover, as the first character of the third line of the first fragment seemed to be KU, I ascribed this fragment, with an interrogation point, to King Kurigalzu, while I placed the other fragment, as unclassifiable, with other Cassite fragments upon a page of my book where I published the unclassifiable fragments. The proofs already lay before me, but I was far from satisfied. The whole problem passed yet again through my mind that March evening before I placed my mark of approval under the last correction in the book. Even then I had come to no conclusion. About midnight, weary and exhausted, I went to bed and was soon in deep sleep. Then I dreamed the following remarkable dream. A tall, thin priest of the old pre-Christian Nippur, about forty years of age and clad in a simple *abba,* led me to the treasure-chamber of the temple, on its south-east side. He went with me into a small low-ceiled room, without windows, in which there was a large wooden chest, while scraps of agate and lapis lazuli lay scattered on the floor. *Here he addressed me as follows:*

'The two fragments which you have published separately upon pages 22 and 26, belong together, are not finger-rings, and their history is as follows: King Kurigalzu (1300 B.C.) once sent to the temple of Bell, among other articles of agate and lapis-lazuli, an inscribed votive cylinder of agate. Then we priests suddenly received the command to make for the statue of the God Ninib a pair of ear rings of agate. We were in great dismay, since there was no agate as raw material at hand. In order to execute the command there was nothing for us to do but cut the votive cylinder into three parts, thus making three rings, each of which contained a portion of the original inscription. The first two rings served as ear-rings for the statue of the God; the two fragments which have given you so much trouble are portions of them. If you will put the two together you will have the confirmation of my words. But the third ring you have not yet found in the course of your excavations, and you will never find it.' With this, the priest disappeared. I awoke at once and immediately told my wife the dream that I might not forget it. Next morning I examined the fragments once more in the light of these disclosures, *and to my astonishment found all the details of the dream precisely verified* in so far as the means of verification were in my hands. The original inscription on the

votive cylinder read 'To the God Ninib, son of Bel, his lord, has Kurigalzu, pontifex of Bel, presented this.'

The problem was thus at last solved. I stated in the Preface that I had unfortunately discovered too late that the two fragments belonged together, made the corresponding changes in the Table of Contents, pages 50 and 52, and, it being not possible to transpose the fragments, as the plates were already made, I put in each plate a brief reference to the other. (Cf. Hilprecht, *The Babylonian Expedition of the University of Pennsylvania,* Series A, Cuneiform Texts, Vol.1, Part I, 'Old Babylonian Inscriptions, chiefly from Nippur.')

H.V. HILPRECHT."

At the time Professor Hilprecht told me of this curious dream, which was a few weeks after its occurrence, there remained a serious difficulty which he was not able to explain. According to the memoranda in our possession, the fragments were of different colours, and therefore could have scarcely belonged to the same object. The original fragments were in Constantinople, and it was with no little interest that I awaited Professor Hilprecht's return from the trip which he made thither in the summer of 1893. I translate again his own account of what he then ascertained.

"November 10th, 1895.

"In August, 1893, I was sent by the Committee of the Babylonian Expedition to Constantinople, to catalogue and study the objects got from Nippur and preserved there in the Imperial Museum. It was to me a matter of the greatest interest to see for myself the objects which, according to my dream, belonged together, in order to satisfy myself that they had both originally been parts of the same votive cylinder. Halil Bey, the director of the Museum, to whom I told my dream, and of whom I asked permission to see the objects, was so interested in the matter, that he at once opened all the cases of the Babylonian section, and requested me to search. Father Schell, an Assyriologist from Paris who examined and arranged the articles excavated by us before me, had not recognized the fact that these fragments belonged together, and consequently I found one fragment in one case, and the other in a case far away from it. As soon as I found the fragments and put them together, *the truth of the dream was demonstrated* – they had, in fact, once belonged to one and the same votive cylinder. As it had been originally of finely veined agate, the stonecutter's saw had accidentally divided the object in such a way that the whitish vein of the stone appeared only upon the one fragment and the larger grey surface upon the other."

Professor Hilprecht is unable to say what language the old priest used in addressing him. *He is quite certain that it was not Assyrian, and thinks it was either English or German.*

The fact that the Babylonian spirit appeared to Professor Hilprecht in a dream, whereas the Egyptian spirits appeared to me in trance, is not a point of great importance: it merely evidences the different degree of nervous or psychic constitution between us. What others experience in the dream-state often occurs to me even in the waking state – whether it be some person or event rendered perceptible at a great distance or some vision of a happening which has yet to materialize out of the future. The little-known truth is that *both* states exist simultaneously; dream and deep-sleep are ever-present even in the waking condition.

A point of interest is that both the Babylonian and Egyptian spirits addressed us in tongues more modern than their own. I do not profess to explain this: it is certainly illogical; but whoever has had some protracted *personal* experience of psychical research discovers in time that the dream and spirit worlds beyond our own sometimes laugh at our three-dimensional logic. Next to be noted is the correspondence between Professor Hilprecht's dream-self being led by the priest to a windowless treasure-chamber of the temple and my own spirit-self being led by the other priest to a windowless passage which opened on a chamber in the vicinity of the Pyramid, or Sphinx, where ancient Atlantean records were stored.

Those who do not believe that spirits exist may conveniently omit this account, for its validity has mainly a personal value. "Sir, every man has the right to his own opinion!" said old Doctor Johnson. I can hear his ponderous feet treading noisily down Fleet Street, while he addresses this sententious remark to the faithful Boswell. Though we may agree with his dictum, the worthy doctor's corollary, that every other man has the right to knock him down for it, is open to question! The Egyptians were a strictly practical and extremely matter-of-fact people, yet they did not hesitate to believe in the existence of spirits. We, however, have grown wiser.

This does not mean, and must not be misunderstood to mean, that I am approving, much less advocating the modern cult of spiritualism in any of its forms. I have little to do with it now, although I took the trouble to include it among my early investigations of the occult. The only spirit-teaching which I consider safe, reliable and uplifting is that which leads us closer to God and further from enslavement by earthly things.

Misunderstandings of one's work are pardonable but I distinguish between them and the malice of detractors.

It is fortunate for me that I do not need their good opinion. My researches into the loftier realm of divine Spirit, as opposed to faulty spirits, have not left me dependent on that changeable barometer. Thank heaven that we do not have to carry certificates of character with us into the presence of the One Arbiter, who alone knows all and therefore is alone competent to judge all, and that in so far as men reveal their incredible pettiness when we draw near, so does the Supreme reveal Its ineffable magnanimity when we approach It.

If I do not need the world's fine opinion, refuse its praise and scorn its censure, I am not so indifferent as to forget the good admonition of One whom I ventured long since to adopt as one of my masters, even though his body has vanished from this globe. "Bless them that curse you," he said, "and pray for them which despitefully use you: forgive and ye shall be forgiven." And so, without resentment, I commend these ignorant traducers to the care of their Heavenly Father.

But I have no intention of being martyred on a cross of my own making. I have broken the age-old silence of the Mysteries, as I was bidden, but I am under no compulsion to continue to do so.

I must return to the volume under consideration. Fourthly, those who have read *A Search in Secret Egypt* will remember the awe-inspiring message given to me by the Adept who used the pseudonym of Ra-Mak-Hotep to the effect that ancient Egypt left an invisible legacy to present-day Egypt, and indeed to the whole world, the exact nature of which very few understood. This legacy includes spirit-entities and psychic forces which, although they have lain in tombs carefully sealed and hidden from the prying eyes of the profane for so many thousand years, still retain a high and even terrible potency for evil.

Sceptics have laughed this idea to scorn, unable, in their naive unawareness of the subtler forces at work in the world about us, to give countenance to the thought that things apparently "dead" can, and do, exert a living influence upon our immediate present. From the occult and psychic point of view it is a true saying that "the past lives in the present". A striking confirmation of this is contained in the following account of a queer experience which came to Monsieur Cellerier and was related to me by one of his friends.

Monsieur Cellerier is the head of the Laboratory of the Museum of Arts and Crafts in Paris. In October, 1932, he was asked by the Conservator of the Egyptian Section of the Louvre Museum in Paris to verify, by means of the instruments available to modern science, the authenticity of a small statuette in painted wood which the Louvre authorities desired to acquire for the Section at the price of 80,000 francs. M. Cellerier accepted the invitation and began by a series of purely physical experiments to establish the kind of wood used, the authenticity and age of the painting, etc. These experiments were carried out by his assistants, under his supervision, and the conclusion reached as a result of these preliminary researches was that the statuette was perfectly genuine. However, a mystery clung round the origin and history of the little statuette, and the scientist, his curiosity piqued, decided to submit it to the ruthless penetration of the X-ray. This was done but nothing extraordinary was revealed. He then proceeded to subject the statuette to the play of ultra-violet A.L. rays. It should be noted that these rays used in the laboratory at Paris are of excessive power and intensity, at least ten times greater than those used by doctors for the therapeutic purposes. No sooner had the rays touched the statuette than, to M. Cellerier's great astonishment, it became suddenly luminous and seemed to disappear and *give place to a new human form, made of light.* The cause and exact nature of this phosphorescence could not be determined. The wood and the painting had to be dismissed as possible causes of the strange glow which seemed to emanate right from the heart of the statue itself, to actually *be* the statue in a very real sense

Who can tell exactly what it was that powerful ray had unwittingly revealed, knowing as we do that such rays are able to pierce the grosser forms of matter and penetrate the finer; knowing that what we call electricity is, even in its simplest manifestations, one of Nature's most mysterious forces, and that in its highly concentrated forms, as in this ray, it becomes a definitely occult force?

The mystery was never solved and has not been solved to this day. The little statuette in question stands today among the later acquisitions in the Louvre Museum. Many may go and see it, attracted by the magic which surrounds it, but to few or none will its precious secret be revealed. Such statuettes were generally placed in tombs and magically treated to act as mediums between the spirit of the deceased and his mummy. Who knows, the Louvre figure, too, may be the temporary house of one of those elemental spirits mentioned by Ra-Mak-Hotep, conjured up by one of the magicians so frequent in those far-off days of Egypt's glory and linked with the little statuette, there to live until the appointed hour for its release into the world of men?

Fifthly, I am well acquainted with several unpublished proofs of the Adept's assertion, but in line with my desire to quote only acceptable and undeniably authentic testimony, I again reprint a newspaper cutting:

"A small piece of bone is being blamed for the chapter of accidents which has befallen its owners, Sir Alexander and Lady Seton (says a Reuter's message from Edinburgh). The piece of bone, declared to be part of the skeleton of a Pharaoh, was brought as a curio from the Tombs of Gizeh by Lady Seton last year. Since then a series of misfortunes has happened to the Seton home in Edinburgh. First of all, illness attacked the family and staff. The various members of the household and visitors complained of a mysterious robed figure which roamed the house at night. Two mysterious fires have broken out in the Setons' home. Glass and china in cabinets near the case containing the bone have been smashed to atoms during the night. 'That bone is going to be replaced in the tomb we took it from as quickly as possible,' Sir Alexander stated in an interview, 'and Lady Seton is making the trip herself to ensure that it gets there.'"

Let this be continued, by way of contrast, with part of the actual statement made by my informant, the Adept Ra-Mak-Hotep, as published in *A Search in Secret Egypt:*

"Those who broke open the tombs of ancient Egypt have released forces upon the world that have endangered it. Both the tomb-robbers of long ago and the archaeologists of our own days have all unwittingly opened the tombs of those who dealt in black magic. Wherever the embalmed body was that of a person with some knowledge of magic or else under the protection or guidance of some one with such knowledge, spirit-powers had been invoked to protect those tombs and punish intruders. These powers were often exceedingly evil, menacing and destructive. They existed within the closed tombs for thousands of years . . . every such tomb which has been unsealed lets out, like a flood, a rush of pent-up, noxious, evil spirit-entities upon our physical world. Those influences can bring only harm to the world, even to the point of destructively affecting the destinies of nations. You Westerners have no shield against them, and because they are invisible to you, they are none the less potent . . . whether it heeds it or not, let the world receive this message: let it not meddle with tombs whose psychic nature men do not understand. Let the world stop opening these graves until it has acquired sufficient knowledge to comprehend the serious results of what it is doing. Let this warning go out through your pen. Even if it be scorned and ignored, my duty and yours shall have been done. Nature's laws do not pardon ignorance; but even that excuse shall have gone."

Without further comment, except to note that the Adept's warning has not passed unheeded, I reprint also the following item, which appeared in the London *Sunday Express,* exactly thirteen months after publication of my book.

"EGYPT PLANS TO RE-BURY THE PHARAOHS
MIGHTY KINGS WHO WERE ONCE 'ON SHOW'.

In a letter to the editor, Mr. H. de Vere Stacpoole, the famous novelist writes:

'I heard recently that the Egyptian Government were going to re-bury the Pharaohs. It was a scandal even desecrating their tombs, and I think it brought bad luck on the world.'

At the Egyptian Embassy in London the *Sunday Express* was informed that the Government of Egypt are now actually considering re-burying the Pharaohs.

The *Sunday Express* understands that the proposal now being considered by the Egyptian Government is to build a special mausoleum for them either at Giza, near the Pyramids, or Heliopolis.

The mausoleum would be an underground one, similar to those made by the ancient Egyptians, and the kings would be sealed down under the earth never again to be seen by the eye of man."

Sixthly, further criticisms have been levelled against the Adept's astonishing assertion that there are entranced bodies in certain hidden tombs which have lain there for thousands of years. Quite frankly even I at first found this statement difficult to credit. The thought that there might be the figures of men below the desert sands who had attained almost endless years, living in defiance of the natural laws of bodily decay and the ravages of time, staggered me also. But I have since become fully convinced of its *possibility*. And my belief is borne out by a striking scientific discovery, an account of which appeared in the Press and is reproduced here:

"Members of the Soviet Academy of Sciences, probing in the Siberian ice, recently discovered at a depth of fifteen feet a number of primitive insects and small sea animals. These creatures are computed to have lain dormant since 1000 B.C. Notwithstanding, they have now, by means of scientific thawing, been brought back to life. Immediately on resurrection, all showed an eagerness to resume their normal functions; even the eggs located beside them have been hatched; and from the frozen crawfish, Professor P. N. Kapterev, the leader of the expedition, has already bred ten new generations.

As an example of Nature's refrigerating powers, this research triumph is amazing. *But scientists attach a far deeper significance to it. They foresee that if insects can survive for 3000 years, man might well accomplish a similar feat.* In America, Dr. Ralph S. Willard, in his campaign to extinguish degenerate cells, has frozen a disease-attacked monkey solid, put it away for a period in an ice-box and then thawed it without the little creature showing any ill-effect."

Let this account be placed in juxtaposition with the following statement issued by a famous medical research scientist, Dr.

Alexis Carrel, of the Rockefeller Institute:

"There is a very remote possibility of postponing for a long period of time the death of a few individuals. It is known that certain animals such as the small anthropoid, tardigradum, stop their metabolism when they are dried. A condition of latent life is thus induced. If, after a lapse of several weeks, one moistens these desiccated animals, they revive and are capable of leading normal life again. *Some individuals could be put into storage for long periods of time, brought back to normal existence for other periods, and permitted in this manner to live for several centuries.*"

We shudder at the thought of death; what wonder that the fabled Elixir of Life attracts as ever the imagination of man? We would prolong, if we could, our span of life to legendary limits. Yet none save certain rare Adepts possess and guard this secret.

Such are the six 'confirmations'. A minor point may be also mentioned. I referred sceptically to the world-shaking events that were supposed to occur in September, 1936, as the inauguration of a new era, according to the expectations of the British-Israel cult, and ventured to assert that although measurements of so large and so concrete a structure as the Pyramid had been dragged in to support these and other claims, I could not find sufficient evidence to warrant such extraordinary assertions as were being made by the leaders of this cult. That fateful September passed over our heads in much the same manner that other months of these overstrained years have passed. I regret the disillusionment which must have come to the large English following of this cult, but the Great Pyramid was built with a nobler purpose than that of mere fortune-telling – on however large a scale

– and part of that purpose I unveiled in my book.

Yes, *A Search in Secret Egypt* startled not a few readers. That man lived and moved in an unseen world which interpenetrated our own and of which spirits, both human and non-human, were the invisible inhabitants was a thought not altogether new to them, for both manhood's bibles and childhood's fables made reference to such a world; but that this world was still an ever-present reality, as real as Broadway in New York and the Place de la Madeleine in Paris, was news that exploded in the minds of some with sudden force.

The fundamental lesson of this book, however, is the lesson of man's survival after death. He steps out of the body, as one steps out of a prison, and does not perish with it. For man is mind, not matter. If this book has done nothing more than to remind the modern world of those vanished and forgotten Mystery-cults of antiquity, wherein this truth was vividly taught and amply demonstrated, it will have justified its existence. *When man will comprehend again that he carries his life onward even after the grave claims his body, he may halt his hurried existence and begin to acquire a nobler sense of responsibility. Yet even then, it must be remembered that mere survival is not the same as enduring immortality.*

Finally, one thing which the company of both educated and simple Muhammadan Egyptians did for me, and which I in turn endeavoured to do for my readers, was to correct the false, stupid and unjust conception which I, in common with most Europeans, had formed of their noble religion. Islam is a great faith and has been admirably suited to the lands wherein it first spread.

§

The book which gave me the least pleasure to write was *A Message from Arunachala,* which was so unpopular that it has never got very far in circulation, whilst its title unfortunately led to a little misunderstanding of its contents. It is a book of pointed criticism, unconventional in form and spirit, unshapely in literary construction, an indictment of the materialistic foundations of our modern civilization and therefore necessarily destructive in tone. The drawing of such a picture of the spiritual darkness of our times, stroked in a few jerky phrases and broken paragraphs, was a task as disagreeable to me as its result must have been to my readers. It is my aim in life to be definitely constructive, to help in building up a new and better world of fruitful ideas, yet somehow I could not escape from writing *A Message from Arunachala*. I felt, as by a complete compulsion, that it had to be done, and in truth I hope never to write such a work again. Moreover, owing to my time-pressed circumstances at the period of its production, it was left somewhat crude and unpolished. It was a bit of rough iron-ore; I had not the time then, nor have I the desire now, to work it over into some more attractive article.

Because I aired a few flippant jokes in between the pages and sought to lighten my weightier aphorisms with sparse and brief efforts at wit, some readers took offence and looked askance at the whole message. Life is full of tears for the thinker, and if perforce he dips his pen in the cupfuls he collects, should he not keep a few smiles up his sleeve wherewith to sprinkle his sad pages? Why should not philosophers be frolicsome on rare occasions? Need that necessarily make them less sincere? Even if life were nothing more than time's miserable interlude in the blissful existence of eternity, it will become a little more tolerable if we pass through it to the musical accompaniment of a few laughs.

The bitterness of that little volume was too extreme and some of its social criticisms were deliberately exaggerated so that I might drive home my points more forcibly – I freely confess that now I would certainly greatly tone down its pages did I have the will to rewrite it – but the tragic history of our epoch, with its chaos and futility and strife and bloodshed, its tense, uneasy peace, its menaced future, no less than the fools' festival in which we find ourselves, may perhaps be cited in part justification. "The Soul may sit lonely and sad, surrounded by mechanical miracles," wrote Zangwill, and my book reflected that kind of sadness. It did endeavour, however, to show that the vicissitudes of present-day politics and society cannot change the eternal truth of man's spiritual royalty in Nature, and the second part did endeavour to provide some helpful and constructive hints for spiritually illuminating ordinary daily life, and perhaps that may be a further justification of its existence

§

It is perhaps nothing else than the logical fitness of things that I should have carried my Indian quest of spiritual truth a stage further and gone into the wild region and long horizons of the stupendous Himalayas themselves. For the 1500-mile long rugged range which eternally watches India has been the Holy Land of its peoples, the sacred region where their fabled gods and famous spiritual teachers, sages and yogis, lived and, people say, even still live, and where intrepid devotees still tend the lamps of their lofty sanctuaries.

Himalaya is to the Hindus what Palestine is to the Jews and Christians. Pilgrims still plod patiently up the narrow, winding trails to the great shrines of Amarnath, Badrinath, Gangotri and Jumnotri, enduring various hardships, and risking accident or illness, for the sake of being in a region which their most ancient traditions have linked with holiness and which must ever impress itself upon their eyes as the most beautiful and the most impressive in all India.

And so I, too, settled for a time among these lonely mountains, whose untouched grandeur made me weep with shame at my own unworthiness. I selected the little kingdom of Tehri-Garwhal State on the Tibetan border as the setting of my spiritual endeavour, because there, amid the grandest mountain scenery of the whole world, one could find that utter remoteness from civilization which was essential to my purpose at that time. I too went there on a pilgrimage, albeit of a different kind from that upon which most pilgrims usually go. I went into utter solitude, living alone with nothing else for company than the wild beasts of the massive forests, the lofty deodar trees and the snow-clad giants which towered overhead. I tried during my stay to practise what was indeed a form of yoga, yet it was nothing more than the yoga of complete stillness. I let body and mind slip into the most quiescent state it seemed possible to attain. I wanted, in the words of the Psalmist, to "be still and know that I am God."

During my travels among the superb peaks and deep ravines and during my residence in their solitudes, I kept a journal, a kind of unconventional diary, in which I wrote down from time to time descriptions of the sublime scenery around me, as well as reflections upon various topics which came into my head. In addition, I noted in it something about the spiritual experiences which I underwent during my adventures into stillness. Selections from this journal came into print and made a bow to the public under the title of *A Hermit in the Himalayas*. My publishers called it a literary cocktail – so varied were its contents – and doubtless they were right. Anyway, I hope that it paid my tribute of homage to the grandeur of the Himalayas and to the divine atmosphere which I found among its granite heights – so remote from a railroaded world!

§

Such are the works which have passed out of the pointed tip of my pen. Each has its distinct and separate message for those who care to ponder over its lines, and not merely skim over its pages, whilst two at least have shown the world what wonderful knowledge lies hid in holy India and mystic Egypt. People who expect me always to write in the same vein and upon the same theme do not grasp the fact that these writings are simply different facets of one and the same crystal – all express the truth as I have found it. This is not to say that all have equal value, because there exist different degrees of truth; the latter is ever relative to our understanding: and it is man's duty to seek the highest as I hope it shall be mine to know and express it in a future work. This, again, at once lays its comprehension open only to the few, because the masses desire and comprehend truth only when it comes dressed up in impressive veilings and heralded by loud trumpetings. Hence they perceive, not so much the truth, but its robes. Hence, too, my desire to present in these books some of these varied aspects before I finally mount into the rarefied air of the sublime ultimate verity, whither, I know, few will care to mount with me. *Yet that verity is the sole cause of our being and its realization the sole purport of our incarnation.*

However, it may be that these works, these intimate thoughts, and these published reports shall not be without their use. When I witness the spectacle of a world not long since plunged in deadly combat and now preparing to plunge, if the adverse elements conquer and destiny permits, in still deadlier combat that can lead only to general self-destruction, I am tempted to think that I have not written quite in vain. I know that some thousands of people wring from my writings the faith that justice, however delayed, must in the end be done, that man's very self is unkillable and therefore immortal; they find therein a little light on their path, a little inspiration wherewith to assist their endeavours after a nobler life, and a little consolation to mitigate the weight of their worldly burdens. And when I read and hear the distorted doctrines that pass current for philosophy, the unreal and intolerant practices of religion, and perceive the relentless pressure of a cruel materialism upon rich and poor alike, I am glad to have borne witness to a few eternal verities which the prejudices of the age can never destroy.

Once again the inner bidding has come to me, to take up the following work and to do it as an act of service, and in the face of such imperious command my own personal will falls powerless. I have therefore obeyed and in the obeying have tried to enter into my task in that spirit of devoted service which was demanded of me. These pages, this gospel of inspired thought and action, this exposition of the way towards Overself – to me one of the grandest and most important conceptions ever held before the mind of mankind, and one of unearthly beauty – are a fitting sequel to my earlier writings. I call it the grandest because we *live* only when we touch our sacred Source; otherwise we merely exist.

Moreover, the three years which have elapsed since *The Secret Path* was written have been years of wider experience of these deeper truths and of considerable expansion in personal realization. My understanding of them is, I hope, now more profound and I therefore feel myself in a better position to handle the subject more comprehensively, more accurately and with a clearer vision of the true relation of these truths to our practical, everyday existence. *The Secret Path* was merely an introduction, an incomplete outline, but in the present work I endeavour to elaborate more fully the same technique, to formulate a complete method of inward thought and inward living, and produce a precise and definite exposition of this difficult theme of divine self-comprehension. Hence I can personally testify to the worth of the spiritual methods explained here; not by theory or hearsay do I understand them, but out of first-hand knowledge gained over a long experience.

Because I have sought to work out the thesis of this volume a little more philosophically, scientifically and analytically, than in my previous volumes, because, more than ever, I wish to show how the truth concerning human existence may be philosophically and rationally reached, I have deliberately adopted a different style throughout this work, although never departing, I hope, from the language of common-sense, that is to say, from the language of life itself. I have soberly and seriously substituted the impersonal for the personal, the coldness of calm analysis for the heat of passionate conviction, and I have had the hardihood to use a dry, semi-academic style which is not my normal wear. For the same reason, I have avoided as far as possible all unnecessary reference to the occult, the psychic and that obscure, 'borderline' knowledge and so-called superstition to which the mysterious nature of the constitution of man has given rise, but which science disdains for the most part to sift. In any case, this domain is infinitely less important than the divine and holy. One memorable word from the lips of Jesus or Krishna or Muhammad is worth all the wonderful feats of the occultists.

I endeavour to lay bare in these pages some of the secret, subtle, but definite laws that govern the working of man's inmost mind, his soul, so far as I have been able to ascertain them. All education, whether of the primary school or of the university, is but elementary if it takes no account of the sacred self and the unfolding thereof. Obedience to these laws will put us into tune with the best in life.

One point to which attention should be drawn is important, because it reveals the difference seen in truth when one takes up a higher standpoint. *A Search in Secret Egypt* preached the doctrine of psychical survival, a doctrine whose value is purely relative to that of the physical body, because it was intended to reach an order of minds more held by that body and by the personal ego. It did not teach the doctrine of spiritual immortality, which is quite a different matter. The former perpetuates the personal ego, the latter dissolves it.

In the present work, which is intended to reach a rarer type of mind, the standpoint taken is consequently higher and therefore the necessity of surrendering the ego to the Overself is underlined; this alone is the true doctrine of immortality.

Every writer or teacher must perforce take up a different position according to the grade of development of the mind with which he is dealing. Therefore, if I declared in *A Search in Secret Egypt* that *x* was true, but now write in *The Quest of the Overself* that *y* is true, neither statement cancels out the other: it simply means that I am writing now for readers in a different or higher grade of development. Even so, the purpose of these pages should not be misconstrued. They are designed to show a yoga-path suited to Western people, a path whose fruit is serenity of mind, control of thought and desire, and power to utilize higher forces of being. In short, they show how to achieve certain *satisfactions*, but they do not attempt at this stage to solve the mystery of the universe. That which our leading scientists are still vainly seeking and forgotten philosophers have given up in despair of ever finding, has been the treasured possession of a rare few in India since that dateless antiquity when this wisdom was whispered by word of mouth alone and in whose shadows its origin is utterly lost. *It is beyond the reach of ordinary yogis,* yet the training of yoga is a necessary mental and moral discipline which prepares one to receive the priceless jewel of absolute TRUTH. When peace of mind and concentration of thought have been gained, then only will one be fit and ready to embark on the quest of Ultimate Truth. We are still in the process of unveiling a subtle and startling wisdom which not one person in a million has yet grasped, and a codified scientific teaching whose irrefragable certitudes have yet to be developed for all time.

Archaeologists excavating in Egypt have discovered a leaf of a papyrus book – that of Oxyrhynchus – ontaining eight sayings of Jesus. The discoverers assigned the probable date of their papyrus as about A.D. 200. Among these sayings there exists a sentence of striking force, whose remarkable similarity to the constantly repeated message of the philosophers of antiquity is noteworthy.

Jesus said: "And the Kingdom of Heaven is within you; *and whomsoever shall know himself shall find it.*"

The book is one help toward knowing oneself. The portrait of self which it produces may be unfamiliar to most of us, but whoever heeds it sufficiently will find ultimately that the soul is not unknowable. The man who thinks that these statements are merely fanciful speculations and that these experiences are merely mental hallucinations, suffers from the delusion of what is but a day in world history. Materialism, as a plausible explanation which has never properly succeeded in explaining life, may prevail for a time but with further time it will fall down with crippled feet.

May this age not be so alien to a true life that it cannot give hospitality to a few of these thoughts!

2

THE MYSTERY OF MAN

The first, and for some considerable time one may say the ruling, thought which vividly dominates an infant child's consciousness is the awareness of *I*. The last thought which moves with the spirit of the tenement of the brain at death is also that of *I*. During the intervening years between these two points of birth and death – years which make up that composite picture of commonplace events, unrehearsed comedies, occasional tragedies, brief sunshine and lingering shadows that we call life – the chief preoccupation of most human beings is with that same *I*.

Strange as it may seen, this *I* is shrouded in mystery, rooted in obscurity and more ignorant of itself than of anything else in the world around it. Yet man is not naturally conscious of this ignorance; such consciousness comes to him only when he starts to become curious about his sense of identity and to think about himself. Then his chief puzzle becomes himself, rivalling that of the Sphinx, and his greatest problem likewise himself. Whenever he has the courage and initiative to question life and keep on questioning it, to interpret his human experience without previous preconceptions, he will be amazed at his inability to understand the Truth, the full truth concerning his relation as an individual to the great Life-Force in which all things live, move and have their being and of which he himself is but a single expression.

Feeble laggards though we still are in the immense and silent cosmic evolution, we must remember that the universe reaches its supreme visible manifestation in the human kingdom, whose complex character embodies most of the elements and principles which are to be found in the simpler manifestations. Thus in the successful analysis of man we may hope to find the first key to the universe itself. Indeed, in the general world-conception of current science the objective universe is fast falling back towards a set of symbols offered by Nature to human consciousness. The Law of Relativity has shown matter and time indefinitely to be such derivative concepts, and the Quantum Theory has carried us so far away from the old-fashioned 'mass' explanations of matter that the acute scientist must sooner or later perceive that the limit of scientific research will not be surpassable without *first* surpassing the present limits of human awareness.

Dean Inge has somewhere said that "from the astronomical point of view we are only creatures of a day." It is one of the sad results of scientific as well as philosophic research, that we become deeply aware of the transient nature of the multitude of forms which constitute a universe. We are forced to meditate upon the fact of mortality and are sometimes appalled by the idea of the futility of all human endeavour. Hence the existence of every religion.

Out of man's efforts to comprehend his real self have arisen all the religions, both great and small, many philosophical systems and a few sciences, as well as those obscure and now vanished secret lores and ritual-paths which were paved in secrecy and which led into the Mystery-temples of antiquity. Yet, in spite of all these historical strivings, the number of people who can confidently assert that their understandings of, and control over life suffice them, is amazingly small, so small indeed that most of us flee from ourselves and have reluctantly accepted the bankrupt belief that the mystery of human life was never intended for man's solving. We accept its incomprehensibility and have become resigned to the thought that we can never completely transcend our spiritual ignorance and human weakness. Such is the perpetual bewilderment of the human mind when pondering upon itself. Yet surely this attitude of resignation, this timid fear of challenging existence for its reluctant secret, which sometimes unhappily degenerates into sloth and indifference concerning the spiritual aspect of life, is unworthy of man, who is today apparently the most intelligent and the most powerful of all creatures.

The normal man's knowledge of his own ego is more or less limited to the commonplace realization of his body as a complete organism made up of flesh, blood and bone. Somewhere in the upper part or head of that organism there is a mass of grey and white matter called the brain, within the tortuous convolutions of which the process called thinking takes place, producing impressions, ideas and arguments. Furthermore, he also knows that within this body various feelings such as those of aspiration, sex, love, hate, jealousy, fear and so on arise from time to time and move him to appropriate action on the physical planes, according to whichever of these feelings dominates the others. For the average man, these things constitute his 'make-up', his 'I'. He is aware of little else in himself and he makes this limited conception suffice for most of the contingencies of his everyday life. And, truly, unless one starts to reflect upon the matter, one may very well pass through life and find such a conception moderately satisfying.

Yet consider for a moment that a man is nothing more

than this fleshly frame and then try to perceive the full implication of such a statement. Here is a creature entirely
composed of various physical substances and chemical elements in different degrees of combination, tightly held
together within a bag of skin, yet these inert and apparently
unintelligent substances – such as carbon, nitrogen and phos-
phorus – which we find in man *do* when thus combined
manifest a living principle, a strange vitality and capacity for
intelligent purposive thought and self-conscious action.

Is this not an extraordinary mystery?

Has any scientist yet solved it? The answer is none. Why?
Because no scientist in any country of the world has, as yet,
been able to assemble these constituent chemical elements of a
man's body into one homogeneous creature of his own fabri-
cation, which lives, moves, talks and acts like a man. On the
other hand, many scientists have issued their opinions, have
built up clever and ingenious systems and theories, mostly
materialistic in basis, which profess to explain man. The test of
every theory, however, must finally be either in the experiments of the laboratory or the experience of life itself. When
one of these scientists can create a man by the art of chemistry
he will have proved his theory – not before. Science, knowing
so much of other things, still lags in comprehension of the
unseen life-force which expresses itself in the human kingdom,
but it is headed truth-wards and one may well be optimistic.

Sir James Jeans in his Presidential Address before an
annual meeting of the British Association for the
Advancement of Science said: "Science has given man control
over Nature before he has gained control over himself. Thus,
in respect of knowledge, each generation stands on the shoulders of its predecessors; but in respect of himself, both stand
on the same ground. These are hard facts which we cannot
alter. If there is an avenue of escape, it does not lie in the direc-

tion of less science, but of more science – Psychology holds out a hope that for the first time in his long history man may be enabled to obey the command, Know Thyself!"

The Hindus, who have enquired deeply into these matters for many thousand years before the first Western scientist started to think, have built their doctrines generally on the tacit assumption of the existence of a universal spirit which interpenetrates and transcends simultaneously the world and the creatures who dwell therein; they assert, therefore, that the human spirit possesses in itself the revelation it seeks. Thanks to an education which follows scientific lines inasmuch as it takes nothing for granted, we can accept no such statement. We can begin only by affirming that which we know to be indisputable, the fact of self-existence. We may, indeed, feel that we are surrounded by a higher order of life than the merely material, but because it eludes our perception we must regard it as illusory. And so modern man has become that curious creature which feeds at the breasts of Divinity and yet knows it not! This spinning globe could not turn on its axis if there were not the propulsive energy of a higher power at its core, but to the educated mind it is nothing more than a subject for geological investigation!

Man is in no doubt as to the existence of his mind – modern life makes too many demands upon it for that – yet he persists in disregarding the oft-repeated assertion of the psychologists, now backed by ample proof that the major portion of this mind – and hence of himself – functions without his conscious knowledge and that this hidden portion influences him to a far greater extent than he either realizes or will admit. Although he engages in the most colossal material enterprises, such as frequently bring drastic changes to the face of this planet, he seems to lack either the will or the desire, or both, to engage in the no less necessary enterprise of discovering the whence and whither of his own life. Although he indulges in a fevered activity throughout the day, and frequently even into the night, it never occurs to him to try to deepen his experience of life by turning his attention inwards and exploring the sources of his own being. He would rather sink elaborate shafts to discover the material gold lying in the bowels of the earth than trouble to seek the rarer treasure which lies buried in the deep recesses of his own being. He does not seem to realize that it is of supreme and momentous importance to him that he should attempt to discover the source and drift of his own life-current, *because it is through its ever-present agency alone that he is enabled to carry on those external and worldly activities in which he is so deeply immersed.* Self-knowledge, therefore, is the supreme science.

Nevertheless, there always have been, there are today and there always will be some people who *do* attempt to swim ashore out of the drifting tide of daily events; who endeavour to find a vantage point of solid ground above the whirlpool of external things, from which to regard this mystery of life and mind. Generally, they only do this under the pressure of great sorrow, emotional crisis or other upheavals, which temporarily drive them in upon themselves and make all the activity which centres around the 'I', the individual ego, seem futile and meaningless. Strangely enough, it is when people reach that point when "life no longer seems worth living" that they begin to become really interested in the spiritual aspect of life, whereas before they had only been interested in the material; it is at this point that they turn to religion for consolation, to philosophy for comprehension, and when these two do not attract or suffice, to strange and unorthodox cults for heretical glimmers of light.

Yet, to whatever source they may turn for inner guidance and enlightenment, they will always find themselves ultimately face to face with the mystery of the self, which is ever demanding, albeit silently, their profounder investigation. It is therefore imperative that man should realize this and make self-understanding one of the primary motives of his life. Until he does this, religion, philosophy, higher psychology, and in short, all avenues of non-sensuous knowledge, will continue to confuse and baffle him.

Life has certainly created man, but the mysteries involved in his creation have by no means been revealed to him as yet. It is therefore not surprising that Nature's profoundest and most tantalizing secret is also her most important one. However, let us not hesitate to question her.

In his eightieth year, when he was drying after a bath, rugged Scotch Carlyle looked mournfully down at his withered ancient limbs and began to shout frenziedly: "What the devil then am I?" and to pluck at his flesh.

The writer will give an answer to Carlyle's oft-asked question.

Interrogation is the door which leads to revelation.

A silent revolution has been taking place in physical sciences ever since the Great War. The naïve materialism of the nineteenth century no longer appears credible, and is pitifully out of date, while the theory of relativity, the quantum theory and wave mechanics are transforming our view of the universe. When the solid atom was broken up into electric charges and then dissolved into pristine ether, the materialist was robbed of his matter! We are beginning to expound the doctrines of the ancients, the teachings of Babylonia, Egypt and India, but we are doing so by the light of modern scientific progress. Evidence accumulates that science is beginning to say the same things as those forgotten ancients, albeit in a different way.

In his published books and articles the writer has repeatedly predicted that this twentieth century will witness the widespread unveiling of life's secret in a rational and scientifically accepted manner. It is not without sufficient reason that this prophecy is made. Only then will the human race begin to co-operate intelligently with Nature's hidden plan of our universe. It is not by chance that a distinguished scientist like Millikan has to confess: "We have found in our life-time more new relations in physics than have come to light in all the preceding ages put together, and the stream of discovery as yet shows no signs of abatement."

Yes, it is not so long ago that the world was explained by science in terms of mechanical engineering. Matter was simply solid, unchangeable substance, a collection of solid atoms, and nothing more. The universe was a machine; there was no mystery about it. Now science is giving an explanation in terms of mathematical physics. The universe has become a set of symbols possessing mathematical relations. Thus we have journeyed from the material to the mental. When all the present researchers have had their say, we shall be ready to take the next step forward. Physics will join friendly hands with metaphysics. And then science will explain the world in terms of philosophy. The universe will be neither merely mechanical nor merely symbolic. The advanced thinkers are already approaching conclusions which the present work foreshadows and which the writer's future work shall more plainly unveil.

It is not by mere chance alone that renowned scientists of the nineteenth century – men like Kelvin, Poincaré, Rayleigh and Helmholtz – who lived into its last decade, had the mortification of being forced to alter their earlier conceptions of this universe in face of the startling discoveries which were suddenly made. The Röntgenrays, the electron, and the quantum were three revelations which deprived every cocksure materialist of his solid supports. They broke down his mechanistic structure, too, and started a train of investigation which is leading our present-day bewildered physicists right outside their own special realm.

§

How, then, is man to start about piercing this mystery of the *I*?

The writer does not deem it worth his while to embark upon a general statement of the condition of spiritual seeking in our day, nor to estimate the positive values and inhibiting limitations of the various and manifold creeds and cults and philosophies which, whether traditional or innovatory, exist among mankind in response to that seeking. Such a survey would draw him into the unavoidable activity of weighing them all in the balance of history, principles and practice, with results that might entail the wielding of a critical pen. This he declines to do, for there is far too much useless criticism in the world already and far too little of useful constructiveness. Let him therefore attend to his own business, interfering with none, and working with a spirit of goodwill toward all, glad that other lights exist to show man where to tread more safely amid the uncertainties of existence. In this spirit, alone, does he offer his own contribution, hoping that it may serve some as he would have been happy to have received similar help during the darker days of his own apprenticeship to life.

Who or what is the Soul? Is immortality really true? What is the meaning of eternity? And where is heaven? There are no quick and convincing answers to these questions. These are problems that also preoccupied the sages and seers of antiquity, and especially of the Orient. They delved deeply, found their solutions and gave expression to their discoveries in language and style that suited their land and time. The ancient lores and primitive cultures contain genuine and correct answers to these riddles that trouble the modern mind also.

Moreover, these sages made it possible for others to reach the same discoveries by themselves, because they worked out methods of religious approach or psychological techniques which were the key to vital personal experience of the realm of spirit. Such methods were indeed effective, but are now somewhat too remote from our own tastes, temperaments and circumstances.

The reclusive yogis of India, the bland sages of China, the powerful initiate-priests of Egypt, the God-ravished Sufis of Persia, the vanished Druids of early Britain and the chief Inca priests of America, among others were custodians of psychological knowledge; they knew of a certain Way, and some among them practised it. It yielded them astonishing spiritual transformations. Their feebler descendants of today have mostly forgotten or ignored that Way and only a rare few practise it. Salvation will come to us of the West when we re-learn this method – now nearly lost in the shadows of darkening antiquity – revise it to suit our own environment, restate it in modern terms and re-embrace its *regular* practice.

This need of a modern revision is essential. Archaic accents require an interpreter. For instance, experience with many people shows that the old Indian mode of discussing and answering these questions in talk and in writing, *seems* too far removed from our mundane affairs, too alien and unfamiliar in tradition and temperament to be of much use and attraction to Europeans. In reality this is not so, but because external forms need to be respected, we Westerners need a more modern and practical method of presentation of the same truths as have been taught since time immemorial by bearded yogis on Ganges banks and revered Rishees in Himalayan caves. When presented in the ancient manner they seem to possess an unreal character and an utter impracticability of being applied in the teeming world which surges around the great cities of

London, Paris and New York. Moreover, if we have to learn a new technique, we need not waste our time and energies in learning a new terminology.

We can no longer feel a kinship with the mysterious people who solve their spiritual problems within the high walls of pylon-gated temples in Egypt, nor believe that the grotesque architecture of Yucatan is an expression of spiritual aspirations like unto our own.

Supreme among the ancient lores is the Indian, *because it still lives when others have perished, and because India is the land which has mothered the deepest thought of man,* as Egypt was the father of his most marvellous magic and Greece was the parent of his highest efforts at creating beauty.

Every philosophy and religion which has appeared in Europe, finds its counterpart in those which dot the long history of India, whilst in addition the latter land has possessed secret systems of mental training nurtured by the yogis who roam through forests or dwell among mountain recesses. At the head of these reclusive men stands Patanjali, who provided the first recorded textbook of yoga methods. He is honoured as the founder of the system, indeed, by many Hindus, but in this opinion they are undoubtedly wrong. Yoga, in essence, is nothing else than the indrawing of man's mind toward his inner god-like self; it is not an artificial system but a fact of Nature, which has been discovered involuntarily by other men, and there were certainly those who lived prior to Patanjali in other lands (prehistoric Egypt, for instance) who practised this turning-inwards toward their divine self. His book was never intended for indiscriminate publication, but was expounded and explained verbally only to selected pupils; no others could have access to it.

What was thus taught in private was not altogether dissimilar to what some Grecian philosophers taught in public, for the same substratum runs through the mind of the world from east to west and teaches the same ancient path to all alike: *Man, Know Thyself.*

For example, Socrates himself practised methods of absorbed meditation which Patanjali's doctrine of direct contemplation plainly inculcated. Both culminated in the trance state, Socrates demonstrating this personally by passing at times into a contemplative trance.

Once he was walking with his friend Aristodemus to a banquet. He lagged behind in a fit of abstraction, fixing the mind on himself, and Aristodemus arrived without him. A servant was sent back to look for the sage, but came and reported that Socrates stood fixed in the portico of a house and did not answer when called. "Let him alone," said Aristodemus. "This is a way he has of retiring at times and standing wherever he may chance." Socrates arrived later. Again, Alcibiades mentions that on one occasion, during a military campaign, Socrates was found by a soldier standing still in one place where he had been since early dawn, fixed in profound meditation. At noon attention was drawn to him and the wondering crowd thereafter watched the sun go down but Socrates still kept to his trance. There he stood all night and at break of day he offered up a prayer to the sun and thus returned to normal activity. This is precisely the same as the *Nirvikalpa Samadhi* of the Hindus.

Hindus who have been following the practices of Patanjali in an unbroken line of tradition since pre-Socratic days, have had identical experiences. The writer has seen several instances of similar trances among living yogis of today.

But however interesting these primordial ideas and practices of the past may be to the readers of the present, the fact remains that they were especially suited to their own primitive epochs, and not ours, to their own simpler surroundings, and not those intellectual backgrounds and complex environments which hem in the modern man. Revision and re-adaptation and alignment with science are indeed called for. Whilst we must honour the wise men of antiquity with the utmost respect and whilst the best exponents of spirituality still exist, if rarely, in the countries of the East rather than of the West; whilst, too, we ought to give India our profoundest homage and respect as the Mother-land of comprehensive religion and grand philosophies and remarkable yogic techniques, we of the Western hemisphere need to remember that the ancient forms of spiritual approach are difficult of application in our own lives and circumstances, with their new necessities; we are forced, whether we care to or not, to take from antiquity and from its legatees in the Orient of today only so much nutriment as we can digest. We must re-work this knowledge, now so remote-seeming, into a fabric of practical utility to ourselves. Wisdom is not less wisdom because it is inspired with twentieth-century freshness.

Such a task is not easy. On the contrary, it is fraught with the widest difficulties and the present writer would not have dared to pretend his competence for it had he not been assured of the direct guidance and helpful counsel of living Oriental Adepts and Sages. Some of them, too, recognize the necessity of expressing this hoary knowledge in modern terminology and of readjusting its demands to the conformation of the conscious outlook of the twentieth century, without, however, yielding one iota of those fundamental conditions which must for ever mark all genuine spiritual self-discipline.

This is no aspersion on either antiquity or the Orient; on the contrary, what we have gained in width they possess in depth, and it is a question which of the two dimensions is the more desirable. We ought not to lay a flattering unction unto our souls merely because we inhabit the Western hemisphere and flourish in the twentieth century. Where the primitives penetrated the sources of human life, the moderns have extended their research over the entire terrestrial globe whereon that existence subsists. Where our pre-medieval forefathers asserted that real knowledge came from within, we declare that it must come from without. However, we have to get on with the inexorable business of daily living in the environment wherein we find ourselves; so let us henceforth endeavour to mingle the best of both East and West, ancient and modern, so far as we can.

And the writer does claim after long study of various yoga systems and philosophies, their most valuable element has been abstracted and incorporated in the present work, yet no demand whatever is made of the reader to familiarize himself with unfamiliar abstruse Indian or other modes of expression.

He will find here the quintessence of the best Oriental techniques expressed in words which are familiar and comprehensible to Occidental minds.

§

In ancient times advanced spiritual methods were almost always described only for those who had renounced the world and its temptations, who had withdrawn into monasteries or convents, or who had run away into the desert, the jungle and the mountain cave. Such escape is not only impracticable for the vast majority of people in this modern age, but one need not hesitate to assert that it is even inadvisable. Yet not a few of us are no less troubled by the insistent claims of the spirit than were those ancient people. The way to a higher life can, and must be found, in and through the world, not outside it.

In preparing a technique, therefore, which is based upon such belief the writer is well aware that it may not be a perfect one. Yet he is convinced that for the vast majority of normal people, who are not consciously seeking the Absolute Reality, the ultimate goal set for human reach, but will be content if they succeed in achieving a wise, and controlled life, the technique here given is completely adequate. The discipline demanded of them is neither too lofty to cause them the discouragement which comes of frustrated effort, nor too difficult to make them turn impatiently aside. It is something which is definitely within their compass. Nevertheless, men who are too absorbed in the glamours of excessive greed, the hot vapours of inordinate passions and the whirlwind of never-ending activities, may disdain it as being a vague and vapid matter of no account. Let it be so. But just as life triumphs ultimately if secretly over death, so shall the spiritual life and all that furthers its development and enrichment finally but openly triumph over our contemporary soulless materialism.

The answer to man's deepest queries is, finally, that a certain effort is demanded of him, a certain spiritual and personal practice which acts through an inward process somewhat in the manner of a pneumatic drill, which bores slowly and steadily through the earth of his being until eventually it strikes the solid rock of the True Divine Self seemingly buried so far below the surface. This practice has something of the nature of prayer in it, something of the nature of sustained intellectual effort along a single line – generally called meditation, but also termed mental quiet and concentration in these pages – yet at the same time, paradoxically enough, its most advanced phase is an utter absence of any effort whatsoever. Through such practice, persistently and hopefully performed, man may eventually discover his own deathless spirit, even whilst living in this body of frail flesh, for an unbroken line of witnesses who have lived in different countries of the world from the prehistoric border-line until this era of civilization's supreme zenith, testify to this truth.

We must clarify our minds upon this subtle and obscure subject. Mental mastery, indeed, cannot be constrained within the limits of a set of fixed rules and formulated principles like most of the other arts. The more advanced practices are too delicate, too elusive, to be taught properly through the inanimate printed page, and must be learned in the time-honoured way, i.e. from a competent personal teacher. Such a teacher is hard to find in this meditation-scorning modern age, while most of the aspirants themselves fail of acceptance even when fortune brings them within his orbit for a time. This happens because they really fail within themselves to pass the silent tests which the laws under which he works impose upon them – tests of their intuitiveness, spiritual ripeness, keenness and fidelity. Nevertheless, it is quite possible to study and master the elementary and intermediate stages of meditation without the help of such a teacher, and such instruction can easily be communicated through writing. And although it is not possible to condense into a few pages what has been discovered during a lifetime's research in this most important of all topics, it is with the object of providing simple, impartial and practical explanations of the art that this volume has been written.

There exist quite a number of ways in which we can start the exercises and each way possesses a particular appeal, or brings results more readily to one person than to another. Considered from the point of view of the final goal which is to be obtained, one method may be as good as the other, provided it suits one's personal make-up, temperament and inclinations.

Normally, man jogs along quite unaware of what depth lies below the surface of his being, like a floating iceberg whose greater part lies hidden beneath the waves. Professor William James, the renowned Harvard psychologist, considered the discovery of the subconscious mind one of the greatest discoveries ever made by man. It meant that we are conscious of only a small part of what goes on in our minds. Ninety per cent of our brain action goes on entirely without our knowledge *in the subconscious. All methods of meditation, therefore, are based on a certain principle, and that is, the throwing of the conscious mind out of gear by means of some physical, mental or emotional device, in order to make us aware of its deeper levels.*

Owing to the infinite diversity of individuals there is no one fixed method of approach for all. Therefore the wise man will not quarrel about the way of attainment; he will allow to all a perfect freedom to choose the way that suits each best, well knowing that the ultimate attainment is, and must be, identically the same. There is but one higher power throughout the universe and whoever contacts it today will find it exactly the same as it was two thousand years ago and as it will be two thousand years hence. The divine essence does not change, but man's ideas about it do.

The form of meditation most familiar to Western people is that of religious mysticism. The great saints of Christendom, such as Augustine, Justin, John of the Cross, Teresa, Thomas à Kempis, and George Fox have told how they have risen to wondrous heights of religious ecstasy and glimpsed holy reality by repeatedly contemplating the mental image, life and teachings of their sublime Leader, Jesus Christ, frequently combined with rigidly ascetic self-disciplines. Needless to say, the effectiveness of such a form depends partly upon the possession of a deeply religious temperament and partly upon the intense reverence which wells up during such silent mental worship.

A man may, by intense devotion to God or one of God's

incarnated messengers, actually lift himself through the power of his purified emotion into the same divine experience wherein he, too, can feel his personality melting away into the larger being of the Soul.

In this rational, all-enquiring and rather sceptical age, however, there are large numbers of people who do not feel attracted to such a path. No religious Personage excites their deep reverence or joyous worship, although he may attract their sincere respect. Religion and its sanctions have lost their power to convince and such people often exist in a semi-critical, semi-indifferent spiritual atmosphere. Intellect, rather, receives most of their worship, while the cold figure of Science stands pedestalled in their shrines. One should not blame them. The value placed upon religious dogmas and hollow forms has served to make a sophistry of Truth; it has turned jugglers in theological lore into the masters of mankind.

Who would exchange a visible seat on the Stock Exchange for a problematical seat in Paradise? This is the Age of Doubt, and we might as well admit it. Those who tremble at the sceptical chill which is in the air, are really trembling for their half-held creeds, for their rickety framework of inherited dogmas, and for the smug comfort of a faith which can be honoured without being followed. So let us not be over-pessimistic about the doubting proclivities of our time, but rather thank heaven for their existence, for perhaps we shall now begin to get at the truth of things.

This does not mean that there is not something of real worth in religion. Close all the church doors throughout the world, burn down every mosque, raze the temples to the ground and destroy the synagogues; discredit the origin of every dogma, show the shameful side of the history of every creed, and prove with perfect syllogisms that Moses, Jesus, Muhammad, Krishna and Buddha never existed – still there will rightly exist in the human soul a spiritual hunger which will remain unappeased until the old religions are restored or new ones formulated.

Why?

Because man has not lost, cannot lose his source in the Absolute.

He has lost his *awareness* of it. Religions remind him of this loss. That tremendous awareness must be recovered.

But is there no way whereby these doubting persons may practise meditation and win the mysterious Truth and Peace which it promises us?

Such a way certainly exists.

The Western peoples possess analytic minds; that is the striking characteristic which has forced the writer to conclude that an analytic path alone is today best suited to them. We have analysed everything that is composed of chemical substances; it is time to analyse ourselves. The path which will accord well with this tendency that is so deeply ingrained in modern man must be based on the use of reason.

Furthermore, considered from the point of view of freedom from theological accretions there is a path available which the writer can recommend to those who wish to cut loose from all 'isms and cults. That method is the Path of Introspective Self-Enquiry. It allies the rationality of analysis with the power of meditation. It peels off the constituents of human personality, like the outer skins of an onion, until its true lineament is revealed. It is an ever-open path which leads to the centre of man, and therefore anyone may travel it. The writer has himself practised it and learnt its basis in the mystic East, where he now pens these lines. Quite a number in the East possess a natural genius for meditation, having been fortunate enough to have been trained in the habit since childhood. But the Western temperament does not easily forsake activity for meditation, and so he has been compelled to make considerable revisions, adaptations and additions to the instruction which he has received, in order to pass it on in a form both acceptable and suitable to the people of his own hemisphere.

The method of approach here shown is a psychological and philosophical one, a method particularly chosen so as to accord with the scientific outlook of the modern world. This one practice of self-enquiry stands in a category apart. It is unique because it can be practised by anyone, anywhere and at any time. Almost all other practices bear some denominational label or other, demand forbidding self-disciplines, require a profound faith on the part of those who take them up or need lifetimes of laborious effort and energy of prodigious magnitude. This art of self-enquiry, however, is simple, direct, primarily intellectual and utterly free from any connection with any particular religion or cult. The Muhammadan as well as the Christian may practise it equally well, and not less successfully than the Buddhist; the labourer may likewise take it up no less than the social dilettante. Therefore this art of self-enquiry is the only practice which will be recommended here.

This path is no imaginary way with imaginary result; it offers realizable facts and not chimeras. One will contact the soul by acquaintance, and not merely by hearsay. Its fundamental basis has been known since the days of hoary antiquity. It is true that other ways, short cuts, exist, but such are not for the student working without guidance; they may be revealed only by a competent teacher to the few disciples whose worthiness and fidelity have been tested by time. The grace of such a teacher must be won or earned by intense devotion before initiation can be claimed.

Those who care, then, may take up the path of spiritual self-enquiry, which because of its intellectual basis and because it is entirely free from any bias, has been the only one which the writer has expounded for popular practice for some years. He does not imitate the old orthodox ways of mysticism and yoga, but constructs a simplified and abbreviated technique definitely built up for our own epoch, an epoch wherein the life wholly devoted to meditation is wellnigh impossible and where most people are forced to live in constant activity.

The author realizes that the workaday world of the average European has no time or patience for the long disciplines undertaken by Oriental seekers, nevertheless, he also realizes that there are practices of real worth contained in those disciplines, and they have accordingly been extracted. Few can make meditation a full-time job nowadays, few can give much more than a half-hour daily. The path here presented is for such people, not merely for the dreamers or cranks, but for practical business men, office and factory workers, or professional men, no less than for those monastic-minded ones who are ready to renounce the world.

He has had to think out analytically every step of the way from the normal every-day state of man to interior spiritual attainment, and repeat this again for the gradual return into daily activity. He has sought to write this book scientifically, carefully analysing his sensations at every step of his own practices, watching in himself the changes during the periods of entry into and emergence from mental quiet and the trance state; and studying the process of resuming ordinary activity whilst guarding against the loss of inner stillness.

Whoever accepts these truths and practises this method will liberate his mind from its restlessness, give it peace, train it to look inward, and sharpen its concentrative power. Armed with this equipment, he will be ready, as hinted in the previous chapter, to enter upon a still higher path, the path to Ultimate Reality, Irrefragable Truth. At the very least he will experience a great renewal of soul, a vernal springtide of light, and his life will bloom with unseen asphodel.

It is said of Emerson that a certain person, a mere humble washer-woman who was half-illiterate, was among those that frequently attended his lectures. And when she was questioned how much she understood of the transcendentalist's sublime utterances, she said: "Whatever else it might be that I cannot understand, he tells me this one thing, that I am not a God-forsaken sinner and that I can really be a good woman. He has made me feel that I, too, am worth something in the sight of God, and not a despised creature, as they say."

If these pages could convince the present-day equivalents of this washer-woman in a like manner, to deride the witness of their present degeneration and to prophesy their ultimate arisal into a diviner condition, the writer would be happy indeed.

3

THE ANALYSIS OF THE PHYSICAL SELF

The first fundamental point to be considered before we can usefully proceed further is to make clear to ourselves what is meant exactly by *self*. Unless this is settled we will not have more than a vague notion of what it is that we seek.

We know that we *are*.

We possess this notion of self-existence through an insight which is spontaneous, direct and indisputable, and through the direct experience of every moment of our waking lives. The data of science are less sure than this primal certainty that we exist. We cannot escape from self nor think ourselves out of existence. *Even to doubt our own existence would be to presuppose a doubter.* Even if we made the mind an utter blank, *we* would remain to behold and be aware of the blank, to *witness* this new phase, immediately we returned to the normal state. For we are gifted with the unexplained mystery of consciousness.

From the humblest jumping frog to the highbrow contemplating philosopher, the fact of being alive means the fact of being oneself. Nobody needs to be a philosopher to declare with the French metaphysician Descartes: "I think, therefore I am," or to hold with his German confrère, Immanuel Kant, that the self is a necessity of thought, for everybody naturally assumes his own self-existence as the most unquestionable of facts. Argument and discussion about it seem utterly super-fluous. Behind this foundation fact of self- awareness one cannot go.

But if the existence of the 'I' is the most certain of propo-sitions, its real nature is the least certain. To say, "I am," is mere description, and an easy enough feat; to query: "What am I?" demands *explanation*, and the most difficult of all feats. Let us consider for a while this brief question, *What am I?* The answer, it will be said, is very simple. Name, personal identity, is a sufficient answer.

"I am S—M—," for instance.

But does that suffice? For S— M— is the most variable of creatures. His 'I' does not carry the same significance every time he uses the word. In the morning, when he is bidding good-bye to his child who is leaving for school, *I* means a father; one hour later, when he is bidding good-bye to his wife who is leaving for the shops, *I* means a husband; two hours later, when J— M— visits him, *I* means a brother; three hours later, when he is dictating a trade letter to his secretary, *I* means a business man; and so on.

Then again, changing the standpoint, we feel ourselves to be completely identified with the flesh body when we are eating a meal after having been hungry for some time; one hour later, the flux of experience has changed that notion and we are so absorbed in anger with someone who has deeply offended us, that we feel ourselves to be a bundle of choleric emotions; two hours later we settle down into a comfortable chair and bestow our attention upon reading a serious scien-tific book, concentrating so intently that we identify ourselves for the time with the mind.

There is thus an endless list of possible ways of looking at oneself.

Which of them can justly be singled out and proclaimed as the true *I,* the real self?

How, then, can we get at the precise meaning of the word *self,* the meaning which shall be most valid for all times and all occasions? *The most logical way would be to distinguish that which is a fixed and common factor of all individual human beings, that in every man which does not change but itself perceives all changes of personality, the unique* knower, *but not the multitude of the known, the root-self of all our changing phases of selfhood.* To achieve this purpose we must commence a course of analysis of our conceptions of human personality which shall probe everything in us and stop at nothing.

Is there something in us which remains identical amid all the varied experiences of life? Is there some essential condition of all these experiences which holds the highest value for us? For we feel somehow that the *I* who sees the surrounding environment, who speaks and is spoken to, who thinks and feels, does possess some inner but elusive identity which is not transient and not fluctuating, and which is in some sense our centre.

This, indeed, is expressed by the very word which one applies to oneself, the short word 'I'. That word is unique in the dictionary because it can never be applied to someone else or to some other thing; no man can call another 'I'; it can only be applied to its owner. For it expresses one's innermost, one's profoundest but unconscious realization that the ego is fixed in the depths of one's being.

Let us close our eyes for a while, retreat into the realm of analytic thought, and begin the systematic exploration of the self for a fuller significance.

We shall start our enquiry with that which is most familiar, most obvious and best known – the material body that we wear. When we say 'I' do we mean the physical self? *Am I the body?*

Yes! That is the obvious response which leaps first into the mind, a response which common logic and ordinary experience impulsively dictate. We are all born unconscious materialists because Nature's first travail over us for the first quarter of our lives is primarily and necessarily concerned with the building up of a highly organized separate physical medium through which each man may get into more or less effective touch with the planetary playground which she has prepared for her child, and in which he may gain crystallized experience of himself. Almost all our thoughts – however varying be the affairs with which they are concerned – are ordinarily slipped like beads upon the thread of this single conception: "I am the body!"

Yet objectify the body as though it were a stranger's, and lay it on the mental dissecting-table for dismemberment; examine it piece by piece; it reveals itself only as a combination of bone and flesh, blood and marrow, sense-organs and internal organs. Not one of these *parts* is the self for, obviously, one's consciousness would then be limited to that part.

The principle of human consciousness does not undergo any diminution during the years between birth and death, even when bones are fractured, hands cut off, legs amputated or paralysis holds the entire body in its grip. Nobody feels his 'I am' less under such awful conditions. Even if we identify the self with the brain, we must remember that a blow on the head which blots out all memory of the past – some have lived memoryless for months through such a cause – does not blot out the sense of 'I', which persists no less than before. Even one who is attacked by such a disease as meningitis and becomes an imbecile, will find that his self-consciousness remains the same as before.

Search where one will, nowhere does the self seem to inhere in any individual portion of the body.

Is it discoverable, then, by some curious alchemy, within the body as a whole organism, within the total assemblage of these organs, limbs and parts co-ordinated for investigation? Is it to be found in the totality of the five senses – sight, hearing, touch, taste and smell? Take the case of a man who is deeply preoccupied with some problem. He may be standing just in front of an object or person and yet if he is asked, "Did you see that object?" he may reply, "No, I did not notice it. My mind was elsewhere." This example demonstrates the fact that eyes fail to exercise their function, although they have unimpaired capacity to do so, *when the self is otherwise engaged.* Similarly, one may speak to a man whose mind is absorbed in something that deeply interests him at the moment, and he may not reply. If he is asked, "Did you hear what I said?" he will frankly confess, "No, I was absent-minded." This reveals that the sense of hearing will likewise cease to function, although the physical organ remains perfect, when the attention of the self is not joined with it. The same line of reasoning is applicable to the other three senses. The conclusion is that since both the separate parts and separate senses of the body are not the self, then their totality – the entire body itself, the aggregate of senses and limbs and organs – cannot possibly be the conscious real self.

An interesting illustration and further proof of this point may be cited from the experience of one of the writer's teachers. The latter is an elderly man who makes no pretence to mysterious powers and who lives a perfectly normal life. He possesses, however, a highly developed mentality. Not long ago a large unsightly boil grew upon his right arm, and on consulting a medical friend he was asked to have it removed by a surgical operation. On account of the latter's painful nature and the advanced age of the patient, the surgeon was about to use chloroform as an anaesthetic, but the teacher refused to have it on account of dubious heart action and his advanced age. He quietly told the operator to wait five minutes and then begin to cut the boil away. Next he gazed steadily at his arm and firmly told himself, "This body is not myself," several times. The idea became so powerfully implanted in him that although he continued to look at the boil, *he did not see the surgeon take up his knife and cut the diseased growth nor feel the slightest pain!* Only when the operation was completely finished did he become aware of what had happened, noticing the trickling blood for the first time, and experiencing the first sensations of pain as he resumed his mental identification with the physical body.

During all the time of this analysis one is aware that something *within* this body, which one calls oneself, is conducting the examination. If the self were the totalized body alone, one would have still to explain the following problem:

Who or what is the self which is itself aware of possessing the body?

Does not recognition of owning a body-self imply a second or higher self who is the recognizer? And is not this second self a purely mental one, transcending the flesh entirely? For the real self of man must be the ultimate Subject of all his experiences and from the mental standpoint the body is an Object which we experience and observe.

When we reflect about the physical body, as we are doing now, we unconsciously imply something in the background behind the body, something that is the body's witness and is definitely aware of it. We are the *perceivers*, not our perceptions. The intellectual cognition of ourselves is *entirely different* from and entirely foreign to the physical sensation of possessing a body. Said the great Hindu sage Prabhu: "Know yourself without losing your awareness. . . If the body be yourself, why do you say, 'My body', etc? Everybody speaks of his possessions as 'my clothes, my gold', etc. Tell me if anyone identifies himself with the saying: 'I am the clothes, or I am gold', etc? You are mistaking a superimposition for a fact. Consider the case of a man saying: 'I lose my life.' Is there one life to lose another life? 'Life-breath' is the primary meaning of the word life, whereas self is the secondary meaning. Self is Being-Consciousness. 'I think' or 'my body' signifies association with the faculty of thinking or the body only. The body is alien to you."

Therefore the self is real, from the physical standpoint, but it cannot be identified with a part or the totality of the body, in strict truth.

§

Let us yield a point, however, to those who claim that the body is all in all, and for the sake of analysis assume that this is so, and consider the data furnished by its sleeping state. For we must not remain satisfied with contemplating man in his waking condition only. We must dig deeper for the self, into dream and dreamlessness, as we dig into auriferous earth for gold. Only in totalizing the data of all three states – waking, dream and deep sleep – can full truth of self-consciousness be known.

Here is a creature who, throughout his daily activities, exhibits all the qualities of conscious intelligence and vitality, yet is, according to the materialists, composed of nothing more than chemical substances which, specialized in the brain, give birth to consciousness. Here is a creature who, after the approach of night, finds himself involuntarily plunged into a totally different condition of being – the condition of sleep, when the waking senses are obscured and the body itself lies inert upon its bed, whether of luxurious down or humble straw, with the eyes fast shut, the limbs utterly motionless and only the involuntary bodily functions, such as those of the heart, the digestion and the lungs, continuing to be active. The life principle, the vital force, appears to be reduced to a very low ebb.

What has become of the intelligence which the man manifested in a greater or lesser degree throughout the day? This, too, to the observer seems to be quite inoperative. One may address a question to the sleeper and receive no reply. He does not know anyone, is not aware of any visitor and cannot understand one's questions. He may be approached with a dangerous weapon and one might seek to injure or even to slay him, but still his dormant intelligence is unable to rise to the occasion and save him from the threatened onslaught.

Thus, we have the seemingly strange paradox of a creature who manifests life and intelligence to a substantial degree during the day whilst he is awake, and yet, at night when asleep, seems incapable of physically manifesting these qualities in any conscious manner. Indeed, the conscious self dies nightly to our world in sleep, whereas the physical body continues to live, for the heart beats and the lungs throb. Therefore the latter cannot constitute the permanent real self.

Yet, we must ask ourselves, "In what respect is this sleeping body chemically different from the same body in its working state?" Precisely similar components still form this human shape; the various elements are still present, with only a slight alteration of their proportions. The nitrogen, hydrogen, carbon, etc., which combine to form its flesh have not disappeared, although the *qualities* of conscious intelligence and voluntary activity have all but gone. Why is it that during the waking state this body has the power to enquire into and reason about its own nature and existence, whereas now that power has departed? The only complete answer is that the reasoning mind has departed from the body; the proof of this answer lies in the fact of the dream-state.

The combination of intelligence, thought and feeling and life in a single focus manifests in the physical body as what we usually call the personal ego, the individuality. Yet if during sleep the consciousness of the body, *its physical focus,* disappears, we know that in the dream-state the combination still persists and the sense of personality still endures. The congeries of impressions, memories, feelings, thoughts, desires, fears and hopes which compose the waking individuality also still persist. Moreover, it functions as fully in its mental creation as when it possessed a body, for all the five senses still operate; one sees, hears, smells, touches and tastes in dreams. One's new dream world seems for the time the only actual world, and one never suspects that this is less real than the waking state. One is guided by thought and stirred by desire, as before. One meets friends, enemies and strangers. One flees from fancied perils and enjoys definite satisfaction in these dream-events. One moves, travels and even flies in dreams; one talks, loves and even argues during these vivid visions of the night. Although the physical self is seemingly dead, the conscious self has come into another kind of awareness of its own existence again as a dream-being.

When the physical-world manifestation of this combination disappears, the latter often reappears in the subtler world of dreams. However fantastic many dreams may be, enough are sufficiently rational to show that *this conscious intelligent ego indubitably continues to exist even in its altered form of a dream-personality,* for it possesses the identical group of ideas, impressions and memories which it possessed in the waking state.

We have set up a criterion which declares that the physical world is the only real world, but a dreamer who is dreaming a coherent and sensible dream would be entitled to dispute that statement because to him his activity in the dream world is no less real than our waking activity in the physical body, and because Nature herself is responsible for this rhythmic process of activity and sleep, of waking and dreaming. Dream experiences reflect a real consciousness, no less real than that reflected by waking experiences, however fantastic the dreams themselves be. Thus, and in this connection alone, the test of reality is self-awareness. It cannot therefore be justly said that all other conditions than that of wakeful activity in the physical realm are personal hallucinations, for the phenomena of sleeping and dreaming are purely natural ones, common to the race as a whole and not merely to certain individuals. *Never during sleep does the insentient body declare that it is the 'I'*. Why? Because the *I* is super-physical, i.e. mental, and has left it entirely for a mental world. Thus the ego's real existence is for the mind, and not the flesh.

The body does not exist for a sleeping man, merely because *he,* the mental ego, has vacated it. The contention, therefore, is that the personality still exists and still continues to function in this state of dream, *quite apart from the physical body*. In brief, the personal ego is a thing separate by Nature and independent in expression from its physical instrument.

A simple comparison of the two states will suffice to show that, because the dream-self cannot use a physical body for its travels and to this extent differs from the physical self, there must be a constant unchanging element present in both which enables the waking ego to remember its dream experiences. This substratum must therefore be the real self as compared with the physical body, and of non-physical "substance". Such substance can only be of a mental nature.

The self is *not* the body, but *a conscious entity, that which becomes one with the body when fully plunged into* it – such is the concept which a thinking man might admit to himself, were his mind not bemused by the theories temporarily current at this epoch of planetary history.

If this last statement is untrue, then we have to accept the momentous implication of its disapproval. For, if intelligence could not be separated from the body, if the soul could not hover like a captive balloon over its tenement, if consciousness could not be freed from its fleshly focus, *there could be no such condition as sleep: man could not become unconscious of his physical body and he would be destined throughout the twenty-four hours of the day and night to remain aware of the body in which Nature had so hopelessly involved him.* Even the effort of Nature to repair bodily tissues and wastage at night would have to be done with man as the unfortunate, and perhaps unwilling collaborator, for the boon of rest would be denied to his mind and he would have to remain consciously aware whilst these processes of recuperation continued within the body. *Herein man may perceive the wonderful wisdom and benign mercy of Nature.*

This implication is of such far-reaching importance that the reader must think it out clearly for himself and not allow himself to be hypnotized by the naive and chimerical opinions of an orthodox materialistic view, now becoming old fashioned and out of date in the face of the newer discoveries. It is by such courageous and independent thinking that a man may ultimately effect his own liberation from the bondage of spIritual ignorance.

Sleep and consciousness could never be at war with one another if man were nothing more than the collection of atoms which form his fleshly body. The war arises because *he is not only a body,* but also a force – something far subtler than physical matter.

The fundamental personal self is finer than the physical

body, and bears the light of consciousness into it; otherwise there could be no separation between the two in the state we call sleep.

That is how a spiritual seer would view the subject. However, such a concept does *not* necessarily imply immortality, or even survival of the body after death. It concerns the living body only, and has nothing to say, for or against, the possibility of such a separate consciousness continuing its existence when the death-struck body is no more. That possibility will be considered shortly.

§

One may now examine the afore-going answer from other angles. to see if it still holds true.

There exists a group of abnormal conditions generically called trance. Modern scientists who have investigated the phenomena of hypnotism and psychical research are also familiar with various phases of these conditions. A multitude of cases has been recorded and described in psychological journals and books, most of them resulting from experiments done under strict test regulations. That the condition exists is nowadays indisputable; that in the deeper phase of trance a veritable and nearly complete separation of awareness from the body – occasionally voluntary, but usually involuntary – can be effected is equally indisputable. Those who have not themselves studied along this line and who care to investigate with an open mind the literature existing on the subject will be surprised at the quantity of evidence which has been accumulated during the past hundred years by the vanguard of scientists and doctors who have been courageous enough to investigate the domain of what they curiously term "abnormal psychology".

Men of University training and manifest impartiality,

men like the late F. W. H. Myers who won more honour at Cambridge than any other student of his time there, have conducted an immense number of enquiries and experiments in these obscure regions and in a thoroughly scientific attitude. They have published the results obtained. Whoever is patient enough and has time enough to wade through these volumes *can find evidence aplenty to satisfy him that the consciousness of man is indeed separable from his fleshly body during his lifetime,* even though this separation is mostly only vaguely and flickeringly brought about in the dream state yet clearly and strikingly under unusual conditions, such as the swoon induced by great stress of emotion, and so on.

The names of other researchers into the phenomenon of hypnotic trance, especially, who have persisted despite the fierce incredulity of those who have never troubled to make such investigations, include Dr. James Braid, a Manchester surgeon; the French priest Abbé Faria, who learnt something of this art in India; and the French neurologist, Charcot, who conducted his experiments in the Salpêtrière Hospital, Paris; Dr. Lebault of Nancy and Professor Bernheim, his pupil; the German Doctor Moll, who wrote a good historical summary of the subject as far as it stood in his own time; the late Alexander Erskine of London; and Dr. Esdaile, who was in charge of a Government Hospital at Calcutta and performed three hundred major surgical operations and many thousand minor ones without using an anaesthetic, yet without causing pain to the patients, by mesmerically driving the consciousness out of the body at the time.

Persons hypnotized into profound trance have utterly forgotten their bodies and found themselves present at events occurring at a distance or witnessing far-off scenes or watching people to whom they have been sent; although their own bodies were left far behind, they did not fail to carry with them the full sense of personal but super-physical existence.

There is nothing really new in hypnotic experiments, as they were often practised as far back as the times of the ancient Egyptian priests and the early Chaldean soothsayers. But the experiments of antiquity now possess little evidential value for modernity.

If such researches show anything at all, if their implications may be analysed, they show that the conscious self is not the body simply because in the deepest and hence rarest degree of hypnotic trance both may be split apart and displayed as two separate units. The entire portion of the mind which embraces self-consciousness is thereby rendered autonomous.

Real trance of the third degree is a much rarer phenomenon in hypnotic research than any other and less frequent nowadays in the West than it was during the nineteenth century. In the East it is still produced by a species of self-hypnotism used by yogis and faqueers and African negro "medicine men".

In that condition the hypnotic ('magnetic' or 'mesmeric' were the terms used by earlier researchers) subject entered a state of torpidity arid rigidity which possessed the appearance of death. He became deaf to all sounds and as silent as the grave. The pupils of his eyes were turned upward. When the subject returned to waking consciousness he or she would affirm that complete *physical* unawareness had reigned during the period of entrancement. On the other hand, and more commonly, in the shallower states of trance there would be a transfer of the centre of personality, when the subject would be able to retain some control over the vocal organ and could describe at length scenes or events at a distance, which he declared he was witnessing at the moment, or persons with whom, he asserted, he was then consciously and clearly present. Hence, the hypnotic state in its lighter degrees corresponds to the dreaming condition, whereas in its profoundest degree it corresponds to deep sleep.

A representative case of the lighter kind is related by Erskine. He put a patient of his under hypnotic trance, as a test set by Sir Arthur Conan Doyle. The patient's mind migrated across space into Lady Doyle's flat at Westminster, London, reported her as sitting in a room there and described the room in detail. The report and description were both proved correct! Telepathy does not explain such a case, for Erskine describes another incident where the hypnotized person was able to give a three-hour report of the movements, journeys, actions and conversations of his father, an official of the Portuguese legation. The latter afterwards admitted the complete correctness of the written report. Yet neither hypnotist nor son had any knowledge beforehand of the official's whereabouts or intentions!

The evidence of the separability of mind and body suffices to support the contention that the self is not the body, for it shows that the ego can function in every way as completely in hypnotic trance as in normal existence, save that it is unable to manipulate its physical instrument, the body, owing to the inert condition imposed by hypnosis.

Wherever there is concious intelligence there must be life activating it. We see, too, from these experiments that life accompanies the mind in its dissociation from the physical body awareness, without, however, involving the death of the body, for the exit is but temporary. It is thus clear enough that mind and life may manifest *through* the flesh, as the electric current manifests through the bulb, but are not completely dependent upon it for their own existence; indeed, they are really quite capable of being independent in their functioning, as the normal state of sleep and the abnormal state of hypnotic trance demonstrate.

A further argument – and one more easy to rebut – comes to hand with the results of modern investigation into psychical research and spiritualism. It may appeal to far fewer minds, because the whole mass of testimony is so varied in quality, ranging from astonishing evidence down to nonsensical vapidity and obvious charlatanry. Yet, when the reports of these phenomena are sifted impartially, a certain residue of genuine fact can be discovered which indicates the survival of personality even after the physical body is totally destroyed, as in cremation.

The Society for Psychical Research has collected numerous accounts of apparitions, phantasms of the dead, séances with mediums, and so on, for more than half a century. Sir William Crookes, Sir Oliver Lodge, Professor Hans Driesch and Sir William Barrett – all distinguished scientists – after extensive investigation and using the services of mediums, were forced to conclude in favour of the spiritual hypothesis that the dead do survive and may even be communicated with under certain circumstances. One medium whose services were much used by Sir Oliver Lodge was the late Alfred Vout Peters, who happened to be a friend of the present writer. Peters was born with most rare and remarkable gifts; he could not only plainly see the "dead", but also converse with them and obtain messages from them for the bereaved. He spent a good deal of life travelling throughout Europe, giving proofs and evidences of the reality of survival to numerous famous persons, including, as he once jokingly remarked, "half the crowned heads of Europe!"

A single instance of his powers for which Mr. Wallis Mansford, Secretary of The London Institution, bears public testimony, will suffice. Mr. Vout Peters, in 1922, gave the following message to Mr. Mansford: "With you is the spirit of a young man of extraordinary physical beauty, clear-cut features, thick hair, intellectually brilliant, strong magnetic personality. I see him in a beautiful garden, wearing a flannel suit. He had had a mannerism of sitting in the chair with the arms folded and facing the back. Have you not a photograph of him in your home in this position? The spirit with you is one who died abroad during the War fairly young. The climate is warm and in the closing hours he suffered from thirst. An anniversary associated with him is very near."

Mr. Mansford replied that he had no such photograph, but on reaching home he searched among his papers and then discovered a picture of Rupert Brooke, the famous soldier-poet. The latter was depicted sitting in a garden in exactly the posture mentioned by the medium. Mr. Mansford was greatly interested in and attracted by Brooke, and it was the latter's mother who had given him the photograph. As for the descriptive part of the message, everyone knows that it fits the poet's physical appearance perfectly, while regarding the truth of the final words, it might be mentioned that Brooke died on a hospital ship in the Mediterranean, his birthday anniversary having occurred only five days before Peters spoke about him.

The existence of such men as Peters, few though they be amid the host of self-deluded or deluding persons who take shelter under the genuine fact of mediumship's existence, is a reminder of primitive faculties discarded and lost through the right and inevitable evolution of mankind's intellectual and physical faculties.

Those who do not keep their minds static know that the whole field of hypnotic and psychical research has now begun to assume some degree of respectability even in the most academic circles. Half a dozen universities in different countries have announced courses in psychical research, whilst Dr. J. B. Rhine has been carrying out laboratory investigations at the

Duke University in America into extra-sensory perception to a point where the reality of telepathy and clairvoyance has been established in a manner which definitely brings it within the scope of approved experimental science. Indeed, Professor William McDougall, the distinguished American whose researches into abnormal psychology are well known, has not hesitated to claim that Dr. Rhine's work has given biological materialism its heaviest blow.

Hundreds of other authenticated cases exist in recorded form for those who care to investigate the literature. These researches show that a non-material world exists in which the conscious self or spirit of man can function intelligently quite independently of its body and even when the latter lies in the grave.

There are many whose minds have a rooted objection to considering the themes of psychical research or spiritualism. They are partly justified by the obvious humbug which seems inseparably allied to the real and the genuine in this realm. If they are religious, then the black bogy of devils hides behind these experiments; if they are scientifically minded, then the whole thing is charlatanry. In short, the subject itself being unacceptable, all evidence connected with it is deemed totally inadmissible. However, even such people can take up the query, "What am I?" in its relation to the body without resort to study of the literature of spirit-intercourse. For there exists a curious line of testimony whose facts are beyond dispute and whose implications are clear. On different occasions and in different places in Asia and Africa the writer has encountered yogis and faqueers who could exhibit the exceptional power of suspending the breath and stopping the heart and blood circulation, and who could even emerge alive after being 'buried' for some hours or days in an airless coffin or below ground. He has carefully examined their feats in order to sift the impostors from the genuine owners of such exceptional powers. He is completely satisfied that these powers truly exist. Yet he does not wish to put forward such personal evidence in this connection; although one of these yogis was lately buried in a sealed cemented stone tomb for no less than forty days, independent and less disputable testimony exists – all dated as recently as 1936.

The first is a cutting from a reliable Indian newspaper, *The Madras Mail,* British owned and edited by an Englishman with a lifetime's experience in sound journalism:

"BURIED ALIVE FOR THIRTY MINUTES
YOGI'S FEAT WITNESSED BY 15,000 PEOPLE

MASULIPATAM, Dec.15 (1936)

A remarkable feat of Yoga was exhibited by Yogi Sankara Narayanaswami of Mysore on Sunday evening in front of Sri Ramalingeswaraswami's Temple in the presence of a gathering of about 15,000 people. He was buried alive for about half an hour.

Lt.-Col. K. V. Ramana Rao, I.M.S., District Medical Officer, who acted as observer, took a letter from the Yogi before the ordeal, stating that he was performing the feat on his own responsibility.

The Yogi was seated in a box specially prepared for the purpose and let down into a pit, which was covered with earth. After about half an hour, the box was removed, when the Yogi was found sitting in it in a state of trance. The Yogi regained consciousness half an hour afterwards, when he was cheered by the people."

The second comes from a friend, Major F. Yeats-Brown, who served for twenty years in the Bengal Lancers, an Indian Cavalry Regiment. He published these statements in the

London *Sunday Express:*

"Resurrection of the 'dead' is a fairly common exercise in Indian magic. I have seen it done twice. The adept undergoes twenty-four hours of secret preparation, which consists in purgation, fasting, and 'swallowing' air.

Before the trance state is induced, the adept is in a state of oxygen intoxication. Then, pressing his carotid arteries, he passes into unconsciousness.

His disciples bury him.

On one of the occasions when I was present, the adept remained thus for an hour, on the other occasion he remained in the death-trance for only fifteen minutes.

Doctors who examined the 'corpse' stated that there was no sign of life. When the given time had elapsed, the adept came to life.

It is not an experiment fit for public view, the rigid body unstiffens, the set lips relax, and from them issues a groan that none who have heard it can forget."

The third is from the *Sunday Times* of Madras, February, 1936. It runs as follows:

"CONTROLLING HEART AND PULSE
A YOGI'S STRANGE FEAT

In the presence of Col. Harty, Civil Surgeon of Ahmedabad and several other doctors, a Yogi named Swami Vidyalankar performed the strange feat of controlling his heart and pulse for a pretty long time. He suddenly stopped his heart and pulse, while squatting on the floor with eyes closed. During the period his heart was auscultated and an electro cardiogram was taken. The tests showed that he had complete control over those organs.

He also showed several other feats, including that of remaining buried in a pit for *25* hours."

The evidential value of this last case lies in its occurrence in the presence of an educated Englishman, who happened to be both an Army man and a *qualified surgeon.* That rigid test conditions were therefore imposed one may be sure.

Anyone having the time to probe more deeply and willing to spare the trouble of searching for records of these cases over a number of years may be sure of reaping a remarkable harvest, despite the fact that the writer is well aware that several yogis, although possessing miraculous powers, escape all publicity because they avoid cities.

What is the final implication of such cases?

Is it not that the bodily life-breath is not the real self? Do they not offer clinching proof that although *physical* vitality may be suspended and breathing brought to a cessation, still the personal existence, the 'I', can re-manifest after a while with undiminished and undamaged self-existence?

Is it not that the body may become a literal corpse without impairing the survival of the individual personality?

Is it not that the life forces, which have been lending the body its vigour of movement and activity throughout the day, are not necessarily the product of bodily tissue and muscle? Their relation to the body may simply be, as in the illustration used earlier in this chapter, that of the electric current to the lamp.

Is it not that the *I*-awareness subsists throughout life, whereas the body-awareness has only been a content of this deeper consciousness? Had the latter been associated with the body as a permanent property of it, then it could not have become dissociated at any time. For example, heat is a property of fire. Wherever we find fire, heat is invariably associated with it. We cannot imagine such a phenomenon as cold fire. In the same way, had the self been a function of the bodily organism it could never have been dissociated from it as in deep sleep, hypnotic trance and faqueers' burials. In other words, the *real man himself,* the soul, if one wishes to call it such, is emphatically not his body. The self cannot be seen by any material microscope.

We do not realize that the moment we withdraw self-awareness from the brain it is nothing more than a piece of inert matter, like the meat in a butcher's shop. Without that self-presence it could not produce a single thought, it could not formulate any idea, whether of itself or its surroundings, whether of abstract qualities or of things material.

The materialists who contend that intelligence and life are products of physical organs are entitled to hold such views, but because they cannot create either intelligence or life in their laboratories, there is no reason why their theories should be held as being more firmly established than those of the seers and the sages who hold the reverse to be true, that is, that the current of intelligence and life inhabit the body and is not created by it. Moreover, these seers, these sages, claim to have discovered the proof of their statements in the only way such proof can really be obtained; by actually separating these two qualities – or, in other words, the personal ego – from the physical body. They have done so, according to their testimony, throughout the ages. Therefore such theories as involve the assumption of the existence of a spiritual and non-physical element superior to all chemical elements are at least worthy of investigation. Nay, they are worthier because they offer the proof to whoever will fulfil the precedent conditions and then faithfully and patiently work within himself for it, whereas no materialist, no scientist can offer a contrary proof other than a purely theoretical one.

Until such time as a scientist can create a human being

and thus demonstrate the truth of materialistic theories, the explanation which is here offered, that of an immaterial Overself to which the physical body is subordinate, and of which it is an outgrowth, of a state of enduring Consciousness against the background of which physical sensations reveal themselves in an independent existence of their own during the lifetime of the body but no longer, is just as much entitled to the respect of intelligent persons as any other of the plausible theories put forward up to now. Moreover, this theory *does* claim most unhesitatingly that its proof is at hand, within every man's own mind and heart, and that, by faithful practice of the method to be unfolded here, he may assure himself of its truth.

Why, then, should we fear to desert the common materialistic view which seeks to pin down the individuality of man to the familiar physical world alone? Why should we not accept the visible signs and hints which both Nature and experiment provide, that the flesh is but a house and not the whole of man? Whoever will have the courage and patience to let his mind think along such channels, untrammelled by conventional ideology, will ultimately be rewarded by the discovery of the eternal truth about man. To rest content with current scientific and philosophical theories which may and will be completely changed within a couple of decades or proved by the next generation to be either incomplete or erroneous, is to exhibit inertia and cowardice in one's mental life. Truth is not for the slothful or the timid.

§

Am I the body?

One must now turn to the last and loftiest consideration of this question. All the previously given arguments and answers may indeed be dropped, for one may ascend to the domain of pure thought, from physics to metaphysics, where a single true concept suffices to dispel the illusion that the self habitates in the body and nowhere else. That the latter idea cannot be correct is marvellously exemplified by the state of deep dreamless slumber or even of unconsciousness (fainting, blank trance and swoon), for then the self vanishes utterly from the body. To every man in this state the insentient physical body is fully eclipsed and forgotten – to be *rediscovered* only when he returns, awakes and remembers.

The mistake of Western philosophers lies in their lack of coordination of the three states of waking, dream and dreamless slumber for their investigation into the truth of self-consciousness. Partial data can only yield partial results. A totality of data can alone yield perfect truth. Psycho-analysis, however, has begun to step forward in the right direction by its enquiry into the source and meaning of dreams, although the results of that enquiry are still a matter of strong dispute.

Life exists in the embryonic stage before one can say 'I'. The mental condition of the embryo is exactly like that of the adult person in deep slumber. In the latter condition every part of the physical body remains intact yet the 'I' has disappeared, the sense of personal being is no more and all awareness has ceased, even though we know that self-consciousness will surely return again with the dawn and that the disappearance is only temporary. We perceive that the conscious intelligence which manifested through the ego must nevertheless mysteriously exist and will return intact and unchanged.

The entire personality, with all its gathered memories of joy and sorrow, its accumulation of intellectual knowledge, its egoistic consciousness, is absent in deep sleep. The ego has vanished completely from the physical body, as at death: it has not even the form of a dream-body. That is the essential point to place before oneself now. Not the slightest trace of self-consciousness remains anywhere in the body or the mind. Self has separated from the flesh in its own mysterious way. Deep sleep thus reveals that the body is no absolutely necessary basic for the existence of man's personal self.

Herein lies the final proof – necessarily metaphysical for we have crossed the boundary of physics and passed even beyond the borderland of spirits and the region of dreamselves – *that the soul, the profound essence of selfhood, the subtlest of the subtle, abstracts itself from the body and returns in deep sleep to its high home in a non-material world of being,* a world so subtle that it escapes the network of nerves flung across our bodies.

The answer to our quest is, therefore, that 'I' am something apart and different from the flesh.

The body is not the self.

What, then, is the body?

It becomes, obviously, an instrument whereby one cognizes the objective world, a world entirely different from the inner world of selfhood with which we are one. We feel this external world to be entirely apart from us. The sensations which register themselves on our minds are our sole links with the objective world. Or, as Bertrand Russell is compelled to confess: "What the physiologist sees when he examines a brain is in the physiologist, not in the brain he is examining."

The philosophical scientist can dismiss the vivid redness of a red external object because he knows that its colour is really in the mind. Similarly, we can intellectually dismiss the external body from our sense of selfhood because we now know that the latter is really to be sought for within the mind's and heart's depths, as there is nowhere else where we may search for it. And it is about the only thing in the world whose real existence is indubitable.

Other thoughts of a like nature will occur to one's mind when engaged in this novel form of spiritual self-analysis and one may pursue them all to their logical conclusion and apprehend the real fact in its integrity, i.e., although we persuade ourselves by habit that we are the body, self-examination shows that this is not true. Advanced thinking draws the sense of 'I' inward and proves that the self is a real entity distinct from the flesh, and that by oneself is really meant something more than the bodily appearance. Both modern discoveries and ancient tenets conspire to confirm this truth.

How, then, do we derive the opposite sense and how is it that the generality of men think otherwise and repudiate this truth? How is it that almost everyone customarily but falsely identifies himself with his physical frame? The answer is now clear. The real 'I' has permitted part of itself to associate with the body and vivify it, and therefore the sense of 'I' quite naturally continues within the body.

The truth is always attainable by the wonderful power of reflection, only we need to bring the latter to bear upon it in a special way.

For all these reasons – and these alone – our souls press against their prison bars of flesh and cause us unutterable yearnings and indefinable longings. For none of us really cares to be doomed to fatten crawling maggots or to become mere dust. Nor shall we, for we are not transient flesh.

4

THE ANALYSIS OF THE EMOTIONAL SELF

Having placed ourselves under cross-examination and searched man's temporary tabernacle of flesh for his ego, for the root of his personality, we have found that the body is used by the self merely as a temporary tenement. It must be something that is intrinsically immaterial. We ought now to turn the conscious process back upon self and see whether this invisible visitant can be found within that other large component of the structure of man – motion. We need to put to ourselves once again the question of what we are.

Strictly speaking, emotions cannot be entirely separated from thoughts. Both arise from a common root – the mind in its larger sense. The distinction between them in ordinary life is really due to their ever-varying predominance, but both are invariably present. The emotions could not exist apart from their setting in thoughts. For the purpose of precise psychological enquiry, however, we may treat them as separate.

Am I emotion? Am I the loves, angers, desires, passions, fears and joys which frequently move me? Such is the further question one must ask oneself as one pushes into the recesses of one's own ego and watches its workings.

Emotions of every kind possess us at different times –

from the heavenly to the demonic. Muradali, the Indian Court Musician to an Emperor of Delhi, wrote the following song as unconscious spokesman of Everyman:

> "O King, for you I go from door to door,
> Song's mendicant, me desolation sore
> Greets as a shadow on either hand, O gone
> The glories, and the palace floors upon
> Animals prowl. But who can take away
> The wild, wild beasts that on my lone heart prey?"

We are swayed alternately by a whole catalogue of emotional changes. Most striking, indeed, is the comparison between a man's body and his emotional states. After all, his body remains fairly stable and rigid whereas his excitements, desires and passions are in a constant state of flux. The body changes its appearance but slowly from year to year, whereas a man's emotions may, and often do, change quickly from hour to hour. This instability of emotion, this rapid fluctuation of mood, is the birthmark of man's emotional nature. The ancient seers compared its ebb and flow with that of the element of water, whilst they compared the fixity of his body.

One is joyous and hopeful today, but unhappy and fearful tomorrow. One is ever the victim of this emotional flux, which moves hither and thither with that of the element of earth. The comparisons are both true and apt, with the attractions and repulsions which bodily experience and mental activity generate.

The outbursts of sudden anger and the uprushes of sexual lust may make one commit actions which later bring remorse, and therefore the feeling that those actions do not represent, but rather misrepresent, one's true self.

Even the general mass of one's personal nature tends to

change over broad periods of time, so that the person of twenty years hence may well be someone who would shrink with shame from the suggestions which now make pleasant appeal.

The fears which afflict one today may disappear in the course of some days or months, perhaps never to return, but one knows that the sense of selfhood, of 'I', will not disappear. It alone is the enduring reality of our lives.

Amid these changes, sometimes bewildering, is there one stable emotion which can be grasped and of which one can assert: "This am I?" One may range through the whole gamut of human emotions, through love and hate, jealousy and fear, timidity and courage, sadness and ecstasy, but not one single emotion can be seized upon of which it would be accurate to declare: "That is myself!" For one is indeed a composite creature emotionally just as one is a composite creature physically. One experiences these transient agitations and feelings, but not of any can it be said: "This is the unchanging self." What one may say, however, with correctness is "The ego *experiences* hate, love and jealousy." One may perceive at different times the tiger, the parrot and the ape within oneself, and at other times the angel and the saint, but as long as these variations are but variations of emotion they are not the 'I-ness', that is the basic self.

When one represses a passion, what represses it? The deeper sense which represses it is thus implied. Moreover, the mere fact that one says, "I feel this" or "My anger – " instead of "My emotions feel this" or "My emotions are angry," indicates immediately that the 'I' is naturally characterized as something separate from ordinary feelings: it implies it to be that which undergoes the experience of such feeling. This cannot be otherwise; for if a man *is* any particular emotion, or even set of emotions, *and nothing more;* if he derives his notion of selfhood from the particular noble urge or ignoble impulse which happens to move him at the moment; if the fluctuating feelings are his root nature, he would alter his mode of speech accordingly and not refer to it in the *possessive sense*. The feelings, therefore, are mine, but not *me*.

I am happy, I am miserable, ignorant, worn out, I see, this is mine—these and other such ideas are superimposed upon the 'I'. The notion of self persists in all this, because no such idea can ever be conceived of without the notion of the ego upon which it is superimposed.

Wherever he uses such phrases as the afore-mentioned ones, *man unconsciously pronounces the truth that the ego is really independent of his emotional nature* and remains as its background.

The fact of my awareness of emotions does not mean that they constitute my self. The existence of someone who feels is one thing whilst his self-awareness is quite another. This difference is of great importance and needs to be properly discriminated. Emotions which come and go cannot be the continuous self. That the latter *must be constant and everpresent* is indicated by the fact that doubts of one's own existence never arise. If it were not always present, one might sometimes doubt such existence.

Thus, behind all these changing moods there remains the unchanging feeling 'I'. It is the only static thing among them. This feeling of selfhood inheres within man so strongly, persists so deeply at the very centre of his being, that he is forced to admit that of all feelings this is the only lasting one. His moods come and go, but, ordinarily in the waking state, the mood of selfhood never goes. All emotions, in the end, are but surface agitations on this ocean of 'I am'.

Here one may find confirmation in another quarter. In the deepest slumber we never feel angry, lustful, joyous, etc.

Hope and hate, along with the whole brood of emotions, vanish when one enters this condition. All personal emotions disappear as though they had never been. One loves nothing, hates nothing, desires nothing. Were the emotions one's real self, they would subsist continuously: they would necessarily be felt throughout the deep sleep state and could never be blotted out from consciousness. So long as life exists without a break, we know that self must exist, without a break, too. The dissociation of emotion and selfhood in deep sleep proves that they are separate by nature.

Thus the emotions which are produced in me are inconceivable without the existence of myself to feel them, of a subject to whom these emotions are objects. I have these emotions, but even if I were to banish them, as in trance, faint and deep sleep, I still continue self-existence. Therefore the true beginning of my life is not emotion but my mysterious elusive and still deeper self, the *witness* of my anger, love, fear and hope. The idea of a continuous underlying self is essential to, and implied in, every emotional mood, the emotions are strung on that self like pearls on a string.

Another way in which this result can be comprehended is to compare the pictures projected on a white cinema screen with constant flickering of various emotions, the white screen being the 'I' which is aware of them. The real ego is emotionless.

More observations might be added here, but it is unnecessary to repeat in full analyses which have already been applied to the physical self and which may also be applied to the emotional self; they require mere back reference.

Such metaphysical thoughts enable us to pierce to the true root of the matter, and show that the emotional states – whatever else they may be as alternating phases of experience *within* the self – are not themselves, either individually or in totality, the real being of a man. The conviction which every man possesses of his personal identity may continue even without the existence of emotion to strengthen it. His identity would thus remain a perfect one, despite the loss of all emotion, because its reality could not admit of any degrees and could not be divided into parts.

This is an argument, yet is also something far more than that. It is an attempt to put the reader's mind upon a trail of accurate analysis which will induce within him a change of attitude as regards his own self-understanding. It is an effort to make him more clearly conscious of what is going on inside himself, in his heart and mind. When such reflections frequently pass through his mind in a series of definite and consecutive thoughts guided by the lofty faculty of reason and grasped in a spirit of searching enquiry, they become intellectual instruments for the attainment of genuine self-understanding. Such is the remarkable power of *deep* reflection, when properly pursued and regularly undertaken, that it can not only turn a man's outlook into new directions, but what is more, it can turn him from a false outlook to a truer one. Although we have seen that man, analytically viewed, is not, indeed, a creature rooted in emotion ultimately, but in something deeper, nevertheless for all practical purposes we generally behave as though the reverse were the truth. We take our emotions for our true selves and are first swamped and then swept hither and thither by the alternating ebb and flow of their waters. We permit ourselves to inhere within these feelings, these sympathies and antipathies, that daily visit us, and thus we come to regard them, at least as far as our ordinary everyday life is concerned, as ourselves, and unthinkingly accept them as criterions of life's deeper values. Such thinking as is here attempted thrusts the dagger of truth into our complacent illusions.

§

Seated comfortably, shutting out those sensations and impressions of one's immediate surroundings which normally engage one's mind throughout the day, one sets oneself to explore the inner nature moment by slow-slipping moment in the quest of self-understanding. This is the best yoga. And if, so far, the results are on the negative side, inasmuch as, by a process of elimination which has left out of psychological counting first the five senses, then the bodily organs and functions, and finally the body itself as well as the entire range of emotional experiences, one has only discovered what the self is *not,* even that is a preparation of immense value, for it has removed distorted or false notions of what it is. By eliminating the untrue, that which will eventually survive will be the true.

The question will be asked, "Is this intellectual self-analysis to be repeated day after day in precisely the same form?" The answer is, "By no means !" The student should not make every day's meditative analysis a mere duplicate of that which went before; he should above all strive to be creative and original in his arguments, to contribute new points of view to the process of self-examination which he is conducting.

The method of introspective self-analysis presented here is merely intended to provide the reader with a broad basis for his own individual thinking. He must expand and enlarge it according to his temperament, knowledge and education, and travel slowly and carefully by himself upon his own feet. Here, he is given direction only; let him move forward in the fullest independence of thought, becoming a creator on his own account. Therefore, it is not necessary to go on repeating the same old arguments again and again when the student feels that he has worn them threadbare. On the other hand, unless he has penetrated into their fullest meaning and inward content, his attempt to go forward too prematurely will frustrate itself and eventually end in failure.

If the student will therefore bear these cautions in mind he may proceed during his reading and thinking to question himself, to analyse his personal structure by clearly formulated thoughts which should be slowly shaped in order to give them their precise significance and due weight. And then these thoughts should be linked together in a chain of reasoning of the strictest logic.

It would be absurd for the reader to follow blindly this intellectual formula of self-analysis. What is here given should give an impetus to his own thinking and evoke for him an atmosphere of a special kind. Apart from this he should also try to work out his own individual line of analytic thought.

The method and argument presented here and in the earlier book, *The Secret Path,* are suggestive only. They are not to be blindly imitated, but are merely intended to give a direction to the aspirant's own efforts and to open new vistas of thought for him. His reading must be made the subject of an inner experience, with its concomitant high tensions and relieved releases. He must think out these points for himself; he must thresh and re-thresh the problem of his ego until his own mental dissection makes its structure clearer and closer to him. He must attempt to originate new arguments of his own to expand and enrich the themes by his own creative contribution and not merely limit himself to them. He must look back into his own everyday human experience and endeavour to draw from it such lessons and such explanations as will assist him in his purpose of self-understanding.

For the object of all this thinking is to awaken within him a mood of soul, a mental atmosphere and even an emotional condition of aspiration towards Truth which will provide an appropriate stage for the entry of illumination. Hence the futility of mere parrot-like repetition of what one has read or heard. The student must make a real effort to think deeply, to press with sharpened intellect into the very heart of his own nature as a human being and to take the arguments and facts of others merely as lamps by the wayside. *He is the traveller and he must do the moving.*

His endeavour is, therefore, to think his way through the problem of self and to arrive at the hidden basis of his being. He has to become a detached observer of his own nature, to see his own personality stand before him almost as though it were a stranger, and thus form a correct estimate of himself. How is this possible if he does not attempt to break away from the settled convictions of everyday life, with their unphilo-sophical and fundamentally unspiritual basis? Without such independent thinking how can he hope ever to become prop-erly convinced of the truth that the body is but a house for the ego, or discover later that the ego is but a drop in the ocean of the Overself?

The student need not limit his mental quest to the minutes when he is seated in his quiet room. He may also profit by those odd moments during the day when one fre-quently finds oneself at leisure either when travelling, in the office, in the factory or the home; at such times also he may call to his mind some echoes of the inner quest. He need then not merely take up the line of argument as to the abode of the self, but rather adopt a purely questioning attitude; it is as though he should suddenly say to himself, "Who is this being who walks in this body or thinks in this mind?" But he should then cease to trouble for a response, slowly dismissing the question from consciousness without waiting to obtain an answer. Everything will later be brought about by the subconscious mind in its own time.

Such an occasional and fitful practice is very simple yet

very helpful. Its potency lies in its reference for a reply to the *x*-factor of our nature. The more the student turns his attention towards his own subjective processes and habitually brings himself to seek this factor, this unknown mysterious Overself, and to verify its existence, the more quickly is he likely to get into contact with it. The form of this question may be varied, but its basis should always be the same, that is, a turning inward in self-enquiry.

5

THE ANALYSIS OF THE
INTELLECTUAL SELF

Dissection of the body and the emotional nature has yielded no ultimate trace of oneself. Man, dissolved of his flesh, becomes mind. Therefore, one must now track the ego still further, struggling to discriminate between it and the veils that cover the real 'I' consciousness, rendering the mind analytically *self-aware* and observable to introspection; thus turning to the last great division of man's nature, his intellect. There exists a relation between mind and its contents which must now be unveiled.

First of all, it must be made clear that the word intellect is here used only to signify the assemblage of thoughts, ideas, notions, impressions and mental sensations which pass through consciousness. It is not here used to indicate the far higher faculty of the discriminative selective *reason*, of that which evaluates thoughts and acts as the arbiter to judge between them and their truth.

What am I? Am I the thinking intellect? Properly used, this question may be solved by turning reflection in upon itself; for thus it becomes in time one's password to salvation, because in thought we move closer to the stuff of reality, and not farther.

Almost all the arguments which were used in the case of the body and the feelings may equally be applied here.

Very important is that reflection which points out the natural, automatic and instinctive use of the possessive sense when referring to one's mind. Thus one never says, "My brain thinks so and so," or "My brain is going on a railway journey to Los Angeles," but on the contrary right instinct compels one to say, *"I* think so and so," or *"I* am going on a railway journey to Los Angeles." When one philosophically observes *why* one uses these forms of expression, one perceives that it is the consciousness of a living interior self – which is intrinsically independent of the brain and therefore immaterial – that dictates them as logical necessities. The thorough perception of this point reveals the reality of the so-called Unconscious and assists to raise it up into the consciousness.

Thoughts spread their wings and fluctuate still more widely and more frequently than feelings, revealing no continuous self in their changeability. Whether one's thoughts arise from objective sources and are based on data transmitted through the senses, or whether they arise from the well-spring of subjective and ultimately unconsciousness sources, they fall under the same law of transiency as dominates the emotions, and hence reveal no continuous selfhood throughout.

Moreover, under the changing influence of external environment one's intellectual capacity differs from time to time during the day, and the opinions held this year may be opposed the next. No thoughts can be guaranteed permanent. Only the thought 'I' will always remain.

The same quality of constant alternation which we found in the emotions is thus equally apparent in the intellect. Indeed, the quicksilver-like mobility of these changes is so rapid and so continuous that no single set of thoughts could ever represent a man. And this weaving and inter-weaving of intellect goes on automatically. Ideas, concepts, percepts, fancies and memories whirl constantly around like revolving wheels inside the chamber of the brain, that wonderful object contained in the apex of the cranium. Thus one's thoughts merely succeed each other and have no continued existence, whereas the self to which they belong is *constant* and maintains the same relation to all these changing thoughts throughout.

Then again one says of oneself, "I think!" thus unconsciously making the declaration that there is someone who exists apart from the operation and who directs the train of thought. Nature, the reality embedded in oneself, thus makes the affirmation that intellect is a mere tool or instrument employed by the Thinker 'I' who is behind it. One feels vaguely aware of a consciousness creating and dismissing, accepting and rejecting, the endless sequence of thoughts, ideas and memories. The experience cannot be a delusion.

There is a certainty about the famous phrase of Descartes, "I think, therefore I am!" which makes it one of the indisputable facts of life. Thought involves the assumption of a thinker.

The world of external objects is something which presents itself to consciousness without any effort on one's part; it is something given. But the world of thought demands one's active presence, co-operation and effort. And as the physical body must be counted among these objects it is clear that it falls under the same head of immediately observed things. The movement of the thought-process is, however, normally unobserved yet it could not continue if one did not play a part in its production. As soon as one makes the necessary inner exertion and stops to reflect on the matter, consciously objectifying this movement in the same way that one has objectified the body, one begins to insert oneself into that deeper element which is the originator of thought, and which proclaims the other-ness of the latter. For all thoughts come to life *within* self-consciousness and cannot arise before that. They are objectified manifestations of it. And thus cognizing that the mind is a thing apart, one proves theoretically the self's separate existence. But such reflections and investigations are exceptional; our lives are too full of personal and external distractions to permit of our becoming *truly self-aware;* and hence one's habitual inability to distinguish self from the activity of thinking and to gain a real insight into one's being.

There is next the already-used but clinching argument that in deep dreamless slumber, in blank swoon and profound coma, as well as in the faqueer's self-induced trance, thinking as an activity totally expires. It is indeed absolutely annihilated for the time. The intellect ceases to function and enters into a condition of blank non-entity. Yet we dare not say that the self has also been annihilated, for its life-current still continues to function within the physical body. Were one identical with this aggregate of thoughts then utter extinction in this way would not be possible without extinguishing the sense of selfhood for ever, yet on awakening the 'I' reappears as the *first* thought. Whence did the mind pick up again this ego-sense which had died during the night? Quite clearly, the latter must have existed latently all the time. (This is the evaluation of experience from the platform of *waking* consciousness only, and not from that of the *totality* of the three states – waking, dream and deep sleep.) *Hence one arrives at the conclusion that the self never really disappears even when all thoughts totally disappear.* Hence, too, both body and intellect exist *within* the self. In short, the answer to our question is: I am not thought but above it! I am something that thinks. Hence the very consciousness which thinks is itself the self-supreme, real, independent and autonomous.

Can the intellect really penetrate into regions hitherto

closed to it? Can it assist one to enter the ultimate and fundamental consciousness? Does it conceal an unknown potency of
perception? No problem is so obscure but that the light of persistent concentration upon it cannot ultimately illuminate it or
find some way to dissolve it altogether. The problem of man's
self can also yield to persistent concentration of the mind upon
it – and does yield. It has already been said that this path begins
with an intellectual search directed within, with the use of a
sharpened but self-absorbed intellect. Such analytical reflections as the foregoing not only provide genuine evidence of the
spiritual nature of the ego, but indeed offer a way which shall
conduct the reflective mind to the realization of its hidden
reality.

One should first appreciate correctly the place of intellect
in one's nature; it is the tool of the self, the means whereby it
enters into touch with the material world. The eye could not
see unless the mind were behind it to act as the seeing agent.
Similarly, the intellect could not function unless the living
principle of the self were behind it to vitalize its functioning.
Intellect is the lower phase and reason is the higher phase of
one and the same mind. Mind-stuff is really a medium, the
intermediate link between self and the material body, and thus
through the latter with the material world.

*It is this central position between both spheres which consti-
tutes its importance and shows the value of obtaining complete
control over it.* Without the mind-stuff one could never become
aware of one's external surroundings for then one's body
would be like an inert, unconscious corpse with none of the
five senses functioning.

If, therefore, the power of the spiritually-attracted intellect to lead a man towards truth is praised here, it should be
understood that what is meant is that it can lead him in the
right direction towards truth until he reaches its own borders.

Thinking of this kind will not run round in a vicious circle but will really assist the student to arrive at the frontiers of Overself, as the constant rubbing of a rope against the stone parapet of a well eventually grooves the stone. It demands a well-trained and vigorous mind to grasp such truths. Mental adolescents cannot do so, but there are easier religious paths for them.

The mind as we ordinarily know it, that is to say the mind which deals with the routine of common daily existence, which enables us to calculate, organize, arrange, describe, work in an office or make something at the bench, read newspapers and express our opinions, or even analyse chemical compounds, can handle such everyday affairs more or less efficiently, but gets out of its depth when it attempts to handle problems which are far beyond its scope. Owing to its innate arrogance and pride, however, it will not admit this limitation, but delivers itself of judgments upon spiritual and psychical (i.e. super-ordinary) problems which are entirely baseless and worthless. Were it sufficiently humble it would realize that some uncommon degree of mental activity is required to match the consideration of such transcendental problems, and it would first set out to find or develop that qualification before it dared to deliver such judgments. Such a qualification calls for a courageous use of reason, a refusal to stop at any point short of ultimate truth, and a determination to proceed along the line of unfamiliar thoughts as far as their most unfamiliar conclusions. More than this, it demands a freedom from personal preconception and from worldly attachment which is uncommon. And lastly, it implies a concentrativeness and sharpening of the intellect to razor-edge fineness, so that it shall be competent to deal with the subtlest abstractions. The value of *ordinary* yoga techniques is that they help one to develop part of these qualities: they foster impersonality, mental serenity, enduring concentration of thought and the ability to keep away all extraneous ideas and emotions and distractions so that the truth about the subject meditated upon may become clear. But such techniques do not develop a shrewder and sharper reason nor the power of prolonged analytical reflection, and here a scientific, mathematical or philosophical training becomes of the utmost value. It is in the joining of mind-stilling and mind-sharpening methods that the right qualities for the discovery of truth become unfolded. Each is incomplete without the other, and therefore can lead only to partial truth. The system presented here aims at combining both.

Thus by a process of peeling off and detaching, as it were, the analysis of self has been brought to this point of recognizing the existence of the ego as an entity whose manifestations possess mysterious transiency, and one that can live, move and have its being apart from the physical body, the emotions and the intellect, when the latter are viewed from the standpoint of self devoid of any content or expression. If investigation has eliminated it from its supposed homes, if the quested self still eludes us, nevertheless we know that it exists; *we feel that our existence is real,* much more real than anything else which can be specified.

One must now advance one's thinking beyond the range of customary experience and begin to envisage the possibility of examining this ego as it really is, unmixed with thoughts and feelings and unhampered by the fleshly body. Few, if any, ever attempt to consider such a possibility, yet this is the way along which we may find the real truth about a man, as well as release from many of the burdens which afflict his soul through ignorance of his real inner nature.

The effect of such analytical reflections when brought to this stage and amply comprehended after sufficient time is to create a kind of revolutionary awakening in the mind, an emergence from night into early dawn. For the mystery of the self begins now to stretch away into unbounded horizons. The possibilities of a more spacious life that seem to open up produce a sensation akin to a thrill of awe and anticipation. For ordinarily the mind is manacled to the body and only when it can be freed from this imprisonment may hope of a higher life dawn.

§

How close to this true ego can one now approach? It is beyond the body, emotion and thoughts, yet it is itself nothing but a single thought – the 'I' thought.

First of conscious thoughts in an infant's mind, it is also the last to inhabit the adult's waking consciousness. When all other thoughts and memories ebb away just before sleep or death, he can only experience this ego-idea in the end. And just as the infant could not think of external objects or persons or even its own mother, until after this primal thought of self had arisen, so the adult eventually drops his thoughts of "He", "She" and "It", just before passing into the unconsciousness which precedes sleep and death, and holds the last thought of all – 'I'.

Whoever makes the attempt to reproduce voluntarily such a psychological situation within himself will perceive that the *thought* 'I' is indistinguishable from the *feeling* 'I' and that both are really one and the same. The final sense of personal selfhood might justly be termed a thought-emotion; it is this thought-emotion 'I' which subsists unchanged and unchanging underneath the ebb and flow of one's experiences and which, indeed, lies at the root of them both. Every emotion one experiences, every thought and memory that arises, comes into existence within the aura of this thought-emotion 'I', and subsequently to it. Here, if anywhere, is the centre of one's intelligence and life: here is the personality.

This personal thought is the stem from which all the thousands of other thoughts branch off. The entire host of ideas exists as one's *own* ideas; personality is the element which is their basic support. The ego is really an enormous nucleus of memories and imaginations; if it is analysed, these are reduced to their root.

Indeed, because all other thoughts are rooted in this first thought 'I' they depend upon it for their own existence. *Hence the intellect itself is nothing more than an endless procession of fugitive percepts, transient concepts, and a name given to a succession of separate temporary ideas, images and memories. The so-called intellectual faculties, such as memory and perception and association of ideas, are simply thoughts. There is no individual intellectual faculty, in reality, other than this single root ego-thought.*

Hence the primary importance of one's ego-thought – the foundation of the intellect and of all trains of ideas.

Even though in actual life one finds it impossible to live merely with this thought-emotion of 'I' and none other, even though one must continually have some other feeling or other thought for it to feed upon, philosophically one must grant that it has an independent existence of its own, because it is the one real and permanent feature of one's being which underlies all one's successive changes. One does not know how long any particular emotion will form a part of one's character, but the ego-thought in which it roots itself exists as long as the self-consciousness exists.

Therefore our investigation demands that this ego-thought must be brought into the sharpest possible focus for minute examination and vigilant inspection. The intellect must look for its originator.

When one attempts to analyse this last residue of intellect one begins a process not dissimilar to that of the snake which coils itself inwards and surveys its own body, but *is unable to look at that part of its body which is its face*. One must now withdraw attention from the external environment and force this truly wonderful faculty of self-awareness to focus itself upon itself, upon something within that is invisible and intangible – a single thought. Thoughts do not arise and take shape before one's eyes as do all things in the material universe. Nevertheless, every individual thought has a life and an existence of its own, albeit infinitely more fleeting and perishing than that of most material objects. Apparently this effort to survey the self-thought is an impossible one – like trying to catch one's own shadow. The I-thought is the last irreducible minimum to which a man may, when resting on his ego, enquire into himself. The character of the ego-thought can only be determined by observing the disclosure it may make of its own nature. This is a task which can be accomplished only by abstracting it from all other thoughts. Nature may not permit this attempt to succeed for more than a moment, but that moment should suffice to give one a glimpse of the real self, the self as it *is* in its own light.

If one examines with careful concentrated attentiveness the course of one's inner life and watches the birth of a thought, as one can do in moments of mental quiet, if one thus dissociates himself from inherence in the intellect itself, it will be discovered that what gives reality and life and value to the thought is attentive awareness. Without the power to bestow attention upon anything man could have no conscious existence in any world, whether physical or intellectual or transcendental. Its importance cannot be overestimated. Indeed, attention is the soul of thinking and the root of perception. When outward-turned, it enables us to become aware of the external world and illuminates its objects. Hence, without turning the faculty of attention inward, one can never hope to become aware of the realm hidden behind thoughts – the realm of spiritual being, the true self.

A change of the field of observation is necessary if one is to effect this discovery. Habit keeps one's attention entirely in the field of external things and the associated mental world resulting therefrom. Images which have their origin, either directly or ultimately, in this field crowd in upon one so incessantly as to prevent the viewing self becoming aware of its own proper nature. One's mind is always travelling. But if one were to refuse to let attention flow for ever into those mental images, and to free it for self-study, one would automatically disengage oneself from the limitations of the intellect and perceive loftier horizons. The habit which compels one to take a materialistic view of the universe exists within oneself as the observer; if this habit could be discontinued – as it can – a spiritual universe would then be able to reveal itself to one's interiorized attention. So long as the multitude of thoughts absorbs one, so long is it impossible or extremely difficult to ascertain that which is *behind* thought.

One must study the working of mind, recognize its ultimate dependence upon attention, and then put this knowledge to the best use. What better use can one hope to find for it than the conquest of the gap between thoughts and the soul and the winning of the wonderful understanding which such conquest promises us?

The quality of attention which makes thinking possible needs to be turned away from the outer world towards the inner, because it is the only means of access towards the fundamental self. Directed to the innermost point of being, it enables one to contemplate one's significance in the light that streams from that self. Attentiveness, indeed, is a manifestation of the essence of man, of that soul which stands higher than intellect, feeling and body. Could one but cultivate one's attention so as to obtain complete mastery over it, at will, one would need no other aid to bring him into the discovery of the highest psychological and spiritual truths, or to enable him to solve the secrets of life, sleep and death.

One's next step, then, is to isolate this ego-thought with the full force of one's attentiveness and hold it prisoner for a while; one must penetrate into its secret and compel it to yield up the answer to the problem: What am I?

For logic, as almost always implied from waking experience, can no longer give a solution. It has reached an *impasse* and can proceed no farther. Argument has but convinced one that the self is beyond argument because it is beyond the intellect. One's quest can end only by its direct perception.

Thus the reader has been led, as by a fine thread, through the world of intellect to the frontier of that sparkling splendour which exists at its core. He has been shown what he may not have hitherto suspected, that just as the external world must be contacted by means of the sense-organs of the physical body, so the inner world of the soul must be contacted by the faculty of attentive awareness freed from the tyranny of *extraneous* thoughts, fluctuating feelings and external sensations.

But disentangling and facing the I-thought does not mean thinking about it. It cannot be achieved if one makes mental statements or argumentative inferences about it. Although the sequence of critical self-observation and reasoned arguments has been a vital help in bringing one to this point, it will only stultify progress if pushed any farther. Mental activity must now yield to mental stillness. The moment one starts such a process one is side-tracked again and falls back into the ever-waiting stream of successive thoughts and ideas which keeps one drowned in multifarious sensations and prevents him arriving at the self.

The only way to penetrate into and grasp the ego-thought at this stage is to drop all discursive thinking about it. *What is required is nothing more than arrested attention, restricted to the field of simple self-awareness* and held behind to remain within itself, within the 'I-in-itself'.

For it has been shown that attention is the soul inhering in thought, *and therefore one plane higher than thought.* Hence concentrated watchful attention alone can regard this ego-thought.

In actual practice, thought cannot regard its own face unless it mounts to a higher point of vantage. But as soon as it succeeds in doing this it should change its nature and becomes pure attention.

What is the meaning of all these statements? What is the momentous implication behind these observations of the thought-process, themselves the resultant of attentive watching on the part of ancient seers and sages?

It is this: thinking fulfils itself in the loftiest degree as an activity when it reaches this point of facing the ego-thought, holding the 'I' firmly, but no longer continuing its normal process of ratiocinative logical motion. But *the power to control the flow of thoughts must be attained before one can approach the 'I'-sense and perceive it undisguised by the multitude of mental waves.*

The proper destiny of thought is attained when it stops here. When it comes into the realization that it must itself now be subdued and give place to the subtler faculty of pure attention, directly confined to nothing else but the ego, to an unwandering awareness which does not move in sequence from idea to idea, but fastens itself irresistibly upon man's primal thought.

Hence, all extraneous thoughts must themselves disappear before one can proceed any farther into the nature of self. Thereupon we have the right to expect the hidden self to disclose itself spontaneously. And we need not imagine this self to be some figment of the metaphysical imagination. On the contrary, because it is the innermost centre which vibrates behind and through thinking, feeling and acting, it must be the highest intensity of our individual life.

This very striving for *awareness* of that mysterious source whence thought takes its rise, helps to prepare the condition wherein awareness is alone possible – that of an intent inward watchfulness which permits the consciousness, however momentarily, to forget to indulge in its customary activity of thinking.

We must bring our cerebral activity to a needle-sharp point of concentration and therefore we need to calm it. When all thoughts come to rest and the mind attains quiescence, it may then contemplate its own self in full awareness, but not before.

Thus our thought has turned inward upon itself. It could not do that immediately we began our quest. First it had to be detached from the body and to view its bodily life as something outside. Then it had to turn on the emotional nature and view that also as something apart from itself. Lastly it has faced itself and learnt to look upon the multitude of thoughts as something objective. The secret of penetrating to the deeper self thus involves the reversal of attention from the external to the internal worlds. Truly speaking, this self cannot possibly live behind us, but rather within us.

There is no fear of being led into a region of sheer fantasy, so long as one is rightly guided, because nothing could be closer, more intimate and more true than one's own selfhood.

When Muhammad was asked by his relative, Ali, "What

am I to do that I may not waste my time?" the Arab prophet answered, "Learn to know thyself!" His counsel was priceless. Why? Let Muhammad answer again, in the words which he wrote down in the *Quran:* "He who has understood himself has understood his God."

For the Biblical statement happens to be true, that man was made in the image of God, but that image *is within him.* It is no mystical absurdity, this. God is ever in the midst of man, just as man is ever in the midst of God. To accept this thought with bored acquiescence, as do those who do not and cannot realize its implications, is one thing; to feel it as a living reality, as a divine force, is another.

The time which is given to study of the composition of our being is not wasted. We are so busy answering all the multitude of problems that arise out of external activities – which are endless – that the major problem of all, "What am I?" remains unanswered. But when we set out in quest of our own soul we are inspired by a higher power – our inherent divinity, which is likewise the best guarantee of our ultimate success. We have in us as much of the divine fire as those sages and saints whose names have starred world history, but they were aware of theirs, whilst we slumber. And because it is a real fact – and not a metaphysical figment – it is experimentally ascertainable as it exists in its unjoined state, i.e. unjoined to the external body, to emotions and even to thoughts. The practical method of this unveiling will be fully detailed in Part II, but meanwhile the reader must realize that these preliminary mental analyses are no less an essential part of the complete system than the exercises which are to follow.

6

BEYOND TIME TO ETERNITY

The foregoing psychological analysis of man has conducted us to the conclusion that the self transcends intellect and that true knowledge of oneself will be possible only if one, whilst retaining full conscious attention, could induce the intellect to abstain voluntarily from its everyday function. It may only be possible to do this for a minute, but that brief period should suffice to give him a glimpse of the reality which lurks behind the scenes of thought.

Such a conclusion is so startling that it might be suspected there is some flaw in the train of thought which has led up to it. Indeed, so curiously personal is this introspective analytic method, so inexorable is its demand that each practiser shall creatively think out his own succession of ideas in a spirit of the utmost independence of the culture of his epoch, that unless one has truly lived through each phase of its progress for oneself its truth will necessarily remain unperceived.

However, it is advisable to approach the same conclusion from angles other than the psychological, and then to see whether it still remains correct when viewed from these different standpoints. Two such standpoints are available; the first is scientific, religious and semi-philosophical and will now be explained; the other is derived from special human experience and will be described in the next chapter. Under the first head we have to consider the question of time, but not indeed as it is seen by ultimate philosophic truth. Such a lofty standpoint cannot be taken up in the present work and demands a space far larger that the single chapter which can be here afforded: nevertheless this book is a preparation for it. Yoga must first grant its enfranchisement to its votaries, before the latter can be led into the inner shrine where the last goddess is unveiled. Even to put into concrete existence upon paper the thoughts which are about to follow is a tremendous task.

The past half-century has seen a slow awakening to the important place which time occupies in man's relationship to the universe which environs him. From the interesting but fruitless suggestions of C. H. Hinton and the acute but incomplete analyses of Professor Bergson nearly fifty years ago to Dr. Albert Einstein's world-famed demonstration of the truth of Relativity, time has become a problem of increasing scientific urgency and one worthy to be dealt with by our foremost Western minds. Certainly the older theories concerning it of Sir Isaac Newton's age have been thrown into the melting-pot.

It might seem strange to suggest that one's hunt for the self should have anything to do with this problem, but will seem less so when it is remembered that every observation of the outside world is made *in* time and that every reflection which passes through one's mind is likewise conditioned by its temporality. If time influences one's thoughts and observations in any way, the real truth about those thoughts and impressions – and finally about oneself, which underlies both – it may not be accurately perceptible unless one investigates the nature of this influence and exposes time for what it is. Hence one ought to understand time if one would understand the self. Strictly speaking, time ought not and cannot be separated from its relatives, space and causation, but because we are here enquiring into man and not the universe, consideration of the latter themes must be omitted.

The average man's attitude towards time does not go so far as to trouble about its minute analysis – indeed it is too deep and difficult a riddle for him – and the ceaseless stride of its flying heels, which succeed each other with regrettable rapidity, are the chief things about it which he deplores. But in the sense that the years heal the seared soul or body. Sir Francis Bacon's maxim that time is the friend of man must be put alongside this thought.

The things that came into our lives with the coming of Time are fit friends of that ancient harridan whose sorry face and slow-moving feet seem like curses set upon the race of man. All that brings us to the wringing of hands and takes from life the sweetness it should have is the black gift flung in our face as payment of the servitude we have given her.

There is much in Eastern ways which will never float across to the West, where the phrase, "Time is money," hangs as a sacred wall-text in many a harassed business man's office. If the Orientals have a lesser belief in the value of time and a livelier appreciation of the reality of eternity, and if their tropical climate emphasizes this appreciation throughout their general attitude toward life, we of the West are unlikely to entertain such views as deeply as they do. We feel too acutely the moment's fleeting impermanence. We may not, for instance, ever arrive at the stage of that stout amiable Hindu money-lender whom the present writer met several years ago in Lahore, North India. He boasted, "Whenever I have an appointment with a client for ten o'clock in the morning, I invariably turn up at the hour of two!" On the writer replying that this was surely bad for business, be laughed and said, "If I turned up at ten, then my client would turn up at two!"

Chronos, lord of time, cuts us all down with his inescapable scythe – men, animals, plants and even planets fall beneath his descending stroke. Is his activity an everlasting one? What is this mysterious element whose flux controls the ultimate destinies of worlds and their inhabitants?

To stitch the verses of a gifted friend, Hesper Le Gallienne, to this prose:

> "Some gather Beauty on the Way,
> Some Happiness and some Despair
> Within the maze of endless years
> That leads to the Celestial Stair.
>
> Throughout the labyrinth of Time
> The æons of Existence sped,
> A strange unending caravan –
> The living and the dead!"

Geologists have been forced to conclude, upon the evidence of the rate of transmutation of radioactive substances, that there are rocks in the earth's crust which are 1,200 million years old. Yet the age of our own earth is young beside that of other stars and suns. Astronomers have computed time-cycles involving 'pasts' and 'futures' of staggering length, but even these are paltry items in the infinite cosmic calendar. One dares not sit down to contemplate the continuity without end of this ever-rolling river of time, this perpetual appearance and perpetual vanishing of whirling worlds, for the prospect of such unlimited changes and vicissitudes bears something that frightens the human imagination and awes the human heart. There seems to be a tremendous mystery behind the endless and irreversible flux of it all until, brooding upon it, one feels at last as appalled at the prospect of a universal life that flows implacably onward for ever and ever through myriads of transient forms as at the prospect of universal death and dissolution! Such a contemplation will leave a man gasping for breath and cause him to clutch with relief at the distinctions which the rotation of the earth and recurring revolutions of sun, moon and stars enable him to devise for his own brief purposes. Such astronomical phenomena provide him with constant intervals regularly repeated in the same manner, and relieve him of the effort to conceive the inconceivable.

Our intellects are limited and finite, they cannot measure more than the seconds and minutes and days of time-consciousness which beat incessantly through their physical organs.

As soon as one attempts to enter into an interior relationship with time one realizes that he lives for ever in the present. Past remembrances and future anticipations are alike unreal bodiless ghosts, which lapse again into dark nothingness, for the present is inexorably inescapable and devours every minute.

The present is always flowing onwards, moving irreversibly in a single direction towards a future which is also always melting into it as a tributary stream melts into the river it feeds. Even this analogy is feeble and partly false for there is no actual movement through space; one can say only that time's movement is unique. In this strange manner we are for ever and inseparably dwelling in the realm of the present as the essence of our existence. The past is but remembrance and the future is anticipation, but the present moment is pre-eminent because of its *reality*.

The present moment, moreover, is the centre between the two extremes of past and future. This will suffice for our analysis and there will be no need to lose oneself in this grand self-expanding amplitude which stretches out like an infinite line as soon as one looks backwards or forwards.

For every past event was a present one when it actually occurred. In the same way every future event will be experienced at the time as a present event alone. *Past and future, when analysed, are therefore seen to be manifestations of present time, resting entirely upon it, and possessing no independent existence of their own.* Therein lies the crux of the whole question.

In other words, time is an unbroken chain formed by successive links of present events only. It cannot be truthfully split up into an absolute past and an absolute future for it is itself indivisible; it is an everlasting NOW. The relationship which exists between past and future has been created by the unifying power of man's memory; it exists in man, not in time.

Because the present is thus ever-existent in both past and future *as their real nature,* all striving to comprehend both, to pry into them or to unravel them, *before* comprehending the true nature of the present is vain and foolish, being like attempts to count numbers without beginning with the number one, the leading unit. The unit is not only the first and foremost of numbers, but it enters into every other number as its basis.

Hence, if one endeavours to ascertain the true character of the present moment first, that will constitute the correct preliminary method of ultimately arriving at an understanding of both the past and future also, i.e. of time in its totality.

§

It is certainly a strange truth that one is immovably fixed in the present moment, that time's secret lives here alone.

Everything one has done in former years and everything one will do in the years yet to come, will be deposited in the eternal present.

The present alone is *real* time.

One must not confuse the present moment with a mathematical point in a line which begins and stretches to infinity. It is nowhere in space, for it is inseparable from the human way of viewing the world. It is something which inheres in man himself, or more accurately, in his conscious attention.

Now because the present itself cannot be observed as something objective, it must necessarily be subjective, i.e. within the consciousness of the observer.

Time is always referred, in the final analysis, to some object or event composed of objects. It takes time to glance at any object, no matter how brief be the infinitesimal flash, because it possesses dimensions of size and the eyes must travel from one edge of it to another and thus bifurcate the glance. Nothing really appears at a single instant but always in time-succession. It is only by such separation in space that any object assumes its form for the beholder. But who can measure the time taken for this process within the present moment? Where does the present moment start or stop? It is impossible to distinguish between these points because the instant one point is fixed that instant becomes a past moment. Hence, we cannot form any absolutely correct idea of the present. Scientifically speaking, the present defies observation and is consequently unknowable. *It possesses no duration, and therefore it is the inlet to a timeless Absolute.* In short, when isolated it is really an abstract *idea* existing within our minds. Thus we arrive at the curious position that "being in time" means "being in the present" and the latter in its turn means "being in timelessness, i.e. eternity." And the sense of reality which we always find in the present moment is derived from this hidden reality of enduring life which underlies it.

A profound mystery is thus contained within the most familiar sides of life. *Hence we are living right here and now in the fullness of true eternal life, only we are quite unaware, quite unconscious of it. The restoration of this missing awareness would necessarily revolutionize our lives.* This is a point of vast and vital importance.

This immediately lifts the whole concept of time out of the material world into the non-material or mental realm. "Alas! not time but we, we are moving onwards," wrote a perceptive French poet. *Moreover, because we are always living through all our experience in the present it implies that we may know time only as a form of self-consciousness.*

The theme is susceptible of illustration from a scientific point of view. Some anomalies in the science of optics drew Dr. Einstein to the discovery that different individuals could hold different ideas about time, as it is shown by clocks, and yet both views would be equally valid. The measurement of time-units was relative to the position and standards of reference of the observer. Moreover, he drew attention to the fact that there are stars whose light has not yet reached the earth. In view of the enormous distance of the stars from our own earth events that happened on this earth centuries ago would be seen – if they could be seen – as current events from some other heavenly body.

Still further, if the rate of revolution of our earth were to alter, the time-sense would alter correspondingly. For instance, the moon rotates in $27\frac{1}{3}$ of our days and if a member of this earth's humanity could succeed in travelling instantly to the moon his time there would hang very heavily because there would be such a considerable retardation in its flow that his moon-day would be $27\frac{1}{3}$ times longer than the one to which he had been accustomed. Hence every man has his own individual idea of time, which is one form of the principle of relativity. Finally, if we could imagine ourselves travelling at a sufficiently tremendous speed, we should come back after a few minutes to discover with astonishment that our planet was older by some centuries.

These four instances show that time has no absolute existence. There is really no such thing as an absolute measure of time, only our mental impressions of it: time is how we *think* it.

The law of relativity is not only applicable to the phenomena of Nature, but equally to the intellect which is observing those phenomena. That intellect cannot help but relate itself to the ideas of the past, present and future, and all its efforts, all its concepts will inevitably move within this framework and no other.

The new scientific conception of time has been forced to admit that no picture of time can be drawn; it cannot really be objectified and therefore cannot be examined as science examines other things in Nature. It can only be interpreted perspectively from within itself.

One cannot represent it properly by a chalked line upon a blackboard, for instance, as one may symbolically represent anything else in Nature from the minute atom to the colossal solar system. For the observer and his act of observation and the drawn line are all so fixed to time themselves that normal scientific observation is vitiated from the beginning. All external things are observed *from the present moment;* but as the latter is not external it cannot itself be observed as an object of thought.

Therefore to fulfil science's latest bidding and get the interior perspective view of the present deeper than the superficial concept of it which one normally holds by racial inheritance, one must now contemplate time as a purely psychological factor – not as something dependent on astronomical measurements. One must cross the threshold of one's inner being – not at all so strange and extraordinary a feat as it sounds.

Such an analysis may be unfamiliar and seem remote, but it is full of significance. Here is a study which, if patiently followed, is sure to be free from the superficiality which would undervalue the mystery of time.

§

In the previous chapter the understanding was reached that the self is fundamentally traceable to a single and persistent seed-thought, which seems to be inextricably bound up with the unending series of thoughts which, in their totality, are called intellect. Being thus involved in an activity of constant mental movement, one normally never has the opportunity to regard the self-thought apart from this movement. One is really enslaved by this constant mental motion, this unceasing flow of impressions from without and ideas from within.

We have also here arrived at presupposing an absolute present, although we are unable to conceive it. A way will now be shown whereby investigation may be raised to an astonishing height. The idea of time is inseparably connected with the idea of motion. It is a sensation of succession. Thus there is a movement of concepts and percepts within the mind, one succeeding the other like the snapshots on a reel of cinema film – a process that continues the day long. There is also a movement of the physical body from hour to hour at the very least, if not from minute to minute.

It is this inherence in a succession of mental impressions and physical sensations, and events as they pass through consciousness, which creates one's sense of time and one's personal memories, because there is no movement without time. It is this eternal sinking of attention in *thoughts other than the 'I'-thought* that prevents one coming face to face, as it were, with one's real self. Therefore, it follows that there is a connection between the two factors and that so long as one is unable to free attention from these thoughts and memories, so long will one be held captive by the sense of the passage of time.

The inability to escape from this constant movement explains why we are not normally aware that the present moments really permeate each other in a timeless Absolute and do not extend side by side, as has been shown. If our awareness could *experience* two moments which were completely identical there would be no transmission of memory from the first to the second, when there would necessarily be a lapse into the Absolute.

A simple analogy will help to explain this. One should imagine oneself to be seated in a compartment of a railway train, which is standing at a station waiting for passengers to alight and enter. Looking out of the window on the side farthest from the station platform, one sees another train which also has pulled up and remains still. Then the guard blows his whistle and one feels that one's train has begun to move. With every second its speed increases, whilst the windows of the opposite train flash more quickly past one's eyes.

But let one now turn his eyes in the opposite direction, let him glance at the side where the platform will soon vanish from view, and one is startled to discover that the full length of the platform is still there and that one's train remains alongside it as before.

A glance back again across the compartment will reveal that it is the other train which has been running out of the station, because it is no longer there!

The second train has been travelling all the time, not oneself nor one's train!

We call this an optical illusion, but it is well to remember that this simple 'illusion' has given rise to mental experience; instead of the true sensation of an object moving before one's eyes, it caused one to feel that one was moving oneself.

This is directly analogous with the situation of the average man. He quite reasonably believes that his life consists solely of a movement through time, through measured moments, days, weeks, and years.

But the true fact is that he, his real self, THAT which is behind the intellect, is not moving at all; on the contrary, it rests immovably anchored in eternity.

Here he is facing a psychological illusion. There is only one way to dispel it, and that is to turn one's head in the opposite direction, as one had to turn it in the train. This turning is effected psychologically by turning attention from outwards to inwards, by directing the mind back to its own source.

The relative nature of time is an unspoken invitation to search for the absolute value of eternity which underlies it, and which is here *now* – not in some far-off future.

The faqueers who have been "buried alive" and whose cases have been reported in an earlier chapter report the complete absence of a succession of thoughts during that hazardous experiment and also the lapsing of any sense of time. In fact, when thought is no more for them, the passage of time is no more either. The mind being still, time is still also.

Because of this interval when he loses the time-sense and experiences a blissful deep dreamless sleep, such a faqueer usually gives a pre-order to his mind to awaken into normal activity at a given hour, and it almost invariably happens that at the precise moment, he awakens. Here is the newspaper report of one recent case which is well known in Northern India.

"YOGI COMES OUT OF SAMADHI (TRANCE) AFTER 40 DAYS

A remarkable case of samadhi, that is, perfect absorption of thought, the eighth and last stage of Yoga – has been brought to light at Rishikesh, the sacred place of pilgrimage near Hardwar in Dehra Dun district, when the emaciated body of a young Hindu Yogi was taken out of a special tomb recently in the presence of thousands of spectators.

On October 10, 1935, he entered the trance in the hollow masonic structure measuring hardly sixteen square feet and about four or five feet high. The entrance to it was closed with stone, which was cemented as soon as the Yogi entered it. A guard was posted at the place to keep watch on him. He was then walled up in his living tomb, and for six weeks great crowds of Hindus reverently waited outside while he performed this, the supreme penance. All during the period he took neither food nor water. On entering the tomb the Yogi, who had already fasted for several days, had left instructions that on the 45th day after he entered it, between 7 and 10 a.m., when they would hear him say the holy word 'Om', they should take him out and massage his body with oil.

This is the third time that the Yogi has taken the trance-experience. In the first trance, one of his hands was partially eaten away by white ants."

The last sentence is significant and unconsciously provides a telling rejoinder to critics who can see nothing but conjuring tricks *in all* the feats of these faqueers. This case illustrates how the stopping of thoughts stops all sense of time, but the corollary is likewise true that as the succession of mental experiences slackens or quickens so the standard of time changes correspondingly. This is confirmed by a little study.

It is known to a few people by personal experience that a drowning person in the flash that precedes total unconsciousness, perceives the whole of his past life moving before his mind's eye. The chief events of every year, from infancy to maturity, are represented and not only seen, but lived through again, summed up and understood. A fifty-year period has thus been experienced within a few seconds.

But even in the waking state it is customary to find that suffering lengthens the hours for us, whereas joy renders them all too brief. A painful illness drags its weary way with slow, tormenting feet through our lives, but ecstatic days pass as quickly as the whirlwind. Two ardent lovers who find themselves separated for only a week feel that at least a month has passed. Hence, we get only the *feeling* of time's swiftness or slowness, and not its mathematical measurement, because we get it entirely as something subjective; i.e. inside the perceiving mind and relative to it.

Such are the tricks which changing consciousness can play with the human sense of time! Similarly, during sleep one may experience a succession of dream-events within a few minutes which would require several hours for their fulfilment in waking consciousness. There are certain dreams wherein one's sense of time is swifter because the intellect is then unhindered by the slower functioning of the physical brain; just as the electrical forces within a physical atom would vibrate more rapidly and intensely if they were to be released from their imprisoning material casement, so the unit of time-perception is speeded up when the perceiver's mind is set free from flesh.

The sea voyage from Bombay to San Francisco may take three weeks to complete if one travels during the waking state, whereas it takes but five minutes if one travels during the dream state. Hence we must draw the inference that time itself is purely a mental condition. Dream-proof is as valid as waking-proof in this particular connection because the sense of real experience is not diminished therein. The dreamer constructs his own mental world and lives within it, whilst even when awake he is living within a mental world because all he can know of the external world is his mental recognition of it. Until the sense-reports are carried to the brain and converted into *mental* impressions, he – or anyone else – cannot possibly become aware of the material world.

An extraordinary proof that a change in the combination of nervous sensations, and of the mental impressions resulting therefrom, will change the human sense of time was afforded by a recent report in the *Morning Post, a* highly respectable London newspaper, as follows:

"Vivid recollections of the prolongation of time have been described by victims of electrical shock and one man who watched a bicycle pass by at a good speed after he had been 'shocked' declared that he could see every spoke in the bicycle wheel and 'it barely seemed to me to be turning'. The same man declared that he could feel every reversal of the alternating current at the rate of sixty complete cycles per second."

Successive sensations pass through one's field of awareness: if they pass through at normal speed, i.e. a speed common to humanity as a whole, they produce the normal sense of time. But when, as in this striking case – when the functioning of time was vividly demonstrated to reside, not in the external physical universe, but in the internal human mind – the brain is abnormally affected, they may be prolonged and pass tardily through consciousness as in a kind of slow-motion camera picture.

It is well known that in the case of a person under an anæsthetic during a surgical operation, or under the influence of a narcotic drug, the sense of time may rise to fantastic limits or fall to equally fantastic proportions.

The moral of these cases is that the sense of time lies in the mind itself, in the percepts and concepts which are its product. Time, therefore, is not outside but falls inside the human organism. It is an idea, not an object to be observed but a concept to be thought, and a by-product of consciousness.

It has no independent and intrinsic existence apart from the mind by which it is conceived and imagined. Its moving-on is one of the essential conditions of ordinary consciousness.

Every external experience which begins at a particular moment, continues for a certain period and finally ends at a particular moment again, measures itself upon the delicate instrument of one's mentality. A fundamental change in that mentality is bound to affect those measurements – raising them to abnormally rapid speeds or reducing them to abnormally slow ones.

Time is a fundamental which underlies ordinary human thinking.

Kant, the German philosopher and one of the greatest of Western thinkers, by means of his own extremely lengthy, laborious but admirably acute reasoning, also established this fact that the panoramic procession of thoughts and sensations through one's consciousness brings with it the sense of time. He concluded that time, in other words, is simply a form of consciousness. He could not, however, grasp as a practical possibility the complementary fact that man might arrive at a thought-free, impression-free and memory-free consciousness – not as a far-off hope, but as a present reality. He explained finally why he believed that the modern scientific method would never bring us nearer to an understanding of the reality behind things and of the eternity behind time. Another and different method was required, but he could not see how its creation was possible.

What his eighteenth-century mind could not see will nevertheless be perceived by some in this twentieth century. A method of attaining higher perception is being placed before it in these and other pages, as it was formerly placed before the truth-seekers of antiquity by ancient seers of India.

§

The foundations of our own belief in the reality of time – as normally known – have been upset somewhat by recent thinkers, who scornfully declare time to be an illusion. They would be more accurate if they described time as an idea.

Our sense of time is less illusory than relative. It seems true and real, we feel that we are traversing it, but it is never really absolute. Everything in one's view of Nature is merely a matter of standpoint; because it cannot escape being related to the observer. A traveller ascending a mountain-side may perceive something which is still high above his head, but which is quite invisible to the plain-dweller below, yet the same traveller may also perceive the plain which he has left if he but turns his gaze downwards. From the standpoint of the unthinking man, time is an undeniable reality. From a higher level, it might be revealed as a mere idea which exists within the mind and which may or may not disappear without affecting one's eternal life, or as a cinema picture which flickers for a brief while over the white screen of eternity and is gone. Anyway, it is clearly a projection on the external world of conditions existing within oneself, and therefore only relative, since they are likely to appear, disappear and reappear again according to one's own inward conditioning

Time is thus demonstrated to be a creation of the human

brain – something which partakes of the psychological order; it may be called a mental concept, a form of consciousness, a subjective movement or a by-product of thought, but without the collaboration of conscious being it obviously could not exist.

So long as one identifies oneself with thoughts, so long will time condition one's existence. That alone can transcend time which transcends the intellect. But it has already been shown that the real self transcends intellect. Therefore that self must transcend time too. Where can finite time exist in a realm, such as that of the Overself, which is above the movement of thought?

The analysis may now be brought to its highest flight: if these mental movements do not exist in the real self, and if, as has been explained previously, undistracted attention is still left over when they have disappeared, then the awareness of the present moment will still continue in that high realm, unbroken by action or thought occurring within it, because that self *is* unbroken self-awareness. The sense of *now* will go on as something absolute, unchanging and infinite – in short, eternal – because there will be no succession, no movement, and no memories in the Overself's consciousness.

The thought-free, timeless self must for ever *be*. It must live; like the present moment, within and behind all time, yet itself paradoxically remain time-free. Consciousness descending out of the Absolute to manifest as thought-movements within the physical brain and reflected into the common and carnal self, becomes involved in finite time; set free from this movement it will abolish its limitation by the finite and regain the sense of its eternal nature.

So long as one wrongly *identifies* himself with the physical body, so long as he even still wrongly identifies himself with the mentality and the ego-memories, so long will he necessarily exist as a creature of time, a captive of past memories, present happenings and future hopes and fears. So soon as, by right introspection and accurate analysis, the truth about time is perceived and *held,* with attention confined to time's source in oneself, so soon shall one enter and remain in the realization that the unknown content of one's inmost self transcends time, is eternal and care-free. Its parentage lies with the angels, for it is divine. That self can never be affected by whatever belongs to time, even though the ego may continue to function *within* it. That is the self we have sought in these pages and to which the writer has made repeated references in previous books as the Overself: the word does not yet occur in any dictionary of the English language, and was indeed coined by him to express something that borders upon the inexpressible, none of the current terms commonly used to denote the divine condition that is the goal of this path being entirely satisfactory. Words like God, Spirit, Soul, and so on, being of ancient lineage, have accumulated around themselves a variety of theological connotations, some of which do not fit in at all with what the author wished to convey. It was necessary, therefore, to find a new word and one which would more accurately, more precisely and less confusingly represent the meaning which he sought to communicate. And if at length the term 'Overself' was finally decided upon, even that was not as completely satisfactory as he could have wished. It tends to convey an idea that the divine state is something which floats over our heads like a cloud, whereas, although that beautiful reality certainly utterly transcends man's personal state and gives him a consciousness of universality, it is paradoxically, mysteriously and simultaneously existent as a point in the innermost recess of his being. However, the writer hoped that the juxtaposition of the two words 'over' and 'self' would reflect this paradox of the transcendent and immanent divinity of man. Strictly speaking, the coinage of *two* words was necessary and one should have been *Overmind,* but it was not desired to go so far at the time. However, the mysterious occult powers of the psychic part of human nature require this Overmind in any accurate explanation of their true source. For the mind does not exist within man; *on the contrary man exists within the one Overmind.* Anyway, the difficulties raised by the coinage of a new term like this were less than those which would have been raised by using one of the already existing terms, which frequently suggest meanings that differ with different people and systems of thought.

The Overself, then, abides in the element of eternity. This is not to say that it must necessarily exist with the whole of its attention spread out over past, present and future simultaneously. That is a false idea, although quite true of the Overmind.

Eternity cannot be a series co-existing simultaneously and stretched between two points in time, however infinitely apart they are. Nor does it exist as the sum total of transitions from past into present and again into future – such a distorted view is a false finality and incorrect, and would render eternal life a horror rather than a benediction because its unfortunate participant would then have to submit to an infinitude of dismal memories, and anticipatory dreads, and to a vast multitude of mental images crowding into his mind and giving him no peace! It can only be an independent mode of being which entirely transcends all concepts of "then, now and after". It is an unbroken whole, a stretch of infinite memory-less consciousness and not an arithmetical collection of tenses. It is the source out of which past, present and future arise and flow, and into which they merge and disappear, *but whether they arise or not, it continues, self-subsisting;* hence the question of totalizing time does not really arise. It is the background of sky against which time may flicker like a sheet of lightning; no arithmetical sum of lightning flashes will ever result in forming the sky. Cross out time and eternity will still be left.

Mankind has divided a portion of cosmic time for practical purposes into cycles of days, months and years; because the train of thoughts, being successive, may also be divided up; but eternity, being in deeper dimension than thought and consequently beyond time, cannot be divided, experiences no successions, is never new and never undergoes the transitions from 'then' to 'now' and to 'after'. Eternity is *ever* here; even at this present moment it is with us and actually contained within it. It is static Be-ness, whereas time is the moving screen of be-coming.

Deep in the interior of each star there is a region where energy loses its direction, and where what physicists call "thermodynamical equilibrium" reigns. Yet this does not prevent the star throbbing its circular way through space. Whereas sequential life, i.e. the life of thoughts, presupposes a time-sense, motionless static life in the eternal Overself annihilates that sense, but it need not therefore be a "dead" existence. On the contrary, it must be *real* life because it is the very core of selfhood and the very essence of consciousness; self and life are synonymous terms, because there could be no self-awareness in a corpse. Moreover, not being subject to the changes of material finite forms its value is imperishable and spiritual.

Incidentally it is because both the will and fate of man ultimately proceed out of this same region of the Overself that the endless dispute between the proponents of the doctrine of free will and the advocates of the doctrine of unalterable fate is meaningless, and can never be decisive. Their dilemma is entirely self-created and does not exist in Nature. Events appear in our lives as a sequence to a two-fold cause, which is itself finally merged into a unity.

Thus this everlasting life of *conscious participation* in the Overself is the glorious possibility which opens itself to our gaze, a life which kills suffering at its source and removes the roots of error.

The question next arises, "How is it to be realized? What is the way of escape into the higher dimension of being?"

That way is being unfolded in these pages – in these analyses, the preparations and practices which are to follow, and finally in the supreme consummation of voluntary self-abandonment to the Overself. The principal feature of the practices will be the right use of mental quiet, which constitutes itself a veritable key for the opening of the door of the eternal.

Educated Western man will be unable to cross the frontier of time – leaving the realm of mortal darkness for that of mental light – unless he is prepared to understand ideas and take up practices such as those which are being revealed to him here, and for lack of which most conventional thinking remains ineffectual to conduct the thinker into the hidden truth.

It has been shown how the mind's incessant movement creates the time-sense and retards one's entry into the timeless Absolute.

Then, *by overcoming this motion one should be able to overcome the tyranny of time.*

The reverse of movement is stillness. The reverse of time is eternity.

One must seek therefore to cultivate the state of stillness, mental no less than physical, if one would conquer time. Consciousness as mentalized movement = time; consciousness abiding in itself in a repose as deep as that of a deep sea free from waves = eternity.

If one were to stop the wheeling revolutions of intellect and reduce all thoughts to the primal one, the 'I'-thought, and then melt this into mental stillness, one would be immediately liberated from temporary captivity. An aroma of immortality would then cling around one's whole being.

If one were to turn the intellect's search and observation *inwards* upon itself and trace it to its *own* point of origin, the ego-thought, one would lapse into the resultant stillness and thus achieve this object.

§

We have found the clue. Out of the stillness whence thought arises, there emerges the first mental notion – 'I'. We must follow up this clue as a dog follows its far-off master by his scent and unfailingly discovers him. We must now summon all our attention and concentrate upon this ego-sense, this notion of 'I', resolutely rejecting the overtures of all other thoughts and of all memories whatever. It we could do this aright, the trail should eventually lead us back to the stillness and there we should discover the elusive mysterious Overself.

The very effort to subdue the thoughts implies that there is someone who subdues them, and hence that one is not the intellect itself. The 'I' is thus clearly placed at a level deeper than thinking.

The use of thought is but a step upon this path; it is here analogous to a horsed stage-coach which is to conduct the traveller in the wide-flung land of knowledge from some insignificant village to the nearest station on a railway line. When the traveller is comfortably seated in a railway coach he has no further use for the stage-coach which he has deserted. In precisely the same manner, when the working of man's brain has brought him to a certain point in his outlook, in his attitude towards life, he is ready to take the further step of deserting thought altogether and taking to another mode of consciousness. Thinking has then served its purpose and to go on prolonging it beyond this point would not only be a purely negative process, but would actually retard his further progress.

Whoever brings his analysis to this point with both concentration and firmness, and is willing to take up the special practices which lead beyond it and which are explained in further chapters, may actually experience as a reality the sense of selfhood utterly divorced from the fluctuations of mood, emotion and intellect. The possibility then becomes a reality, even if only for a moment. But this experience once achieved may be repeated again and yet again until the integrated harmony of such a life provides a new outlook. And this wonderful new state will expose the falsity of that theological misunderstanding which turns the eternal life of heaven into an indefinite and limitless extension of finite time. The heaven of fluttering angels and singing inhabitants is a combination in time. For time presupposes movement – whether in consciousness, thinking or physical activity – whereas the supreme mark of eternity is its utter stillness. All other concepts of this state are wrong. And this eternal life can be found on the familiar earth for the human mind harbours both time and its contrary.

The power to follow this way exists within us all. The current of human thought can be made to turn backward to its sublime source. Thus one may be ferried across the Styx which flows between the world of time and the world of eternity.

When the implications of this method and, more, the astonishing results which it will bring into the science of the twentieth-century psychology, are fully grasped and understood, then we shall witness a revolution in thought no less epoch-making than we witnessed when Dr. Einstein's law of relativity was enthroned in the science of twentieth-century physics. We stand already, as it were, upon the summit of material knowledge, but the entry into this new method will reveal to us *a whole world of neglected truth which shall show forth the universe as God's strange paradox and man as God's secret radiation.*

Many philosophers of former years have unnecessarily and arbitrarily shut the mind within closed limits, while others did not know that the Achilles of intellect possessed a vulnerable heel.

A new horizon is opened up to us when we understand this matter, when we perceive that a timeless existence, *that is, an eternal existence,* may be attained by the inward regulation of thought. Admittedly the reconciliation of a timeless Absolute with the world of clock-marked time is extremely difficult and, in fact, only the master of yoga can do it *practically.* But it is the possibility held before mankind by its greatest religious teachers and its secret lies in understanding that the present moment holds eternity as its ever-present underlying *motif,* and in grasping the fact that behind the moving intellect there always abides the Great Repose.

The intellect works like some machine which constantly dissevers our awareness into an unending series of separate thoughts and sensations, and splits up our interior sense of being into comparatively minute measurements of years, months and days, thus rendering us the prisoners of time when we are, in reality, the children of eternity. Whatever it apprehends is grasped under this limitation and through this instrumentality of time. It is important to understand that these disintegrated fragments are contained within the real self, are perceived and pervaded by the Overself-consciousness during every instant of the present, and that *were it otherwise mankind could never become conscious of these differences of thought and impression.*

If we could paralyse our sense of being in time, we could awaken without difficulty to the sense of being in eternity. Those awed Quaker-quiet moments when we throw off the chains of temporality and sit in worship before the Overself, might thus be stretched out to all infinity.

Because time is the product of intellect, and not of anything external to us, the way to paralyse its limitation is to paralyse the intellect *first*, to make the mind absolutely *still*. The moment we rise above the activity of thinking, we rise also into a supernormal *x*-dimensional region where our conceptions of being held captive by the passing years disappear.

It is this mysterious region which swallows up past, present and future alike! Here alone may be found "the Eternal Now" of the Hindu Sage.

There are many who will assert that such thought-control is impossible and that these notions of a diviner life for man are purely illusory. Their assertions are accurate enough from their limited standpoint, but why should one accept such limitations. Why should one remain in a jail when a key is placed in one's hands, the key which will open the mind's door and admit him to the ampler spaces of liberty. A man ought not to be hypnotized by current doctrines. The ideas which hold sway today are frequently the rejected notions to tomorrow, and only those who have emancipated themselves in advance of their own epoch can help others to do likewise.

The human mind must revolt against itself if it would attain a complete and not merely a partial insight into the nature of things. The common egocentric attitude is natural, but it is not the final standpoint open to man. Eternity is open to a higher 'I' alone. The price we must pay to find it is the price of dropping the lower 'I' – that which counts the seconds and months and identifies itself wholly with the body. Mental quiet is the means thereto. The root of this higher 'I' is within us; the inner obstacle to it lies therein also.

"You cannot speak of the ocean to a well frog – the creature of a narrower sphere. You cannot speak of the thought-free state to a pedagogue; his scope is too restricted," complained that discerning Chinaman, Chuang Tzu.

The attempt to hint at the possibility of a timeless and thought-free existence to beings who have no idea or experience outside the limits of time is fraught with the fullest difficulties. Such a world is really quite inconceivable to the average man who quaintly but naturally believes that, because he is in the overwhelming majority, he is also the normal man, man as Nature wished him to be. Yet the attempt is not without its value because it draws those who heed it to slumbering regions of their mind; their very efforts to comprehend – seemingly at first so vain and futile – give birth to dawning intuition. For we bear within our own natures both the bonds that keep us tied to incomplete or fallacious opinions as well as the means of liberating ourselves from those bonds. He who strives earnestly to grasp the full implications of all these statements will find in due course that his very strivings possess a magical value; they will help to open a new sense for him.

To revert. Eternity exists, but the price of becoming aware of it is that of inward mastery over the ever-flowing currents of thought. The intellect creates time, the Overself absorbs it whenever it absorbs the intellect.

One must begin to acquire a new way of viewing things and a new habit, that of timeless inner repose. One must learn to distinguish between ephemeral sensations and enduring life *even whilst both co-exist within us*. One must release the mind from looking backward to the dusty past or looking forward to the sealed future or being swept away by the fleeting moment and make it understand truly intuitive thought, which is the sensing of the inner voice of the Absolute. Although one cannot directly grasp the idea of eternity with the intellect and must needs take refuge in metaphor, one can, however, indirectly understand it by using the intellect as a springboard. When the leap-over is successful eternity will remain rigid within the heart, because one has become unified with it.

One must reach this higher outlook and live in the eternal, that inward serenity which is the same yesterday, today and for ever, and is unaffected by vicissitudes. This does not mean refusing to profit by the lessons of the past nor moving heedlessly through the present. It means a *perpetual* underlying steadiness at the centre of one's conscious being which neither the past memories nor present deeds of evanescent existence can shake – a steadiness which may indulge in retrospect or in anticipation without becoming the victim of either. But most often such a one will cease to think of events as soon as they have passed; their mental impressions will flow off him like water off a duck's back. For it is better to be indifferent to the future if the reward is eternal life; it is more profitable to forget the past if the same reward will follow. Thus one may continue uninfluenced by self-reproach and unexcited by speculative hopes.

Thus the study of oneself resolves itself finally into the study of one's intellect, and the study of the intellect resolves itself later into the study of consciousness, and consciousness in its turn is ultimately discoverable as the seraphic and secret exploitation of the Present, the mergence of every moment into eternity. This is the divine life which carries one beyond time.

§

There is lastly the religious angle on time. Does it offer confirmation of these ideas? Let us see. Let us look first into the *Old Testament*.

When Moses found himself in the presence of Jehovah, his God, he asked what he should say to his flock of Israelites when he returned to them to become their leader. "Behold, when I come unto the Children of Israel, and shall say unto them, the God of our Fathers hath sent me unto you, and they shall say unto me, What is his name? What shall I say unto them?" was the first of his questions. And God, out of what appeared to be a burning bush, said unto Moses, "I AM THAT I AM!" and further: "Thus shalt thou say unto the Children of Israel. I AM hath sent me unto you."

Now past and future betoken change, *time*, whereas 'I am' indicates the eternal present. Hence the present tense is used in this jewelled sentence of Jehovah, for that *alone* when profoundly understood – points to eternity. There is no time with God. Hence, too, the further declaration – "which is, and which was, and which is to come, the Almighty." We may penetrate this cryptic phrase even deeper. For "I am that I am," signifies in this latter sense the single idea, *I. It is a way of saying that the "I" of man is the God-element in him, and is consequently eternal.*

"I am going", is a phrase which when analysed psychologically offers a curious illustration of this idea. As it stands it represents life under temporal limitations. But when written like this: "I am – going", the space between the verb and the present participle represents the gap between the time-movement and its cessation. Hence, when we can truly say, "I am", and are not forced to add some movement mentally, we rest in a mental calm which is that of the eternal.

Further on in the same book, the Psalmist says: "Be still and know that I am God."

God dwells for ever in the changeless, ever-calm Eternal.

Hence the mastery of oneself through stillness will lead him into the realm of eternity with God: one shall then partake of His eternal time-proof life.

Next, we may glance into the *New Testament,* when the tenth book of 'Revelation' reaches its higher flights, when the mighty Angel who came down *from heaven,* declares therein:

"There should be time no longer."

What can be the state implied in that phrase but that of awareness of everlasting being?

"Now is the day of salvation," urged the messenger Paul in his Epistle to the Corinthians. He knew that one need not wait till death for the eternal existence.

We may read also the words of Jesus himself.

He announced to the Jews who proudly boasted that they were the descendants of the Patriarch Abraham: "Your father Abraham rejoiced to see my day: he saw it and was glad." Then said the Jews unto him: Thou are not fifty years old, and hast thou seen Abraham? Jesus said unto them: "Verily, verily, I say unto you, *Before Abraham was,* I AM." He did not say "I was", but "I AM". "I was", relates to time, but "I AM", represents unchanging reality.

And the profound meaning of Christ's counsel to His followers: "Sufficient unto the day is the evil thereof," when grasped, is no less an injunction to live out of time, to escape from the thoughts which keep us its captive, than His other bidding: "Let the things of the morrow take care of the morrow!" To make one's exit from cares for the future, to cease looking forward or backward, is to enter into the new life of timeless Reality and to feel the taste of true immortality. Thus alone the world-process is given its true worth.

A proper understanding of this theme provides us with a key to one puzzling aspect of the Biblical story of the world's creation. A hint may be found in St. Augustine's "Confessions", wherein he postulates that creation began, not in time, but with time, i.e. there was no time till there was creation.

But thousands of years before the finger of Christianity touched the book of history, there existed that remarkable religion which was its predecessor in ancient Egypt. This vanished cult was not silent upon the same theme. Its holiest scripture, the *Book of the Dead,* which contains the formulæ of so mixed and mythical a character that only by reference to the doctrine and practice of the Mysteries are the most important passages to be properly understood, speaks of the "deceased" initiate who had been united with Osiris, i.e. spiritually reborn, as affirming:

"I am Yesterday, Today and Tomorrow. I am the divine hidden soul!" Such a one has attained the consciousness of eternal being. And equally significant is the hieroglyphic phrase written on a papyrus which has found its way across the Mediterranean to the Louvre Museum in Paris, and which declares that God, the First Cause, is not only "Goodness itself", but also "Lord of Time, who conducted Eternity". If, further, one had travelled to early Egypt to drink from the fount of her wisdom, as the young Plato once travelled, one would have discerned an inscription over the innermost shrine of the titanic temple of Isis containing these truly remarkable words: "I am that which was, which is, and which is to come. No mortal has yet raised my veil." The meaning of the last phrase is not that eternal existence cannot be found, but that its seeker must first overcome that which limits him to mortality, i.e. his perishable personal ego. And this he can do only by overcoming his thoughts. And if the traveller could have penetrated to the perception of the goddess, he would have found her figured with a handled cross in her right hand, a symbol of everlasting life and the key to the Mysteries; a square boat-sail in her left hand, the symbol of breath and hence a parallel to the ether; and Isis' head itself crowned with her hieroglyph, a throne. Thus Isis would be presented to him as throned in eternal existence.

We find in the faith of Hinduism an equal appreciation of "the mystery which time had hid." Says its sacred Bible, the *Veda,* "That Supreme Spirit was, is and will be." But let us look again into these age-old, palm-leaf texts of the *Veda.* "Eternal and changeless is the Supreme Spirit," it declares, and for him who may have any lingering doubt on the matter there is the plain assertion: "What transcends space and time is the Supreme Spirit."

We may peer further into another sacred Hindu work, the famous manual of the yogis, the *Master's Song* (Bhagavad Gita). Herein Krishna, the Hindu Christ, speaks to his awe-struck disciple, Arjuna, and tells how he taught the truths of spiritual knowledge to sages who lived long centuries before and then explains that this was possible because, "I am the Unborn, the Soul that passes not away."

The mathematical figure for infinity is a union of two circles, thus ∞. The Hindu and other ancient scriptures picture eternity under the old symbol of a snake swallowing its own tail, thus forming a perfect circle. When time turns inward, like the snake, upon itself, it becomes eternity. Indeed, what better symbol could be contrived for time without beginning and without end than a line which returns to its starting point, a line which appears both beginningless and endless, which itself infinite encloses a portion of finite space? Past, present and future constitute a complete circle, which we may start to travel at any point without really marking a beginning or an end.

Very clever was that remark of Mahatma Ramalingam, a South Indian Adept of the nineteenth century. "Time is an invention of the mind," he said, "to calculate its own activity during its runnings and flights."

If, lastly, we travel farther East still and peruse the slim classic of the once-glorious but now debased cult of Taoism, the *Book of Inner Life in Action* (Tao Teh King), its prophet, Lao Tsu, reminds us that:

> "Repose is called the law of return,
> The law of return is called eternity.
> To know eternity is called illumination,
> To ignore eternity is to draw misfortune on oneself,
> To know eternity is to be great of Soul."

Thus the Chinese prophet affirmed in sage syllables that *the knowledge of eternity is possible;* he intimated that man is not doomed to be imprisoned in this temporal life, nor is he so spiritually impoverished that the kingdom of heaven is closed against him. Those who regard the very notion of eternity with uneasiness and think that the life of a Sage who lives with his eyes turned toward the eternal is a kind of never-ending boredom, should spend a few months is his society – if they are so extremely fortunate as to be able to detect and recognize such a one under his modest exterior. The experience would correct their mistake and make good their ignorance.

The timeless Overself is the imperishable divinity in us. We are royalties of long lineage, yet today find ourselves wrapped up in beggar's rags. We may become truly immortal, casting off the years and setting time at defiance, when we enter into recognition of this truth. The time to gain this wisdom is now, and the place is here.

7

THE GENESIS OF GENIUS

There exists a mental phenomenon, a state wherein the higher mind which functions mysteriously above our conscious intellect in the Overself, and which is really the one universal Overmind, seems to speak more peremptorily to man and indeed to take him under its direct if temporary command. That state may fitly be called inspiration; it may remain secretly static, or it may dynamically manifest itself visibly in a definite form or product, such as a work of iridescent art. Inspiration may thus exalt a man with religious ecstasy, or direct him towards great achievements, or transform him into a creative artist.

When someone succeeds in crossing the frontiers of mediocrity in any sphere, we generally regard him as an inspired individual, a genius.

All great art, all recorded spiritual revelation, all truly creative and imaginative work, all new material inventions – when hallmarked by such genius – are the outcome of a spontaneous state wherein the angel of inspiration takes a man by the hand.

We see from this classification that nothing is outside the broad scope of inspiration. We cannot say that such and such a thing is too material, for instance, to become the subject of an inspired revelation. Inspiration is a luminous condition which is competent to deal with all things alike, with the highest ascents of the spirit as well as with the most searching investigations into the material possibilities of our earth.

What exactly is this infrequent and admired condition towards which so many aspire but which so few ever obtain? Let us examine first of all how it arises in a man, and later seek the philosophy implicit in its processes. If we take the case of a great inventor who seeks for the solution of a technical problem and practise some psychological probing into his life, we notice that he broods in anguish and ponders in torment over his problem again and again before the authentic solution which has been eluding him finally flashes across his mind and then grips his soul completely during its materialization. In other words, he enters through endeavour and effort into a state of intermittent self-concentration, of ever-sharper attention and heightening interest until his absorption becomes so deep that, it may be truly said, he has forgotten himself and his environment in his problem. Normal perceptions fall into abeyance and the clock ceases to exist. The inventor who refuses to be cajoled into taking his meals when he is nearing the solution of his problem is a quaint figure familiar enough to every reader of biographies. During such a gestatory period, inventors have often been known to lock themselves in their laboratory or workshop, and refuse to see anyone or attend to other matters. The birth of their invention is about to take place and they seek solitude in the same way that a female animal seeks a solitary place wherein to give birth to its child. This is noteworthy evidence of the degree of utter absorption into which these men naturally sink when striving to obtain a revelation beyond the ordinary reach of intellect. They are completely controlled by what seems to be some superior force. The most wonderful material inventions have been discovered in this strange manner.

We must not consider such absorption as being a mere condition of extreme self-centredness alone and imagine that the inventor is merely wrapped up in his petty personal affairs to the exclusion of everything else. On the contrary, the farther he progresses within his mind towards his goal, and the more he meditates upon it, the less is he occupied with thoughts about his personal self, although paradoxically he seems more withdrawn into himself. The price which he has to pay for the solution of his problem is indeed nothing less than the price of absolute self-forgetfulness. He becomes one with his problem – so perfect is his concentration – and whilst doing that, he dissociates himself from his own ego.

But the invention once accomplished and completed. his mind springs back to its personal groove with greater force than ever, and the erstwhile state of inspired impersonality disappears. Thus we may say that one highly important condition which is an accompaniment of inspiration is a state of self-forgetfulness.

We may find analogous evidences of this truth among the geniuses who flourish in the arts. The musical composer who strives to hear within himself the echoes of that infinite beauty which comes fluttering down to earth as a fine symphony, quite naturally seeks solitude at such a time. Not infrequently, he disdains food and all else in the concentrated effort needed to catch those echoes. One speaks here of real music, such as proceeds from and affects the deepest heart of mankind, lingering there long after the last note has been heard, like those last quarters of Beethoven's "Kreutzer Sonata." The composer who is faithful to his call, who knows how to carry on his true business, will never permit himself to be seduced by the world into its numerous distractions when he feels the beck-oning hand of inspiration laid upon his shoulder. Instead, he may become as rigidly ascetic in his renunciation as any ancient hermit has ever been.

What happens to him in the quietude of his chamber during the divine moments when inspiration rewards his labour? Can we not say that he is so intent upon unreservedly hearing those delicate tones that he has become a mere instru-ment which is being played upon by another power? Can we not say, further, that he has forgotten his very personality, his family, his friends or his duties through this absolute surrender to the music which flows into him and in which he has *lost him-self*? What is all this but a yielding up of the obstructive ego?

The truly talented and spiritual dancer will likewise reveal rapt absorption in her graceful spontaneous movements which is the significant sign of her genius. In the degree that she forgets her admiring audience, she understands her true mission of beauty-bringing, of symbolically reminding them of the Ultimate Beauty they are unconsciously pursuing.

If we turn to the work of the painter and sculptor we may behold the same striking phenomenon. A truly inspired painter who seizes his brush and stands for hours before the easel, studying his half-finished work, making deft strokes here and there, covering the canvas with coloured embodiments of the forms which his heated imagination and observation com-bine to create, is not aware of the passage of time nor even of the noises and sights one foot beyond his studio window. Every painter who has considered and judged the nature of the art which he practises, will confess that he lives deeply and happily in such irradiated moments – the deeper self-absorp-tion the happier he is. Such inspired hours are themselves the genuine and true reward of the artist; they bestow a mild but deep ecstasy for which popular applause or high patronage is only a feeble substitute. The actual joy of his work is unconsciously derived from the temporary forgetting of himself.

It is necessary for the artist to fling himself entirely into his theme and to float away in its current as in a stream. To do this effectively, he must forget everything else. He must silence all those claims upon time and thought which spring from all the other departments of his human life and this he accomplishes by entering into a condition of mental quiet. Such quiet, such a silencing of his personal life brings him to the ultimate source from which all art springs and permits him to produce a masterpiece. Hence, Carlyle could adorn his craggy pages with a tiny flower of prose like this: "In all true works of art wilt thou discern eternity looking through time, the god-like rendered visible." The smile of a Madonna, as portrayed in the famous picture by Raphael, may be more persuasive than a score of theological sermons. Who knows how many sceptics she has troubled with new notions about the value of religion?

We must here make a distinction between talent and genius. Genius alone is inspired and works with triumphant spontaneity of production; talent is something developed by the mastery of technique. The technique of his craft must, of course, be acquired by the artist during his earlier years, and to a degree that makes him an adept in the chosen channel of expression, yet this is only preliminary. Technique is necessary for the material nourishment of all art. A great artist needs a grasp of technique no less than his imitators. Genius and talent must marry and give a banquet to the hungry world. The genius who has never studied the technique of his art cannot produce a good work; but on the other hand, the talented man without an inner source of inspiration cannot produce an outstanding work. Thus, if we turn aside for a moment to consideration of literature, it is easy for a practised writer to make his paragraphs heavy with rouge, and then to offer his book upon the altar of Olympus as the sacrifice made by genius. But the gods spurn the false gift and fling it back among the world of men, where, even though it may have a triumphant welcome and be acclaimed by a thousand voices, its life will eventually flicker and pass out like a guttering candle. Skill alone is not enough, creative illumination is also needed.

A great French painter said to the pupils in his Paris studio: "Master your technique and then forget everything about it." He knew that whatever art-work one takes up, one ought first to master all the rules and details about it until they have sunk deeply into the unconscious, and when that is done, to turn inwards and seek inspiration, which must appear and shine through the formal technique. If one does not forget the rules of his craft but has to think anxiously again and again about them, one will be only a talented man and not a genius. If a man must be constantly making reference to rules of technique, in order to produce fine work, then God help him! Inspiration is the essential thing. It throws the artist into a state of creative but quiet ecstasy. It exempts him from the narrow limitations of nerve and brain.

The inspired artist will form his own individual conception of a subject, and it will be truer than the stereotyped product of the art schools, while his productions will be markedly superior.

The Japanese of a less commercial epoch than the present possessed a suggestive word in their language for the idea of artistic elevation – the word *fu-in* which means literally "wind inspiration". When an artistic production had been successfully accomplished under the influence of this inspiration, it was said to possess *kokoromochi*, which signifies literally "heart-holding". They meant by these terms an elevation that was the result of a gracious manifestation of divinity, something imparted to the artist by the Creator. They asserted that such inspiration could neither be conveyed to another man nor acquired by laborious effort: for it was given by divine grace and in no other way. This was the quality they looked for in their most esteemed works of art, in their most graceful pictures, whose beauty seemed to be spun with rainbow-thread. Today, alas, that attitude had dwindled and they are becoming much less critical, readier to accept gaudy tinsel instead of genuine expressions of "wind inspiration".

Among the Hindus, there are traditional scriptures, the "Silpa Shastras", which prescribe practical rules for the realization of the ideal of spiritual beauty through practice in the technical arts and crafts. Their chief artists and artisans attached to temples in former times employed a yoga process before executing their work upon these buildings. Only after they had succeeded in putting their minds into the proper condition of intense concentration were they permitted to begin painting or modelling. Inspiration was the thread upon which these creators slipped the beads of their most beautiful work.

§

We may turn next to the condition of inspiration in the domain of poetry and literature. Every land may be laid under tribute for inspired pieces, thus showing that the quality is universal, inherent in the human race, and not the product of either Western civilization or clever modernity alone. In the Orient, a hundred titles are available, each standing at the head of authentically illumined works. The wise and witty poems of Sadi, the ecstatic prose of Jami's *Lawaih,* the lyrical songs of the burly Sikh Bhavir Singh, the mystic tales of the "Mathnawi", and the priceless *Rubáiyát* of Omar Khayyám, no less than the musical rhythmic sweetness of Sir E. Arnold's poetic translation of the Indian "Song Celestial" (Bhagavad

Gita), offer choice specimens abounding in illuminating metaphors of the poet, which are, indeed, the language of the soul-world.

The same desire for seclusion is apparent here as in the cases of technical inventor and musical composer. It means that a process of psychological turning-inwards is occurring and the writer of genius who seeks to drive an immortal pen will positively resent any intrusion upon his privacy during a creative period when ideas flow like a running stream. Balzac locked himself up inside his room during such periods and, working day and night, had his meals placed outside his door so that he might later unlock the door and take his food without being disturbed by the presence of another person.

One need only read such an extraordinary poem as Coleridge's masterpiece, "Rime of the Ancient Mariner", to feel a mystic influence gradually stealing into one's mental atmosphere and thus understand in how much deeper a measure the poet himself must have been pervaded by the same mysterious inspiration during the period of composition. Again, he fell asleep one day whilst reading a book. On awakening he felt that he had composed two hundred to three hundred lines of poetry during his sleep, and that he had nothing to do but write them down, for the images rose up as though they were things, calling forth their verbal expressions automatically and instantaneously and absolutely without effect on his own part. He got his pen and wrote down that strange fragmentary poem entitled "Kubla Khan". This proves how easily the work does come when the conscious mind is in abeyance.

Such products do not seem to come from a man's common intellect; they seem to come from something higher than that, something which is able to control him completely as he writes his rhymes. He must surrender his little personality and let this higher mind, this Overmind, take full possession of him. When this is really done and the spiritual act is allied with a perfect technique, the world receives a work of outstanding genius. During the moments of complete impersonal detachment, he draws from his innermost a spiritual element which he places into his work and which renders it inspired.

That is why a writer cannot always be judged by his books. Not seldom his habitual state of mind and character is inferior to the plane of his writings. Sometimes he may be wiser and better than his works; but sometimes they are wiser and better than he. Tennyson afterwards confessed that "In Memoriam", his long poetic pæan of personal survival after death, represented an expression of truth which he had not himself adequately grasped or understood, previous to writing it down. "It is more optimistic than I am," he told a friend.

For when inspiration is dominant, it temporarily lifts a man beyond his normal level, but the last word written, he falls back for a period once again to the general state. Hence some of his works may be coruscating stars, the product of inspiration whereas others are the product of his uninspired moods; some may be imperishable masterpieces of the highest quality and others positively bad. If we recognize this as psychological fact, we can then understand why a great genius sometimes produces poor stuff and why many of his swans are mere geese. We cannot expect to find inspiration in every line of a poet's stanzas, nor sparkling truths to fall always like sapphires from his pen.

We hear much of the fact that inspiration is fickle and every poet complains that he cannot control his inner genius or command its arrival. He works by spells and trafficks in moods. His achievements are mostly partial. Ideas fail him; he cannot make headway with his composition; and words fall dead upon his pen. His bright-plumed muse comes and goes without warning at her own sweet will – not his – and cannot be summoned at desire. How often he sits intimidated by the sheet of blank paper before him! Creative moods are intermittent. Inspiration is not constant, man is capable of connected thought but not of connected inspiration. The flowers of genius have sudden blooms and swift witherings.

One needs to frame no theory of explanation for these alternating rhythms: the facts explain themselves. The condition essential to inspiration is not present – that is all. That condition, as we have seen, is intense mental absorption because we habitually live in external activity and personal remembrance. It is not easy to forgo this race-habit. Hence the genius who struggles to give birth to great things lives fitfully, warring sporadically with his own self, sometimes blindly and unconsciously interfering with the inspiration which woos him. He himself provides some of his own obstructions.

His physical activities imprison the mind in the region of effort; lifeless words hem him round and he cannot string them together as in his brighter moments. His ordinary intellect keeps him pegged down to its limitations, not least of which is the vain conceit of its own creative power. Scholarship, however illustrious, is no substitute for burning transcendence. But when he lets this intellect become self-absorbed in concentration, inspiration "returns" and the creative flow proceeds unhindered once more. Let him relax for a while and learn to be still in body and breath, turning the intellect by powerful concentration inwards upon itself, and the divine afflatus will descend upon him anew.

His personal ego presumes upon its own competence to deal with all difficulties, handle all problems, but only when he forgets it and loses himself utterly in the impersonal does the highest possibility of wisdom or beauty or power really come into the ascendant of his horoscope. *This self-forgetfulness, this momentary loss of the personal 'I', is the true cause of this bliss which accompanies the creative state.* For we cannot sew the soft tapestry of immortal art save with the bright orange threads of divine joy. Where is there one man who has stood aside and watched his hand and mind being used for the eternal wonder of artistic creation, without finding that all the gloom he has gathered from his daily contact with the drabber world is flung off his shoulders with the first stirrings of the divine impulse?

The real truth is that personality is only a vessel or channel and that when it wholly absorbs our consciousness, it hinders our sense of divine selfhood and also hinders the creative element which manifests through it so markedly in genius.

"Poets are sometimes the echoes of words of which they know not the power – the trumpet that sounds to battle and feels not what it inspires," wrote one of England's premier poets, Shelley. The curious thing about many writers and artists is that they do not know beforehand what they are going to produce, whilst sometimes the future development of their works takes a different course from that which they had planned. Referring to his last two symphonies at a time when neither was completed, Jean Sibelius, the composer, said that "the plans may possibly be altered according to the development of the musical ideas. As usual, I am a slave to my themes and submit to their demands." This apparently shows that inspiration is something received from the letting-go of personality. If it came from the personal will, all composers would be able to plan every stage of the work. That it is something spontaneous in its own nature, and that therefore all inspired work is delivered to us whole and complete before even the first movement of hand or head has been made, is shown by many instances. Mozart, 'the musical prodigy', as he was often called, related once that in the process of composing his music, "provided I am not disturbed my subject enlarges itself, becomes defined, and the whole stands complete and finished in my mind, so that I can survey it like a beautiful statue at a glance. For this reason the committing to paper is done easily enough, for everything is as I have said, already finished."

Arnold Bennett, the novelist, has told how he usually overcame the stalemate of lost inspiration. Instead of cudgelling his mind all day, his habit was exactly the opposite. He went to the South Kensington Museum in London and looked at tapestries or bronzes, or in Paris he strolled by the Seine and browsed around the old bookstalls. While thus distracting his mind and forgetting his problem, leading his mind away from the subject for which he had been groping, the inspiration he sought would suddenly come to him. The processes of thought had done what they could and attained their limit; to be side-tracked from the work in hand, *the conscious personal ego* had to be detached from it; this gave an opportunity for the deeper subconscious division of mind, i.e. the Overmind, to come into play.

Now it is important to note that had Bennett not been engaged on a book and thus used his intellect already upon the theme, the remedy would not have been effective. *The working mind has something of its own to contribute, its part to do, but once done it should retire gracefully and permit the deeper mind to work through its human agent, returning to activity only to revise and repolish when all is done.* When the first spark falls into the conscious mind, it must be fanned by self-yielding. When, however, as with most intellectual men, the ego remains obstinately on the throne, then it stultifies its own purpose and prevents the inflow of inspiration.

The duty of a writer's intellect is first, by a prolonged effort of intense concentration, to hold before him and in the field of consciousness the particular theme which is to be worked upon; then, when this has been adequately achieved and when it senses the influx of glowing inspiration brought about by forgetting self, it must yield itself up entirely in a state of utter passivity, yet remain as alert and as conscious as ever, and it must interpret the subtle message into thoughts and frame them into the right words.

In oratory of inspirational origin the speaker is not infrequently quite ignorant of the character or even theme of his impending speech. Making all allowances for perfection of technique and vocal organ, something is left over which grips the audience or awes it, something intangible but communicable as an atmosphere. Thus, the late Sir Sahabji Maharaj, leader of the Radhasoami Yogic Colony at Dayalbagh near Agra, in India, delivered remarkable religious addresses to an audience of two to three thousand nightly for several years, each night changing his subject. Not only did he prepare no notes, but he informed the present writer that he knew nothing beforehand of what he was going to say each evening.

Socrates confessed that when it came to the profoundest truth of things, it was not himself that spoke but a voice – his 'dæmon' – within him. Who or what was this voice but that of his inspired mind?

§

When we turn to consider the case of religious and spiritual inspiration, we find the same laws operative here, the same characteristics of artistic creation, albeit in an extraordinarily strong relief. The ancient, medieval and modern saints of Christendom, faqueers of Islam and yogis of India have all had their rapturous experiences of a religious order through processes wherein the phenomenon of artistic inspiration was plain to behold. The artist, writer and inventor have perforce to transmit their messages through the medium of a material instrument, but the inspired saint is under no such limitation and exhibits in himself the psychological changes he has undergone.

For the religious mystic – if he is worth anything at all – exemplifies, by his yearning to surrender himself utterly to his God, the working of the basic principles of inspiration. When through ardent prayer or heartfelt aspiration he succeeds in realizing this, his personal ego sinks into hushed quiescence whilst the Higher Power which he adores seems to take possession of him. He may – and indeed he will – interpret his holy experience with the aid of images, symbols and doctrines pertaining to his particular religious creed, but his essential experience is that of an influx, a merging into a state where the ordinary self apparently ceases to operate and a joyous ecstatic sacred harmony overwhelms his being. He is likely to pass into a trance when this experience reaches its culmination, a condition where everything seems wrapped in God. He has paid the price of true inspiration – the dropping away of the personal self to its lowest ebb of rhythm that it might be engulfed in ineffable exalted emotion.

The Hindu yogi who drives his thoughts into a corner by pitiless concentrative power and then makes a supreme effort to drop them out of his mind altogether, likewise arrives at a state of inspired being where the thinking intellect no longer obstructs the inflow of peace which he seeks. He, too, at the culmination of his quest may enter into a profound trance similar to that of a saint. Although he has travelled along the road of thought-control, whereas the latter has journeyed along the road of exalted emotion, the power which draws them both into the trance-like condition and out of the little personality and limited intellect is one and the same. They are content to enjoy the bliss of communion with that power, to make no endeavour to transmit or express its fine efflorescence through some material medium such as art, invention or oratory; but at the root of both lies the supernal element which spreads its mantle over the latter. It is the same in kind and quality as that which takes possession of genius. Music, sculpture, poetry and architecture were sacred in the eyes of the ancients, to be practised only by special priests of the temples or gifted initiates of the Grand Mysteries in early Egypt, Greece, India and China.

The important thing to observe is that the concentrative activity and consequent influx are precisely the same kind as those of inspired painters and poets; it is the manifestation which alone differs, for where the artist feels an intense urge to communicate his vision or idea and turns back to the outer world to express his experience, the mystic is content to lose himself in his contemplation. Art is a form of meditation, a path to that satisfied state which mystics call God, only the artist calls his deity, Beauty.

The Grace of God, whose coming rewards the mystic's yearnings, possesses its equivalents in the inspiration whose coming rewards the artist's efforts. Both are derived from the same root. When intense concentration melts the personal 'I' in the impersonal universal Overmind, benign Grace descends on the mystic or yogi, and creative inspiration on the writer or sculptor.

Those who become so absorbed in artistic creativeness of whatever kind as to be forgetful of self and surroundings, really arrive at an interior condition wherein they open an inlet to the universal Overmind not very dissimilar to that which is experienced by the seekers after God in their trances. The important difference is that the yogi is turned inwards upon himself, upon his innermost mind, and lets his body remain immobile, whereas the artist keeps his body actively engaged in transmitting to some medium, whether it be paper, canvas or stone, the refulgent images or ideas which hold his mind as under a spell; the degree of mental absorption in both cases may be equal. For the artist is no less rapturously gripped and held by these images which he is transmitting than the yogi is gripped and held by the light of undivided consciousness which he experiences when all thoughts are stilled. Both become unaware of the passage of time when they attain this supreme inspiration, which feeds them from the same holy source, and thus unconsciously demonstrate that time is truly only an idea.

And even people who are neither artists, inventors, saints nor yogis, occasionally have experiences similar in kind, although less in degree, when they feel the power of these visitations to the concentrated absorbed mind. Genius may manifest in the desk-filled office, the goods-lined shop and the thronged Stock Exchange; why not? Is it so circumscribed that it must disdain to appear in a metropolis among those who carry on some of mankind's essential activities? Business magnates who control organizations of vast extent, have not infrequently discovered new policies of the utmost value to them when they have been concentrating in a mental condition of deep reverie upon their business and its problems. The illumination which came and perhaps set them upon the road to striking success, came after deep concentration. This act of concentrating their thoughts with great tenacity upon a single track eventually brought them, even if only for a minute or two, into an inspired condition of self-forgetfulness and mental abstraction from their surroundings, as a paradoxical reaction. But that minute or two was sufficient to give them the desired revelation of manufacturing plan or sales policy.

Moreover, the inspiration which presents a business man with a prophetic vision of what he is to achieve will not necessarily desert him again completely, but will leave a lingering, exalting influence that will help him to carry the work through right from its beginning. Inspiration not only gives the vision, but also the strength to achieve the end. Whoever recognizes and yields to this inner influence will find that the results always justify its guidance. It fixes a certain aim or goal before the eyes during the first intoxicating moments of self-absorption, presses upon him from within, wells up with compelling illumination again and again, carries with it the inspiring sense, the positive certainty of the success or rightness towards which it is leading him.

The parallel between all these diverse manifestations of inspired genius, ranging from the religious to the mundane, is clear. A single principle, an identical source, lies underneath these varying phenomena. Deep within us there is a wonderful and infinite store of knowledge, wisdom, power, beauty and harmony. Genius can call forth these qualities and use them to inspire its work, its thoughts and its being. If one is a lawyer, one becomes a better lawyer and a more trustworthy one and not worse by being inspired. If one is a teacher, one can gain a better understanding of the psychology of the pupils' minds; one will know how to deal with them more efficiently, because one will see their varying individual standpoints. No man can touch his own deeper self without unfolding a sense of harmony and sympathy with others. The barrier between the teacher and the taught will therefore disappear, and the possibilities of the student will have a better chance to develop.

The collaboration of perfect technique and perfect inspiration is needed to produce the perfect and complete genius. If the latter phenomenon is extremely rare among us that is because almost all of us are rather mixed and unequal beings; even our acknowledged geniuses cannot always function at their top level because, although they can always command technique, they cannot always command inspiration. A man can only hope to hold his spell of glowing inspiration for a while and then watch it fade. But this is not to say that the possibility of entering a permanent relation with inspiration cannot one day be materialized. This possibility means that if we will trace out and study the source of inspiration and begin to understand the conditions of its manifestation, it might then be practicable to discover how to make its subliminal upsurge come to us more frequently and how to work out some method whereby we can retain this inspiration more lastingly.

The present writer believes this can be done, that if a man will master the technique of his art or business as perfectly as can be, and also train his mind in self-absorption the combination must unfailingly produce genius in its highest flower. Such a man could produce inspired works always, without exception. Whereas our accepted geniuses are suffused geniuses at some hours of their lives and ordinary technicians at others, only such a combination as here indicated can provide a permanent manifestation and demonstration of mankind's yet far-off possibilities of the genuine superman.

Everything depends, then, upon the degree of self-forgetfulness through complete concentration which one can achieve. In everyday activities one is too wrapped up in the interests of the personal ego which one allows to circumscribe his consciousness to seek to forget oneself, and yet this ego which one thinks so important is after all but a tiny fragment of existence within the infinitely vaster existence of mankind and the world. It acts like a screen that shuts off awareness of the supreme reality, the Overself that feeds our life, because it is nothing but a medley of ungoverned thoughts, and it is only by pulling down that screen that one may come into the transcendent knowledge, powers and possibilities of the Overself. All things have arisen out of that reality, all things are possible by and through its aid, all knowledge lies like a coiled serpent within its embrace. That which debars a man from entering upon this marvellous wider heritage which is truly his, is only this narrow ego, this tiny fragment of conscious being which he has fenced around himself as a kind of prison-compound and out of which he mulishly refuses to pass.

With the close of this chapter there closes also the first part of the work which will constitute the document of this analytic system. Hitherto the reader has been led upon a preliminary path. He has been provided with material for intellectual analysis, and if he will do his part earnestly and obediently he will have properly prepared himself for the intermediate path, which consists of a group of spiritual practices designed to bridge the gulf between mundane experiences and mystical reality. Upon this second route he will be trained to realize, make real in his own life, the spiritual truths which may have hitherto been but faintly illumined intellectual cognitions.

He has been led to recognize the existence of his unknown self, the Overself, which hides in his innermost deeper mind like a shining pearl hiding in an oyster-shell. He has been taught the real meaning of time and the secret habitations of eternal life has been revealed to him. He has been brought to understand how to tap the source of the most valuable inspirations which have blessed the human race.

Finally, it has been pointed out as true from various angles of elevated human experience, that the screen which shuts him off from the awareness of the Overself is nothing else than his own personal ego and his own inability to bring his thoughts under control. Entry into this diviner selfhood is impossible unless and until he can mortify the one and subdue the other – in reality a simultaneous operation, as demonstrated when both were analysed and traced to a single root.

A practical method must now be found whereby this may be accomplished. The method exists and *part* of it has been known to the wise men of the East and the illuminati of the West since the earliest centuries. Altered, adapted and supplemented to suit European and American needs, presented in a form palatable to the modem mind, it is confidently offered in the following pages as a tried and tested heritage of the race which possesses incalculable value.

Part II

THE PRACTICES

8

THE SPIRITUAL CULTURE OF
FINER FEELINGS

The practical mental training which from the next chapter onwards is prescribed in the second division of this treatise, constitutes work on the most important portion of man's being, but the emotional element needs a certain education also. Indeed, to not a few temperaments purely mental methods will make less appeal than those which touch the feelings. Human beings are built in different ways and are naturally attracted to the kind of activity which best accords with their ruling temperament.

Religion particularly is a matter of feeling, and reaches its culmination in religious mysticism. Foremost from the viewpoint of universal occurrence, the religious element has been predominant in the past among the masses of mankind. Worship attains its greater value when it gives a re-orientation of the worshipper's thoughts from his own personality to that of another belonging to a spiritual order and its greatest when directed to the infinite Power which we name God. It becomes truly effective in so far as it evokes the quality of *aspiration,* the yearning to be uplifted from one's common frail condition towards that which is divine and holy. Such aspiration, when it is at its best, really transforms popular religion into mysticism; therefore it may be said that he only is absolutely religious who has become a mystic – all else but touches the fringe of worship.

Devotional persons may practise such a way with profit. They may take the figure and life of their Lord, and meditate upon it as an ideal existence. Revering the picture of this great soul, they should throw the full force of their aspiration towards Him with such intensity that all other thoughts are excluded. The picture should be formed as clearly as possible, with vivid details and living colours, and then the mind may dwell lovingly on the incidents of the personal life of the Inspirer, or on some aspect of His teachings, or a single one of His sayings can have its inner content extracted during contemplation. They must 'see' Him so clearly that for the time He appears to be a materialized figure, no less real than their physical surroundings. They must visualize situations and events until the latter 'become alive' to them. The mystical element of this practice really begins when Christ – if He be the chosen Guide, for instance – no longer appears to be external to them but within, when He is transcended as a *person* and becomes a *presence*. That is to say, His picture should ultimately disappear during the height of devotion, while His very being, His life, should manifest within the devotees as the Christ-self. When that high state of spiritual rebirth is reached, He no longer appears as a distinct and separate being, but the whole personality is merged into Him, surrendered at His call, absolutely and unconditionally. Then is born the Christ-self in its place, a pervading presence that is our true incorruptible inheritance.

There must be a real craving, a heart-devastating love for the Divine Personage before such meditations ultimately bring successful results. One ought to call upon Him for His grace, but the call must proceed from the deepest place in one's heart if one is really to receive it. If He is made the theme of one's sincere aspirations in this wholehearted manner, and enshrined in the silent cathedral of the heart, all other thoughts being dismissed during the time of worship; if one dwells in His spiritual presence during meditation and lets His spiritual presence dwell in one during other activities, a time will surely come when one will have the unforgettable experience of mystical ecstasy. The varied wants and inescapable sorrows, the cares and tribulations of personal life will be temporarily blotted out in the unutterable joy that will overwhelm him. One will discover the true meaning of that much-misused word, love, and will want to befriend the whole world, even at the cost of complete self-martyrdom. Thenceforward, one will seek to do His will, to surrender the personal to the Divine, and one will understand with joy that all created things are moving forward with the evolution of the whole universe toward a stupendously glorious goal.

If, in these devotional contemplations and religious yearnings, tears begin to fill one's eyes, they must not be denied expression. They should be accepted as part of the inevitable price that is demanded. They will help dissolve the invisible barriers between one and the Divine Ideal. *Those who weep in their spiritual exile do not weep in vain.*

It is necessary to explain here, for the benefit of persons who belong to other continents than the Western ones or who hold another faith than the Christian, that identical results have been and can be obtained outside the fold of Jesus's followers, and along precisely similar lines of practice. Many are the mystics to whom the names of either Krishna, Muhammad or Buddha have alone conjured up the deepest devotion of the heart, yet who have won, by earnest aspiration and constant meditation, the blissful ecstatic union with diviner existence. The attractive power of a revered religious

Personage of such a high order bestows positive aid in concentrating the mind and enabling it to overcome faults and frailties. That is why in India and Persia, for instance, religious mystics take even today, as they have taken for centuries past, the physical portrait of their living teacher or mental image of an ancient spiritual master as a focus for their meditation. They derive vital help in curbing wandering thoughts from such practice, while it appeals to the heart and arouses aspiration to frequent effort.

It is necessary to point out, however, that ecstatic bliss is not the final goal with which the meditative life presents us. Such bliss is not the highest criterion of truth, even though it is no distant neighbour of truth. It is true that many mystics have thought so and have stopped their efforts with its attainment, thus inviting that terrible scourge, the dark night of the soul, or spiritual darkness. The meditating mystic must learn not to tarry overlong in the realm of joyous spiritual emotionalism, but rather to transcend it. For there is a higher realm yet to be attained, none other than that utter peace which passes understanding, a realm of wide calm and supreme tranquillity.

Even from those who are not naturally religious and who will therefore remain untouched by this brief description of the aforementioned way, a certain culture of aspiration is still required. In their case, however, it is not necessary to direct such yearnings toward any religious Personage or Principle but toward the idea and ideal of Truth which appeals to them. Although the mind is thus made the principal instrument of attainment in this work, it needs an inner force behind it that shall move it toward success. That driving power must be supplied by aspiration.

The worth of this one factor cannot be over-estimated. To send out repeatedly into the universe a silent or vocal call, desire or yearning for spiritual truth, peace or guidance, is to set stirring into action certain intelligent forces that exist in the universe and that *ultimately* respond, in the exact proportion to the degree of intensity of the aspiration. The universe is not a blindly working machine, but a garment worn by a hierarchy of conscious intelligent beings. *And it is a good time to begin aspiring, if one has not learnt to do so before, when the deep despairs which follow the harder blows of fate create a melancholy sense of the transitoriness and hollowness of mortal existence.*

Whether one is religiously inclined or not, whether one aspires to know the intellectual verity or not, there is still a third form of emotional development which should be attempted. It lies partly through sensitivity to æsthetic impressions, both in Nature and art, and partly through finer ethical feelings and the avoidance of unworthy emotions.

We take a delight in scenes of natural beauty which we cannot take in city streets. Who has not been stirred by beautiful landscapes that need the high-flown language of poetry to do them ample justice? Who has not met those high moments in our lives when we are *lost to ourselves* amid surroundings of impressive splendour, inducing us to become absorbed in their sublime contemplation? More people in this mundane West than we suspect have had an emotional experience either once or at intervals which has made life assume for a while a totally different aspect. The allusion is to those flashes of ecstatic illumination, of contact with a beautiful roseate reality which enfolds the material universe, that descend unexpectedly and leave a joyous or peaceful exaltation in their train. Such moments may come when one is alone upon a ship deck at night surrounded by the vast ocean, or when watching the pink sunrise creep over a mountain ridge, or they may descend with sudden incongruity but compelling power amid the noisy hubbub of the market-place. They come when one receives Nature into one's heart, not as the botanist who dissects a flower or ruthlessly removes its petals to study its structure, but as an ardent lover and friend. They come when we see a landscape through the eyes of a poet, and when we realize that heaven may begin in a patch of grass near home. However they come, one finds oneself forgetting personal cares and anxieties and becoming uplifted into an impersonal view of things which has formerly never been possible to obtain, much less to hold. Time seems to stop, the sense that life is eternal infiltrates into one's mind of its own accord, the physical environment loses a little of its tangibility, its reality fading off slightly into a dream-like substance. An ethereal peace, before unfelt, surges into the heart and brings with it an intense satisfaction which the gratification of no mortal desire could ever bring. A clearer understanding dawns, too, life seems clarified and one senses rather than sees an intelligent purpose at the heart of things. The horror and chaos and conflict which seem inseparable from human and animal existence in this world vanish for a while from one's ken, because in this divine atmosphere to which one has been introduced, their harsh memory cannot endure. The beautiful truth, so impalpable and yet so ineffable, has touched the heart. One *knows* . . . but alas! the experience recedes, although the remembrance of it for ever remains. It cannot be forgotten even if one wants to; its quality will abide and never be worn threadbare as are the normal experiences of earthly existence. Again and again, the sublime memory haunts one and he yearns for a renewal of such divine moments.

What does the recollection of such rare moments mean? Can one gather them anew for himself as one gathers fresh odorous flowers daily from the prolific earth?

The answer to the first question is that behind the self which everyone knows there lies another of which one is normally unaware and which is that mysterious and elusive thing called the soul or the spirit. This Overself is the most secret part of man's nature, yet it is nevertheless the most funda-mental. The impersonal blissfulness of which we obtain such brief fragments is *inherent* in the nature of that other self. Our inspirations, then, are merely crumbs dropped from its eternal feast.

The answer to the second question is "yes!" These beautiful states of feeling, these glorious spells of time can be recaptured at will and lengthened as desired after the full method of self-training described in this book has been under-stood and sufficiently practised, for the right culture of our finer feelings forms a part of this training.

§

One must set oneself to watch for and cultivate certain fragile moods of the heart. Such moods come into most people's lives at different times, often casually and unexpected, but generally for the shortest of periods, and being uncultivated are thrust aside and much of their value lost. These moods are most fre-quently evoked unconsciously through æsthetic pleasures, through such things as listening to ecstatically beautiful music, reading inspired poetry, and yielding to the impressions made upon one's senses and mind by unforgettably grand natural scenes: more rarely, there is a very valuable mood of profound veneration and deep appreciation induced by personal meet-ing with one who has aligned himself to some degree with the Overself.

Whenever such a mood of powerful charm, intense awe or utter peace is experienced it is necessary that one should keep all one's mind upon it and recognize it as an important messenger and listen to its message; one should ponder long and deeply over this message and seek to trace it to its higher origin; one should try to weave its effects into the fabric of one's own character. Because such moods do not come to us labelled with the name of the country of their mystic origin, we are apt to under-value their worth. They are generally of momentary duration and should be recognized at their real worth and their inner essence consciously extracted, for truly, these moments can be turned to high account and the experiences which brought them about will not be vain ones. Everything that helps the love of exalting beauty, that tends to influence one towards a nobler attitude, towards a profounder awareness of life than that which is given by the merely material sequence of changes which composes the commonplace daily routine, should be thus accepted and fostered; it will increase the inner sensitivity to finer forces that is needed on this path.

Nature, the Grand Artist, can inspire in sensitive souls moods as elevating and as profound as any caused by the handiwork of mortal man. One may turn to her kindly arms at any time for relief and succour from earthly misery. She is beauty made earth and serenity and stone. When, for instance, one wanders into the silent depths of a forest and penetrates its throbbing silence, alone with its immensity, one should keep one's attention concentrated upon the first emotions thus aroused and heighten them to a degree where they pass into something of genuine spiritual value. One must begin by being thus alert to catch the earliest sensations of charm and serenity whenever they make themselves felt. Then one must make them the lingering theme of a musing reverie, and delight in them as holy signs. One must sip these feelings again and again with increased joy, and continually turn their taste over on the tongue. Thus even as one walks upon the leaf-strewn ground, a state of concentration may be induced which will deepen gradually until, if one is fortunate, that eternal serenity of the Overself which underlies all our fitful moods may flash forth and give us an unforgettable experience.

In just the same way, one may wander along some lonely stretch of seashore and listen to the breaking of the waves. And then one may sit down for a while on a broken boulder or a dry patch of sand, and there gaze outwards over the vast expanse of blue sea towards the horizon of amethyst sky. One should then open oneself to receive all that Nature has to say. The rhythmic splashing of the waves and the immensity of the ocean both bear a message to man. One must allow this message to enter powerfully into one's whole being rather than try to comprehend it intellectually. Sitting as still as possible with concentrated gaze and heart, and with passive receptive soul, one must let the senses of sight and hearing become the mediators of a higher mood. When this new mood is engendered actually and intensely, one should surrender oneself quite freely and permit it to live within oneself *without, however, making it the subject of intellectual analysis*. Indeed, it is of such importance in the evocation and cultivation of these higher moods of emotion not to bring one's critical faculties to bear upon them, not to attempt to dissect them mentally until after they have entirely gone, but rather to let oneself melt gently into them. Should one interfere, one succeeds rather in cutting himself off from the mood and in dissipating what might have been a precious spiritual experience.

There is a subtle psychological reason why natural scenes which include widespread plains and far-stretching deserts, distant mountain ranges and remote ocean horizons, possess a special power to elevate one's being into a spiritual state. When the eyes *first* behold such a scene and the gaze is fixed on its farthest point, the mind – which is the real conscious seeing agent and which merely uses the visual organs as instruments – projects itself into space until it reaches the boundary. The entire operation takes but a flash of time, for mind travels with amazing celerity. In the result the mind fastens itself upon the distant object whilst yet retaining its hold in the base, i.e. the physical brain. This activity is similar in part to the curious activity of a worm which, while endeavouring to move from one position to another, actually lengthens itself as it is about to let go of its original hold.

The psychological result in oneself, however, is that the moment of first fixing the gaze so remotely lifts consciousness partly out of the physical body and frees the mind from its habitual egocentric attitude. One involuntarily deserts the purely personal for the impersonal with the speed of a lighting-flash, one ceases to be immersed in constant cogitation, all attention being bestowed on the act of beholding, and then returns again to the ordinary condition. But this mystic interval suffices to create the state of the Overself.

If one could carefully and vigilantly catch such divine moments and, not letting them melt away unheeded, nurture them thoroughly, savouring their spiritual flavour as it were, one could on some blessed day slip consciousness completely into the Overself and remain therein for a while. That day would be unforgettable for its ecstasy would be so sublime.

When one approaches some mountain peak aright it may put stillness into one's mind, silence upon one's lips and quietude within one's heart, for peaks and pinnacles carry a purer atmosphere than the plains and valleys. They are less tainted by the emanations of human crowds, less familiar with scenes of human greed, misery and savagery. And in their pointed summits they image forth for us the lofty lesson of aspiration toward a perfect life, the broad expanse of sky which covers them being as the broad expanse of God who enfolds us all. Mountains and hills have for ever been associated with the idea of the sacred and the holy. There is almost no country, no people but has its fable, myth or history linking the two together.

The prophet Elijah fasted for forty days on Mount Horeb to crush his animal nature for ever, and returned with stern and fearless denunciations of the sins of Ahab and the idolatry of his Jewish flock. On that treeless height he gained the unbending force with which he opposed the King and his Baal-worshipping Queen Jezebel. In the deserts of Arabia, Muhammad found his God and his faith during prayer in a cave high up on the side of rocky Mount Hira. The early Persians lit their sacred flames on the highest hills, flames which were kept perpetually alive in symbolism of the eternal nature of Deity, and there worshipped God in the open air, considering their fire-topped hill as a temple. Their prophet Zoroaster prayed on a high peak where Ahura-Mazda, the God, appeared to him and revealed "The Book of the Law", which was to be the divine law-code for his people. Similarly, it was on lonely Mount Dicta that a deity gave King Minos the laws which were to govern Crete. To Tibetan and Hindu alike, the towering snowy giants of Himalaya carry an inheritance of holiness unequalled by anything else in their lands. The Druids of ancient Britain held their hills in high veneration and respect, regarding them as consecrated abodes of divinity. The priests of early Mexico selected lofty peaks, among other places, for their holiest rites. Melanthes, who was far nearer to antiquity than we are, gave his readers the assurance that it was the universal practice of the ancients to worship their highest deity on the highest available mountain.

And in our own time the hills are still resorted to by those who have renounced worldly existence to live a stern ascetic life away from temptation and activity. The Nakshabendi Dervishes who have cut their rocky cavernous homes in the hills that overlook Cairo; the Greek monks who hide from the fairer sex on rugged Mount Athos; their more jovial Italian brothers who have built themselves a large monastery on a pretty garden-dotted hill just outside Florence, no less than Moses spending forty days on Mount Sinai to obtain the Divine revelation of law for his people, or Jesus in retreat on Mount Carmel, his face shining with the spiritual beauty of His Transfiguration as He communed with His Father, testify to the illumination and power which are to be found in the loneliness of mountain-tops.

All Nature-loving and worship surges up, indeed, from the deepest part of one's being; concentration upon the emotions that belong in their origin to the "soul" is therefore a valuable practice. The important thing is to react in the suggested way to the impressions received from Nature.

§

When one leaves the kingdom of Nature and turns to that of art, wherein man tries to copy her variegated beauty, her order and her pattern, one finds further opportunity to train the emotions along the path which will lead to the spiritual opening of oneself. Poem, picture, pose, tune, monument and carving provide, indeed, a fascinating preliminary path towards the divine kingdom and are a force in spiritual evolution.

Art is not merely a decorative addendum to life, although to superficial minds it frequently remains so. It can affect the human being in a deeply spiritual manner; it can be turned to account in such a way as to provide him with valuable psychological experiences. The artist who succeeds is the one who communicates his sensations of ethereal beauty, his ecstatic exaltations, so that beholders partake, understand or feel the same sensations, too. So far from being an idle luxury for those who can afford it, the power latent in great art of any kind is such as to bring one to the threshold of authentic divinity. The great artist, in the exalted beauty of his apprehension, is an unconscious transmitter of values beyond his normal conception.

To disregard for a while the routine activities of common-place existence and to enter into the world begotten by genuine artistic creation, is to experience an expansion of horizons beyond the purely personal, an upliftment of feelings beyond the merely material. One may, indeed, when one learns how, use the productions of the artist not merely for enjoyment but also as a lever to lift the mind into a degree of awareness different from the ordinary.

Whenever one meets with inspired work which has been called to birth at the bidding of an illumined artist, it should be given the most careful and concentrated attention; thus one reproduces in oneself the state of mental absorption which carried the artist through the finest part of his achievement and one may then be able to touch the profound source which he also touched. If one has not mistaken talent for genius, one begins with admiration, passes into adoration and ends with inspiration. The moment of electrifying contact must be looked for and seized upon, the first feelings of uplift or charm must not be thrown away, through heedlessness but, on the contrary, valued as being the threads which, when followed, guide one to the treasured state. It is important that one should not dissipate the exaltation by hurrying away to the next kind of mental impression or physical sensation. Some effort of will is required to keep off extraneous thoughts and emotions, so that the soul is abstracted from personal routine, brought into a higher atmosphere, and kept concentrated on the spiritual vitality with which it is being nourished by the strains of music or whatever be the art-form.

At the supreme moment of such response, one should begin the special breath, visual and heart practices described in later chapters, and go through them very briefly but consecutively for a short while. In this way, the highest profit will be derived from art, so that instead of being a mere means of increased pleasure, it will become a veritable golden gateway to unusual spiritual existence.

If one is fortunate enough to be blessed with a balanced, artistic and intellectual nature, one which possesses a real feeling and sensitivity for beauty and yet sufficient intellectual self-control to keep one's feet from being swept away unduly, one will make better progress upon this path than another who lacks such a nature. Therefore, it may be said, in general, that artistic culture is, in its truest, deepest sense, an asset which is well worth having. One cannot become a real artist or a real appreciator of art without enhancing one's sensitivity to those finer emotions which are above the average.

Music is especially valuable in appealing to the hidden faculty of the soul; these rhythmic bars of inspired sound draw the heart it knows not where. In the beautiful strains of Beethoven's noble *Fifth Symphony,* for instance, or the sublime anguish of Chopin's *Ballade in G Minor,* there is spiritual profit no less than artistic worth for those who know how to heed them aright. There is a divine element in symphony, tune and song which tends to put us into the spiritual state, ecstasy or anguish wherein these great artists created their works. The ascetic who sees in them only seductive snares that make us forget God or that occupy time which might be devoted to religious purposes, is at liberty to avoid these dangers; all are not called upon to follow his fear-ridden path. Beethoven himself said: "Music is the mediator between the spiritual and the sensual life." Yet if he had lived to hear some of the noise which passes for music today, he might have added a qualifying adjective to the first noun.

Nevertheless, one should remember that the type of artist

who loses himself in exaggerated, unbalanced enthusiasms or spends his energies in wild dissipations or who worships in art-temples which are permeated with the atmosphere of a madhouse will be totally unsuited for his path, whilst his artistic productions instead of helping the beholder or listener towards a higher view of life, will actually detract by reason of their distorted nature. One should seek rather those productions which do not drag one back to undesirable emotions, but which, on the contrary, elevate the soul, refine it and bring it to the majesty of spiritual joy. There are indeed men of admitted genius, even of awe-inspiring genius, who have either become psychically distorted vehicles of their inspiration or in their mediumistic helplessness have let their wonderful capacities and gifts be used by the powers of hell itself. When we are faced by the work of such men, we may recognize and confess that we stand also in the presence of genius, but we should unfailingly remember that we stand also in the presence of distortion of truth i.e. falsehood, of an expression of the destructive unseen forces which have ascended from the nether world itself. And perceiving all this, it is wiser not to immerse ourselves in the atmosphere of these productions, but to turn aside and seek a saner and purer air.

Music will arouse precisely such feelings, literature will convey precisely such a state of mind, pictures will create in the beholder precisely such a mood as that wherein they were composed – hence the importance of finding the best art, spiritually-inspired art. We find ourselves caught up into the imaginary world which the artist has created. The great artist should be an interpreter of the spiritual life to lesser mortals. The uninspired materialistic artist is like an electric-light bulb disconnected from the main current.

Moreover, one should deliberately attempt to cultivate those feelings and qualities of character which are helpful to the pursuit of a higher life. All such emotional expressions as anger, hatred, jealousy and fear are highly undesirable. We may not realize it when we are dealing with something so completely invisible in itself as an emotion, but a bitter antagonistic and suspicious feeling can be most destructive in its results not only upon oneself, in character and circumstance and, still more, in shutting out the spiritual light which could help one, but also upon others, for it moves, silently and telepathically, through space until it strikes invisibly against the person who has aroused it. One must therefore not only pay attention and attempt to guard against continuance in undesirable feelings – their first manifestation cannot be helped, perhaps – but one must set oneself to realize that in the inner world, where mind functions telepathically, these things are definite realities. Just as a man would not knowingly harbour a number of savage beasts in his own household, so he ought to strive to keep out of his breast the savage tiger, the lustful panther and the treacherous snake.

There is a great deal that is deplorable in current history, but it demands, not hatred, fear and destructiveness but understanding by a higher light; not an addition of more antagonism and more distortion in an over-antagonistic world but an addition of more constructiveness, more kindliness and more truth. This cultivation of the emotional life prepares the right conditions for the incoming of spiritual revelation and actually fosters it within the active field of daily life. Every time one expresses the sentiments of reverence, veneration, devotion, admiration, homage and humility towards that which is greater and grander in persons and Nature, one helps forward the day when this revelation may arrive.

The question is frequently raised whether or not certain radical and austere changes of an ascetic, self-disciplinary character should be made in one's mode of daily life when one decides to embark upon a spiritual path of this kind. Indeed, most people seem to think that such innovations are expected, and some even tremble in anticipatory dread of the difficulties which will thereby be created for them.

So far as the path which is particularly advocated here is concerned, these fears may be largely allayed. No ascetic changes of any kind are asked for, and no ascetic mandates will be issued. The basic work has to be done inwardly and such outward gestures as may be necessary should come gradually and out of one's own inner guidance, not from any external authority or preconceived conventional ideas on the subject. Far more important than the sacrifice of some physical habit is the sacrifice of mental habit, therefore one may enter upon this path without making any undue exhibition of it so that even those with whom he may be living in the same house or even in the same family may sometimes be unaware that he has embarked upon a higher order of living.

Nevertheless, the fact remains that where it is possible to do so without undue friction or without placing an undue burden upon oneself or one's circle, certain simple modifications in the physical life may be advisable.

It is unnecessary to run away from the world's necessary activity into hermitages, ashrams, retreats and the like. One's harrying thoughts and one's personal ego will run alongside wherever one flees. Salvation is purely a personal matter; the belief that it can be won only in spiritual groups and societies or monastic orders is a queer illusion; "souls are not saved in bundles," said Emerson, and experience verifies his words. On the other hand, temporary retreat for very brief periods is always helpful. At such times Nature herself will provide a better and more harmonious monastery than man.

Another difficulty arises in the matter of physical chastity. Here again people frequently believe that one must renounce all sexual relations as something shameful and enter upon a life of absolute celibacy. If they feel a deep call to such a life, their obvious duty it to obey it. But human existence is broad enough to contain other paths to the Overself.

On this point the writer hastens to clear up a misunderstanding which may arise among some who have read his reference to this point in *A Hermit in the Himalayas*. His note on the subject in that book was quite incomplete, being but a diary jotting, and therefore now needs amplification. All that he meant was that *marriage* was no bar to spiritual attainment and that one could live a normal married life in the world and yet become Overself-conscious. He certainly did not mean that one could give free rein to one's passions merely at the beckoning of desire. On the contrary, he believes that it is by the *sensible* conservation and control of sex-force that man may become a dynamic power in the worlds of matter and spirit.

A higher civilization will perceive in marriage what only a minority of youthful couples perceive today – the opportunity for two souls to mature together for a dual spiritual-material purpose, and physical intercourse will then become but the accompaniment, and not the object, of marriage. The presence of a clergyman and the singing of a church choir do not necessarily make a marriage ceremony sacred; only when both husband and wife comprehend that they must finally find unity in companionly worship of the Supreme Light does their marriage achieve a higher status than that of a civil contract. But this is not to say that complete celibacy, denial of the human relationship of marriage, is the *only* path to spirituality as so many intolerantly and ignorantly declare.

Because this book does not concern itself with moral injunctions, it is essential to warn the reader that mystical meditation must be safeguarded by strenuous efforts to improve character and elevate ethical standards. Without them, there is danger.

9

THE PRACTICE OF MENTAL MASTERY

The ordinary man moves irresponsibly from one thought to another and lightly lets his mind work at its own sweet will. Yet his thoughts are something for which he is responsible and they in turn will react, and are reacting, upon the whole of his material life. The advisability of eliminating undesirable thoughts and of fostering the finer ones is something he but dimly sees. It might seem fantastic and far-fetched to assert that there is any such connection between what a man thinks and what happens to him in the material world, between the condition of his mind and his material well-being, but those who have practised the methods advocated here for sufficient years and watched the results of their practices in their own lives will know that this is not fantasy but the actual truth, and that man's external life is very largely a reflection of his mental world. Unfortunately, so strongly has our age become saturated with materialistic views about life that it has lost to a large extent both the memory and the belief in the subtler mind-powers of man. Such a loss, however, cannot and does not alter the basic fact of their existence. So long as we prefer to continue in spiritual ignorance, so long must we go on groping our way with the cataract-film of materialism over our eyes. The result is much unnecessary suffering and an utter inability to fathom the deeper purposes of Nature and the destiny of our race.

To gain control of our scattered thoughts and feelings is to establish a sovereignty which we have lost. Man must be complete master in the region of his mind if he is to fulfil perfectly the evolution which Nature has set before him. He may spurn the task as not being worth the trouble, but the loss will be his own, for inability to control thought leads by the most mysterious ramifications to all kinds of suffering. For it is a truism that many decisions, events and happenings in our lives are strongly influenced by our habitual mode of thought. Therefore to change this mode of thought is to change to some extent the circumstances and environments of our existence, as well as to attain self-confidence and inner well-being. Moreover, we must perform the inward miracle of conquering the mind, before we can ever perform any outward miracle. No practice therefore could be more important to those who are in any way dissatisfied with life than this of thought-control. And in this practical age, when people always look for tangible results rather than intangible theories, it is surely a powerful argument to say to the world: "Do this! take up this practice and in time you will find the current of your life flowing in smoother channels, along sunnier routes and amid pleasanter scenes."

For these reasons alone, if for no other, the closest attention ought to be paid to thought-life. But there exist other and higher reasons why one needs to re-work the mind anew, for through mind one may penetrate the mysteries of the kingdom of heaven and discover for himself whether the soul exists and what it is really like. A fundamental principle is that the certainty of one's spiritual existence can never come from objective proofs, but only by making an intellectual or emotional venture. Through mind rightly directed the inmost self opens up to him and he crosses its veiled sanctuary into a diviner state. Such direction, termed variously as 'mental quiet', 'meditation', 'yoga' and 'mysticism', re-moulds the mind and compels thought to serve man, not to tyrannize over him. And such is the supreme worth of all practices of mental quiet that Ignatius Loyola, the Founder of the Jesuit Order, once confessed to Father Laynez that a single hour of meditation at Manfesa had revealed more truths about heavenly things to him than all the doctrines of all the theologians put together could have taught him.

If the reader is now ready to begin this lofty adventure of the soul, he must fulfil the preliminary condition. It is this:

One must find, out of the twenty-four hours of the day, a fixed period of about half an hour when one is able to withdraw from ordinary personal activities and be alone, in quietude and stillness, with one's thoughts.

Anyone whose circumstances are so rigorous that he cannot find a half-hour for such a high purpose, may utilize twenty or even fifteen minutes daily. It is not so much the length of time one devotes to it as the quality of one's thinking and the alert, concentrated awareness with which one conducts oneself during those few minutes. But most people who complain of lack of time for meditation usually manage to find time for pleasure, for theatre-going, for seeing the newest cinema pictures, for reading the latest tit-bits of newspaper-gossip, for idle chatter, for tea-parties, dinner-parties and other engagements. Are they, then, never to have an engagement with their divine self? What they really mean is that the trouble and effort and slight sacrifice that meditation calls for do not seem worth the while, and the benefits it promises seem somewhat remote, vague and shadowy. Yet could they but understand the matter aright, they would understand that these little fragments of the day given to mental quiet are the jewelled moments of life, infinitely important because they may yield eternal treasure and precise gains to the patient-hearted. Those sacrificial minutes, which are given to mental quiet, are not given in vain. The Deity thus worshipped well rewards His faithful devotees.

The length of time to be devoted to the daily practice should be decided upon beforehand and will naturally be fixed only after taking into consideration the particular duties imposed upon one by his environment and status. One need not, and should not, neglect the normal everyday duties of business and home in order to find time for these spiritual practices, yet one should not be so foolish as to assert that he is too busy to find any time for them at all. There is no human being who cannot, with a slight sacrifice of trivial activity or unnecessary pleasure, create sufficient time for these practices. Half an hour is a good average period for most people and such a half-hour can always be found somewhere in one's daily programme if the student is really determined to embark upon the quest. If he wishes, he may even have two such periods each day, morning and evening, and although this is advisable where possible, it is certainly not essential.

The times chosen should be such as will cause the least interference in one's daily duties, as well as the least inconvenience to those persons with whom one happens to be living. However, there are certain hours of the day when these practices are particularly pointed to by Nature, and when they will be rendered easier and more fruitful. These hours are roughly early morning after dawn, and early evening before sunset.

The fruitfulness of the early morning period lies in the fact that the mind is then fresh, quiet and undisturbed. The day's agitations have not yet begun to ripple its placid surface. And an advantage of practising at such a time is that its results "carry over" into the remainder of the day, one's life and work being thus conducted within the atmosphere of its lingering after-echoes. Mental quiet provides the finest possible start of a working day. When successful, it puts one into proper relationship with the Infinite and into tune with the universe. Such interior harmony bespeaks an external harmony with all affairs to be dealt with during the coming day. It lessens the likelihood of jarring discords, helps the day to pass agreeably, and creates a store of serenity and wisdom with which to face problems. Inspirations and ideas appear later as its pleasant fruit. Dawn is appropriate especially to those living in Oriental countries. Westerners are at a disadvantage, at this hour, for two reasons. They are then eager to get into the world of activity again, they fret to go out and about and start their daily work; this very eagerness and fretting become serious handicaps in their practice and spoil the fine quality of their meditation. One should sit down to such meditation with a sort of sublime patience, unhurried and untroubled by thoughts of what one is to do afterwards in the world outside. The second reason is that the early morning is often extremely cold in Europe and America and the body's sensations of cold distract attention from one's practice.

Dusk is easier for some people, as then, tired of the day's work, they look forward with pleasant anticipation to rest and relaxation; meditation being a change for the mind and a definite rest. On the other hand, people exist who declare that they are too fatigued after the day's work to be bothered with meditation or indeed with anything except dinner and amusement. Such must fix on any free half-hour of day or night when they are not tired.

Both dawn and dusk are 'junction-periods' according to the tradition of the yogis, when spiritual forces are particularly active in our planet's atmosphere. The periods immediately following sunrise and immediately preceding sunset are the great meeting-points in Nature's timing, when the forces of daily activity meet those of nightly quiescence; and when these two mingle, a subtle pregnant stillness is created which has a profound influence upon the mind of sensitive humanity. At such moments it is more possible and somewhat easier to contact the deepest soul of man.

Once fixed, the hour must be adhered to with determination. Thus a steady time-habit is created which, in course of months or years, makes the mental quiet hour a definite part of the day's programme, so that if it is missed, one feels a lack just as one feels hungry if a meal is missed. It is therefore better to give a few minutes at the regular time daily than a longer period at fitful irregular times. As the mind establishes this new habit of meditation, it will naturally be easier to recur spontaneously to the exercises when the fixed time arrives each day than at any other.

It is inadvisable to choose a time immediately following a meal, for then the body's absorption of energy in the work of digestion tends to make the mind less alert and more sluggish, hence unfitted for the fine and subtle practice of concentration here called for. In fact, the best results will come when one meditates on a light or an empty stomach.

Whatever the time chosen, there are two days in every month which possess a special role in this system. A definite effort must then be made, not merely to keep on with the practice, but also to devote a longer period to it. Such days are when the sun and moon come into conjunction and opposition, i.e. the new and full moon nights. On such occasions spiritual forces are released upon the world and the aspirant must take advantage of them, for he needs all the help he can get and these forces constitute a kind of "grace" for souls ready and waiting in meditation to receive it. We need not be surprised at the existence of such influences in connection with the time-markings of the heavenly bodies, when we remember that the moon influences millions of tons of water to move in the tides of the ocean, no less than it influences the more delicate growth of plants. Why should it not, together with the sun, be able to influence the inner life of man? Psychiatrists have long since established that human feelings are so influenced because many lunatics are known to show both the worst as well as the lightest phases of their malady particularly on these two days of the month.

One must take care, therefore, to practise for an extended period on the evening or night of the new or full moon day, or at the dawn following them. It is worth doubling the half-hour into an hour because then attainment of one's aim becomes easier. The spiritual potency of these two phases of sun and moon was recognized by almost all ancient sages and seers. Buddhist monks still hold their most important ritual on new moon day, while high-caste Hindus regard it as the most sacred of each month, the strictly orthodox among them making it a day of silence, fasting, and cessation from work, followed by a sleepless night devoted to meditation or prayer.

§

Next to be considered on the practical side are the physical conditions. A first rule is to bathe completely or at least to wash face and hands up to elbows before beginning meditation. This establishes correct conditions of magnetic purity. Then there is the question of bodily posture. Standing, for instance, is obviously an unsuitable bodily posture because it leads so much more quickly to fatigue through the effort spent in keeping upright on one's legs. Lying flat on one's back or side, although much better, is nevertheless still not quite suitable because it is habitually the sleeping posture and tends to deprive the mind of its keenness and wakefulness. The best bodily position, then, is one which involves sitting on the haunches, with backbone upright and steady. The best seat, whether upon a floor-rug, in a chair, or on a couch, is that which is comfortable, easy and least likely to distract the mind from its chosen topic to the physical body by reason of mal-adjustment. No physical contortions or yoga pose are required for this path. It may be added that for persons of medium height who dislike squatting the best seats to obtain effective results in these exercises is, generally, a low chair or stool about fifteen inches high. The ankles may be crossed, in which case the hands should be placed one above the other with palms upturned, or the legs may rest upright on the floor, in which case the hands are most suitably placed upon the knees. Beginners who wish to experiment with squatting will be much helped if they provide a support for the back, such as a wall or chair-back. Whatever position one adopts let it be that in which one feels most at ease and unreminded of bodily exis-tence for half an hour. One should assume the same position every time one does the practices.

A further important factor is the avoidance of antagonis-tic surroundings. Environment possesses much influence upon the mind; the chief requisites here are solitude, quietness, uplift, inspiration and the avoidance of extremes of tempera-ture. One ought not to be disturbed or distracted by the physical body during this attempt to penetrate into the inward recesses of being. Therefore, even after having established oneself in a comfortable position it is well to remember that the senses of the body will still be active, carrying on their normal work of transmitting sense impressions to the brain. If one is to penetrate into the mind's depths, these physical senses must be compelled to keep silent. One should therefore practise as far as possible in a place of complete solitude and perfect quietude, and if a room is used this should be locked to prevent sudden intrusion. Better still, if one is living in or near the countryside, some sequestered spot in a forest glade or beside a river bank or on a hill-side should be chosen, where the beauty and silence of Nature may aid one's spiritual aspirations. There is indeed no finer spot for meditation than those quiet places which are Nature's hidden treasures and for which a house-room, where bad emotional atmospheres are often impinged upon the walls, can be at best the substitute enforced upon a town-dweller. However, even the mental atmosphere and emotional influence of a room may be much improved by keeping it in a condition of spotless cleanliness, by brightening it with colourful flowers and inspiring pictures and by a tasteful harmony of wall decoration and furniture. All these things help to put both body and mind at ease and tend to create the necessary inspiring atmosphere. Those who care for it, may burn a little incense, too, but they should take care to use only incense of good quality and of such fragrance as has a personal appeal.

Abnormal cold no less than abnormal heat renders the body uncomfortable and in so doing makes meditation more difficult. In the Western countries there is frequently much cold and unless proper heating facilities are available or adequate wrappings are used, the body's disturbance and discomfort react on the mind and interfere with proper mental quiet. Yet warmth should not be secured by making a room too stuffy, because bad air dulls the mind.

During the time of these meditations the student would do well to keep his eyes closed in order to facilitate concentration and shut out distracting external impressions. If the eyes are kept open. they will transmit to the brain light-stimulations which keep the physical world too much within the field of attention. Both bright sunlight and bright electric light are disturbing, so windows and lamps should be shaded.

Then one begins to relax completely and let go of all physical tensions. In the earlier stages of the practices one would be well advised to break off meditation at odd times and become closely aware of the state of one's body. Is it strained? Are the muscles taut? And the nerves tense? One should correct oneself constantly in this manner and thus form proper habits of posture.

It is helpful to play good music on a gramophone before concentration. Such tunes as 'Stille Nacht, Heilige Nacht', or Schubert's 'Ave Maria' exalt the mind and turn it inwards.

In the previous chapter the writer has already briefly outlined the path of religious mysticism for those who care to follow it. Some others exist for people at different stages of development and of differing tastes and temperaments, but they may conveniently be grouped together under the heading of the Path of Concentration, for they are variants of the much talked about but little understood yoga of the East. Of the dangerous yoga methods, which seek to attract the ignorant by the bait of marvellous occult powers, the less said the better, and people who practise or propagate them do so at their own peril and on their own responsibility. The safest and best of the yoga systems consist in taking some material object, mental notion, *spiritual quality* or personage and concentrating the full force of attention through successive thoughts linked up to it until the mind literally becomes united with it. The chain of reasoning must be severely logical and the special subject of the meditation is of less importance than most novices think; what really matters is the quality of concentrated attention given to it, the power of keeping the vagrant thoughts fixed on it for a given time. Thoughts which lack concentrative power are evanescent, scrawled in the sand. When, after long practice through several years and the exertion of much will-power, the host of mental impressions ceases to whirl through the brain, and the goal of one-pointed mind is attained, a further step appears in view, but it cannot be taken by any who have not gained enough power of mental concentration to hold the attention in an unbroken manner upon a single point, concept or idea, without falling back into psychic mediumship and becoming a channel for beings much lower than the Overself.

This stage is called contemplation and requires the practiser to drop the object or idea or mental image from his attention at the very height of his exercise, without, however, dropping the mood of fixed, unwavering attention which has been engendered. If this be properly done – and it is no easy matter – -the stilled mind remains a state of vacuum for the briefest of periods. There may occur a temporary lapse of memory, a swift swoon of self-oblivion, and then the centre of being is found to have shifted itself deeper, into another plane entirely different from the normal one. In this plane the mind merges into a state of dazzling peace, illumination, understanding, freedom and desirelessness. This wonderful condition does not long remain, however, but passes away almost as imperceptibly and as silently as it came. The contemplator's final task is to repeat the experience of attainment as often as he can, and to prolong these high moods for as long as he can, until ultimately they stretch out over the entire day, unbroken and unbreakable.

At the plane just below that of final attainment, all the different paths of meditation and contemplation merge and unite. The closer they approach to that plane, the more they tend to become alike. It is likewise true that certain conditions of practice apply, at some stage or other, to all the paths – especially the need of concentrating thought.

Concentration consists in stopping this ever-changing habitual wandering of the intellect, and in keeping it steadily directed to a single line of travel, by entering deeply into a special thought. To achieve this it is necessary to ignore the impressions and physical sensations which are thrown into one from environment, to hush the noise of worldly life into mental silence, to keep out the swarm of intruding and extraneous thoughts by practising conscious control of the mind during the half-hour or so of meditation. In short, whilst thoroughly thinking about the chosen subject, there must be a willed resistance to the impacts of perception which come from without and to the uprisings of alien thoughts which come from within. One cannot immediately destroy them or blot them out, but one can set up an unfaltering purpose, an ideal of remaining unmoved by them like a rock over which the waves of the sea dash in vain, unable to dislodge it from its firm foundation. During the first half of one's practice one will feel an almost uncontrollable urge to leave it, to get up and be busy with something else. The mind will complain bitterly about being turned away from its wonted tracks, about the tyranny of being turned unnaturally inwards, while itself glad to submit to the far greater tyranny of being externalized throughout the day. The restlessness of the mind is the general discovery of all people who take up the practice of meditation. This discovery is confirmed by every early effort and leads at first to some disheartenment. The first fumbling efforts leave a sense of failure and fatigue. One understands then that only a small fraction of one's thoughts is one's own, the rest being but an undisciplined, rebellious mob. If one yields to these negative feelings, one is headed for failure. If, however, one accepts the fact that the task undertaken is a serious and difficult one, yet still perfectly possible and worth while, bravely attempting to carry on with the exercise without slackening, there will one day be a reward, when a delightful lull in the tumult of the mind will arise and its outward-turned bent will be broken through.

Hitherto one has unresistingly obeyed this constant motion of the mind and yielded to it; the moment one begins to still its habitual turmoil there is quite naturally much resistance. This is to be expected. One ought to accept, therefore, the fact of its inevitability and instead of giving up the practice, because it seems uninspired and barren, persist patiently and hopefully to make the intellect slightly steadier with each month that passes.

For the mind has been captured by the body and made to serve it; the purpose of meditation is to reverse this position and free the mind from this tyrannous domination so that it may reunite with its rightful master, the Overself. When it eludes one's grasp in meditation and causes outside sensations or forgetfulness of the subject to impose themselves upon one's attention, one should do the brave and difficult thing – ingather it from its wanderings; try to make it introspective and patiently turn its attention back towards it's proper focus, however tiresome this is and however frequently this must be done. *Patience plus indifference to repeated failures is essential to obtain final success.*

The concentration of thought is like riding an obstinate mule which constantly takes a direction entirely its own; every time the rider becomes aware that his steed is straying he must forcibly turn its head back toward the right path. The Overself within is always accessible to us, but our errant thoughts must become its fuel: we have been prodigal children so long that it must take an appreciable time to make the return journey. Therefore patience is needed in these efforts. No one can become an efficient musician in three months, and yet most of us expect to win life's best after a few efforts, becoming despondent because there is no immediate response.

A final note must be added to remove a confusion which frequently occurs in the minds of those who take up yoga, the path of concentration. The maintenance of a line of consecutive sequential thoughts, or meditation, is only the preliminary and intermediate process of this path. It is a transitional state. Advanced concentration, or contemplation, consists in fastening the attention to a single thought, object or person, letting it dwell thereon and not indulging in further thinking about it. Hence, consecutive effective thinking is the initial effort which leads to concentration, but is not final concentration itself, because it involves the passage of a succession of thoughts. True concentration involves only one object, or one thought. We must learn to look upon the intellect as a thought-machine, to be put aside temporarily when it has served its purpose, and not to be continuously tended. Disciplined mental action must be followed by controlled mental rest – the rest which, opening the present moment, admits one into eternity and frees the thinker from the cocoon of thoughts which he keeps ceaselessly spinning.

§

Such exercises may seem at first extremely boring to the average man because he is dealing with nothing tangible, with nothing that he can touch and feel with his hands or see with his eyes. He may have a natural dislike of being torn away from his moorings in the physical world and led to grope in this mental world which seems so shadowy, but which is really of the highest importance to his own well-being. Such thoughts may and must come to him, but let him not yield feebly to their cajoling; let him arise from spiritual sloth, lured if needs be by the thought of the lofty rewards which await him upon this path, rewards which cannot be valued by any material standard alone, for they come in every shape and form – material harmony, emotional contentment, mental satisfaction and above all spiritual wisdom. No price can be set upon these things and they should be sufficient to tempt a man to undertake this daily task of self-discovery, no matter how laborious and how long the task may prove to be.

Obstacles and difficulties exist; they are natural and almost invariably common to all novices alike. The mind inevitably and obstinately wanders away like a mule from its chosen theme or loses hold of its selected picture. Quite often its lapses are unnoticed for some time; then the mediator suddenly becomes aware that he has either been thinking of a dozen different things instead of one, or else that he has forgotten the very subject of his meditation. Can we wonder that the Indian yogis compare the mind with a monkey gone mad and leaping aimlessly hither and thither? Most of us float all day upon a stream of rushing thoughts and desires, or indulge in frantic and foolish haste; meditation is an effort to pull up at an island for quiet self-regaining: hence, the current's opposition to this effort is inevitable.

Once the thoughts have been fired by aspiration and a keen desire to get attuned is felt, progress will not be so slow, and one will then begin to enter 'the concentrated state' with less effort and more frequency.

The student who practises this training faithfully and regularly, setting himself to attain mastery over thought, will reach a time sooner or later when an inarticulate feeling of progress begins to make its presence known to him, and when he begins to struggle out of the vague condition which necessarily attended his earlier efforts. Such a premonition may be trusted and should strengthen his hope and confidence, two qualities that will aid him much on this path. Hope is essential because the failures to arrive at any distinct and striking advance will inevitably be many and may sometimes be prolonged for years; whilst again and again the mind will continually run away from the task he has set it. The man who despite this is still willing to carry on with his practices, who is still willing to keep his faith in their ultimate efficacy, is the man who will one day discover to his astonishment that a sudden and rich interior reward is bestowed upon him for his patience and his optimism.

After all, he need only practise for short periods every day. For the rest of the day, he can go about in a perfectly normal manner, using the intellect as actively as before. The effect of this daily stilling of the intellect will, however, gradually begin to show itself in all sorts of remarkable ways.

The things that will help one most on this path are free – guidance, courage, faith, work and patience still cost nothing, and the reward which waits for those who practise is nothing less than the divine Overself itself, at the most, and mental tranquillity at the least.

Faith and patience are fundamental, not blind faith and lethargic patience but intelligent, reasoned belief and calm trust that the right kind of effort must, sooner or later, produce the right results.

Finally it may be added that some people are specially susceptible to the development of concentration through hearing certain sounds. Oriental teachers of the art place such people near to a small waterfall and bid them keep attention fixed upon its musical note, to the exclusion of all other sounds or thoughts. This unifies the mind with the sound and thus keeps off the former's wandering tendency. A similar result may be attained by concentrating the hearing upon the purring revolutions of an electric fan.

The man who has gone on meditating quietly in the solitude of his private room or in a peaceful forest, perhaps, striving for many months or possibly years to attain an intellectual understanding of himself on the basis of his own independent thought, has been slowly building up all this while a background and stage which shall later become the scene wherein the drama of his spiritual rebirth shall take place. Through the power of increasingly abstracted thinking, he is learning to withdraw from purely material surroundings, to forget the existence of the physical world, and to enter this world of ideas that is a mediate region between matter and spirit. Even though nothing startling and nothing striking should happen during these purely preliminary mental practices, he should nevertheless comprehend clearly that they are preparing the way for a state which makes striking and startling things possible. Everything here as elsewhere in Nature is a matter of gradual growth. The thoughts that seem to end only in vague metaphysical abstractions are really, did he but know it, taking him to the boundary of this land of intellect where fresh guides and new methods of conveyance will be at his disposal. For this reason alone, if for no other, much patience is necessary.

There will also arrive a stage when thoughts begin to assume a deeper importance in one's life than they have hitherto borne. When one pursues a path such as is described here and deliberately attempts so to order his thoughts as to arrive at something beyond his everyday self and therefore something which is of the utmost value, he begins to feel a growing sense of the importance of controlling his thought-life with a more exacting care than before.

Indeed, as his power of inward abstraction and mental concentration grows, he will be surprised to find that the line of connection between his persistent or concentrated thoughts and the events in his outer life can sometimes be traced with surprising clarity. *His thoughts become creative forces.* This realization will then make him careful to entertain less and less thoughts of hatred, jealousy, avarice, fear, timidity and all destructive or useless thoughts generally. He should, on the contrary, welcome their opposites.

When such a state is reached, it is a good sign and demonstrates that the man is indeed making solid progress upon the path, and he will sense within himself, no less than it may be discernible to observers, the emotional balance and inward poise he has achieved as a result of his exercises. And out of this mind-quest comes the lofty grandeur of spiritual calm – so needed by a world in woe, so marked in every man who approaches the Overself.

A curious result of these concentration practices is that extraordinary mental faculties sooner or later may begin to unfold themselves, but it is very unwise to seek them for their own sake. The telepathic power to send or receive thoughts from other minds becomes most marked and may in time become so familiar a part of one's existence as to be regarded as commonplace. Prophetic premonitions of future events may likewise arise naturally and spontaneously within oneself and be fulfilled to a most remarkable degree. The ties which bind one to the fleshly body begin to loosen and the freed soul can fly the world and appear to others in vision or dream. One's own dream-life alters entirely and becomes a coherent rational existence which possesses the extraordinary quality of *awareness that one is in the dream-state*. Thus, the latter loses its vagueness and fantasy and becomes a real continuation of the personal daytime existence. Dream-life will emerge from the chaotic, jumbled and senseless character which it often normally possesses, into a useful sequential and sensible condition.

10

THE PATH OF SELF-ENQUIRY

The stage now being set for one's first meditations, according to this system, one may begin the work assigned to the elementary period. This consists of nothing more than reading and studying a few sentences or paragraphs at a time and utilizing them as subjects for mental concentration until, eventually, the whole of Part One, with the exception of the unimportant Prefatory chapter, has been completed, just as one eventually completes the reading of a serialized story.

Each daily text thus becomes the meat upon which the mediator's mind may feed. The words must form his sustenance; they are to be chewed over and over again and the sauce of his own further ideas added until they have become thoroughly masticated, swallowed and digested; in short, until all the ideas appear acceptable.

The critic will immediately object that this is tantamount to gagging the reader and that it is an attempt to force a set of opinions down his mental throat.

The writer's reply is that without this turning of the mental outlook from its habitual immersion in a preconceived criterion of truth, i.e. physical waking experience alone, no true idea of man's inner constitution can ever be obtained and no progress achieved upon this path.

Right enquiry, unconventional self-questioning, as formulated here, may possibly lead to other and different answers than those which are given, if one refuses to depart from the preconceived opinion that physical frontiers are the limits which surround man. But the adherence to such an opinion is in itself to assume that the chief part of the truth about human personality is already known. That is mere assumption, after all.

The questions which partly constitute this system of spiritual-analysis have not been lightly formulated. *They have purposely been framed by those who already know the answer.* They originated from the minds of ancient seers who looked pityingly upon blinded mankind, groping in darkness, and who designedly put the questions into men's heads as a sort of Ariadne-thread which, when properly followed, should lead their minds through the maze and labyrinth of this world into discovery of the spiritual world hidden within it.

If the answers are here set down, too, it is not from any intention of finding adherents to them, but from the necessity of cutting a path through untracked land *for those who have to follow*. If the writer had not himself been led into the discovery of this spiritual world of being, he would necessarily have looked upon these answers, in the way that so many people do, as mere intellectual opinions.

But they are far more than that.

They are not only correct rational responses; they are also statements of observed fact.

The observations have been made by those competent to do so, i.e. the seers and sages who form the crest-waves of millenniums of spiritual evolution.

The matter may be put more bluntly now by affirming

that a sympathetic perusal of these pages and rumination upon their content until the truth of that which they have to say begins to percolate through the mind by interior perception rather than blind faith, ultimately leads to definite reactions within the innermost depth of human nature. Every page that is included in Part One is directly and indirectly intended to work upon the reader's mind, when he does not hinder the influence by inherent bias, and when he carries its words into his daily period of mental quiet and meditates upon them so intently that the spirit of which they form a vehicle is able to enter into them also. Indeed, he must not only read, but also meditate whilst he reads, perceiving in stray words and phrases significant hints for his own personal guidance.

By such unprejudiced reflection and by such tentative confidence in these observations and conceptions formed out of uncommon experience, *combined with fulfilment of the other prescribed conditions,* the reader may extract unsuspected spiritual experiences of his own, for he will liberate hitherto concealed forces which reside below the threshold of his own personality. Self-analysis when practised on the lines laid down here will provide the essential preliminary intellectual training which deepens his inner knowledge. The perusal must not be executed in an idle, superficial manner such as we use with newspapers and the like; this will be little more than useless; it must be done with the whole force of one's being pivoted in interest upon the point under attention. Therefore, the student will undoubtedly find it necessary to re-read certain portions several times before he can grasp their full content, and it is not until he does grasp it that he can really progress any further on the path.

Even those who are not beginners in spiritual matters and who aleady entertain the spiritual conception of life to some extent, will not waste their time by such perusal because they will be enabled to put some of their own ideas and experiences into an orderly arrangement, thus clarifying their self-knowledge and perhaps adding important facts thereto.

Because this work demands the labour of close thought, it might be said by some critics that a mere "way of thinking" could not possibly effect such a profound alteration in the consciousness of man or give him such a lofty experience. Indeed, a superficial glance over these pages might lead one to such a conclusion; nevertheless, the latter would be a false one. We under-estimate the power of thinking, simply because we are but imperfectly acquainted with the nature of the intellect. Did we but know it, the intellect is itself enfolded by the Divine Spirit and its act of *unfolding* itself towards its hidden source inevitably leads to that Spirit. One ought to be as intent, alert and concentrated in awareness as possible. One should sit down with the feeling, "Now I am going to forget myself, my personal affairs, and throw the whole force of my attention on this inner quest!"

The essence of this method is therefore very simple, although the effort to practise it may require a degree of concentrated abstracted attention which few people possess but which more may acquire. If this quality is at present lacking it can be acquired by persistent practice, just as one can acquire a moderate facility to play a musical instrument by dint of persevering practice. In fact, the analogy is extremely close. In music the ears of the student have to be trained gradually to detect the more obvious differences between notes and tones and, later, the more subtle graduations between them. Similarly the student who practises this psychological and philosophical method of approaching Divinity begins by learning to detect the more obvious differences between himself, his feelings and his thoughts, and later on, the subtler shades of those differences. Finally he learns to "listen-in" and detect the divinity which is the undercurrent beneath his personal ego, just as the student of music learns to detect the existence of a certain basic "motif" in a musical composition.

Thought, therefore, can become a powerful instrument of self-liberation in the hands of those who are taught how to use it properly and in these pages the reader will find ideas, words, phrases, sentences, paragraphs and questions which, if properly pondered upon, will actually train his thinking and enable him to detect and eventually penetrate those mysterious regions of subtle thought and understanding which lie at present outside his mental ken, just as the student of music will so strain his musical faculties as eventually to hear those delicate harmonies that were formerly outside the range of his detection.

The very study of this path to the fourth-dimensional consciousness of the Overself helps one to gain the necessary new intellectual outlook which is itself a part of the system.

The paragraphs in this book are the outcome of a different range of experience and therefore carry liberating and revelatory guidance. The function of this work is to take hold of the mind and place it on a new track; and just as a man who has taken the wrong road may be guided back to the correct one, so one may be led onwards in the directions which Nature intends us to take.

A great deal of close concentrated thought has been compressed into a minimum of space in the foregoing chapters. The shortest sentence may hold the profoundest truth, and therefore the real benefit comes when one works through them with the deliberate slowness necessary to master a new subject. Anyone can read a single chapter in an hour or less, if he likes, but it will take a week or more to study it and perhaps months or more to absorb and master it properly. Had space allowed, the writer would have isolated each separate idea and printed it with a broad division of white space to separate it from the next one, and thus impressed on the reader's mind that careful mental labour is demanded of him to conquer each new thought before he proceeds further.

If such pondering be done in the right manner and with the right attention, every idea presented may become a seed-thought upon which the reader's own mind can work and lead him in time some distance along the path towards the goal – knowledge of the Overself. For these truths will take root at deeper levels and will then slowly grow to the surface of consciousness.

The practical course, therefore, requires the student to carry a few phrases, sentences, or even paragraphs from his reading into the silent chamber of his brain, there to be fixed in the mind, deeply and thoroughly pondered over and made the material for abstracted musings. The active participation of his thought and imagination is demanded. All that has been said in the previous chapter upon the art of concentrating one's thoughts and excluding every irrelevant topic must be remembered in this connection. The mind should be kept calm and deliberate, intent upon exploring each idea to the full, for it is only in such a condition that it can arrive at undistorted understanding.

Every sentence is written with deliberate intent to provoke a certain reaction and to sustain a certain mood in the reader's mind. But only those readers who have adopted a truly impersonal, impartial and correct attitude from the beginning are likely to have this reaction and find their thinking to become spiritually significant.

There is thus a certain energy latent in these pages awaiting its liberation by an attitude of right receptivity and reasoned appreciation.

What Am I? That question must sink itself deeply into

one's consciousness. It must be framed silently and asked with reverence, with earnestness, and later, even in a semi-prayerful spirit.

One must begin to become conscious of and engrossed in this query for a limited time at least every day of one's thought-life. One must attempt to analyse one's nature and, in an earnest and thorough spirit, dissect the notion of selfhood as the anatomist dissects the physical body, until one becomes aware of what he really is. Such analysis must be more than mere grubbing among the human passions, as some modern psychologists think to be sufficient. It must be an effort to delve through a cross-section of human experience, in its entirety, from the grossest up to the most ethereal.

One returns always to the sole factor which is to be placed as pre-eminent, whether in theoretical philosophy or practical life – the knowledge of the self. Hence the Secret Path goes directly to this goal: a mental analysis of the personal self which shall result in a discovery of the spiritual self. Such a discovery can never arise by leaning over the laboratory table. Deep meditation upon the theme WHAT AM I? is essential.

The basic principle of this method, therefore, is to take that query, and try to trace out the nature and origin of the notion of self-hood; analyse the assembled totality of components which one generally considers to constitute one's own individual being; examine, one by one, each separate part of the body, the emotions and the thoughts respectively; and through all these search for that which can truly be said to be the self, temporarily relegating all else into oblivion.

§

This path of self-training is divided into two stages and contains different practices. The first stage is intellectual and consists of analyses which give understanding; the second is mystical and implements that understanding. In the first stage, one sets up a mental current of self-questioning, attempting to ferret out what one really is, and to trace the living being who thinks and feels within the body; whereas in the second the rational thinking mind is switched off, the so-called conscious self is put out of gear so that the mis-called subconscious self may arise.

The components of personality are subjected to rigid analysis during the period of meditation. The body and its parts, organs and senses, are carefully examined in thought with a view to trace out whether the self resides in it and, by various analyses, it is seen that the sense of selfhood is not to be found there. It is then eliminated from the analysis and the emotions are subjected to a like examination. Here again their transiency and the implications of the naturally-uttered phrase, 'I feel', indicate the self to be something apart. The faculties of the mind – imagination, ratiocination and perception – are likewise observed and analysed away; the self is found not to be inherent in any of these functions. The intellect itself is critically cut to pieces and ascertained to be nothing but a succession of thoughts. One watches the thoughts in the process and then endeavours to pin them down to the mystic stillness out of which they arise. Finally the conscious 'I' is traced to a single thought.

Out of the great stillness and blankness at the back of the mind, that thought 'I' is the first arising of the personal ego within consciousness. Out of it has sprung the whole accumulation of other thoughts, which have created the notion of a personal being existing independently by itself. The entire personality has sprung up around this single thought-root. Uprooting this primal thought, nothing but impersonal Life will be left.

If one persists and applies oneself to frequent meditation

on this topic, the effort will turn logic to its loftiest creative use and one will ultimately track this thought to its origin, self to its lair and consciousness to its primal partless state.

At the end of this mental analysis, therefore, the mind must be stilled, so far as possible, and a devotional semi-prayerful mood much be superimposed. That stillness out of which the 'I' has sprung should become the object of this devotion. The 'I' itself is pinned down and rendered inert. All one's attention should be focused upon the mysterious blankness behind it. It is at this point that the electrifying guidance of a true Adept – if one is fortunate enough to meet him – becomes a potent help.

But before we can achieve this stillness, we must curb the inherent tendency of thoughts to wander away and dissipate themselves, and arrive at the fixed concentration of attention which is so essential; hence certain adjuncts to the mental practice are needed and will shortly be presented. First there is a breathing exercise to be followed; this calms the mind. Then there is a visual exercise to be done; this fixes the attention and induces a concentrated state. The cessation of attention in the external field sets attention free in the internal field. That state reached, what will next happen? If the effort has been rightly made a kind of vacuum is temporarily created in consciousness, but Nature, abhorring a vacuum, swiftly readjusts matters. The *mental* investigation now ceasing, there ensures an interior revelation. The banished thoughts are replaced by universal Overmind; this in turn yields later to the divine Overself which steps into the field of our awareness. It brings with it 'the peace that passeth understanding,' as St. Paul phrased it: (A better translation would be 'the peace that passeth intellect.')

Once the leap-over is successfully accomplished, the true self thus reveals itself to the dumbfounded mind. We are then stricken into utter mental silence, for we realize that we stand now in a divine presence. It is an experience which cannot be surpassed. It will break all foolish illusions and dispel all erroneous dreams. Confusion and contradiction will go out with the night. Illumination will flood the dark places of the mind with glorious light. We shall KNOW, and knowing, accept. For we shall discover that the heart of our Being is the heart of the Universe also. And it is good.

Thereafter the task turns from temporary retirement into the creation of a habit of self-recollectedness which is to be resorted to whenever necessary throughout the day and wherever one may be, until it becomes a fixed and prevailing mood when the heart is for ever immersed in the One, even whilst the head and hands are busy with their own duties.

We must remember that cold, unfeeling mentality alone will not suffice during the analysis; this path demands that we put the heart, as well as the head, into it.

At this point it is also important to understand that the mere intellectual duplication of the thoughts given in such a meditative analysis is insufficient; if cold, critical analysis could alone succeed in reaching the subtle realm of the spirit, so many of the world's thinkers would not have become the materialists they have become; no, something more is needed. That something is inner aspiration toward truth, genuine heartfelt and sustained desire to be elevated into the spiritual region. One ought to lay aside all other desires during the period of self-enquiry. That aspiration acts as a propulsive force and without it a dry, intellectual cutting up of one's ego may lead to purely negative results. What is wanted then is deliberately to induce moods wherein thought is fired with feeling, and to create emotions when the mind is lit up by the sparks of spiritual aspiration. Careful following of the instructions will bring this about. In this manner a balanced development will prepare one to advance along this path, and although the fundamental training will be intellectual the essential exalting of the emotions will proceed side by side with it. Thus, there will be evoked in time an atmosphere suitable to the sublime manifestation from within of the divine to which one aspires.

When one has practised over a sufficient period of time, the second stage will gradually unfold wherein the perusal of these pages will become unnecessary and their basic ideas or phrases alone need be mentally revived out of memory and meditated upon. The question as to how long this course of meditation should be continued must be answered by each for himself. It is necessary just so long as one feels that it is required: it is necessary until the fullest intellectual conviction of the truths taught in these pages has been obtained. It is necessary until one finds it so easy, spontaneous, welcome and pleasant that one longs for its daily half-hour and hurries forward to its daily practice; it is necessary until one can drop all the trains of discursive thought and feel an increasing luminousness in the brain, so that all true ideas stand out as startlingly clear sure images or inspired certitudes in this brilliant light. The practice must be prolonged until one can win through the constant clamour of outside impressions, physical sensations and restless thoughts to an inner vigilance which is sharply intense yet seemingly effortless. The state it induces is to be picked up again and again until it becomes habitual: then only may it be dropped.

There should be no hurry, no impatience. Unless the student moves in this mental world with calm confidence and unhasting determination, he will defeat his own ends. Mere superficial thoughts rushing from insufficient data to a vague general conclusion, a haste to get through one's period of meditation and be done with it – all these are factors detrimental to any progress in the inner life; such hurry is not really speed and actually retards the student and prevents him from entering the deeper soul-world to which he aspires.

One should sit down to one's half-hour with the understanding that so-much-time is required for the preliminary 'digging' in the mind until its deeper layers are touched; so much also for the entry into the Overmind; hence one must be ready to wait resignedly for results whilst working for them.

The question of inner attitude is of some importance in this quest, as important indeed as attitude of body. One must undertake the practice of this meditation in a hopeful, confident and optimistic mood, and never waver from that; yet withal one must never forget the paramount importance of being humble. Humility is the first step upon all paths that lead to the Infinite, no matter how different they are, and it is also the last. But one should begin by believing that the Truth *is* attainable, that the mind *can* be conquered, that the opposition of hindering environments is opportunity to overcome them, and that constant effort to find the Soul-light will eventually call forth its Grace.

One should not hesitate to maintain such an inner attitude for the very fact that one has undertaken such a practice is a sign that the Overself is beginning to touch him, to bid him awake. And the Overself's interest is in itself a herald of its coming Grace.

One ought now to strive and grasp the essence of this special method. It is not only the daily rumination over metaphysical truths, for partly this is a process to refine the mind and give it the tendency towards abstraction. Nor is it only the intermittent cultivation of certain delicate moods which exalt the soul, for this, too, is but to gain the uplifting force of aspiration which propels one forward on the inner quest. No, it is equally the creation of an attitude of right questioning. This movement of the mental life into the camp of self-interrogation is one vital difference which distinguishes the present method from all others. Instead of making personal effort the *sole* factor of one's progress, it succeeds in calling upon a higher part of one's being as a collaborator in the work at a certain higher stage of the path. For, the constant question of self, the search for the 'I', when practised in the manner prescribed here, gives adequate ground for such collaboration, because after providing all due preparation, it invites the Overself to take a more active hand in the play *and itself do something to lead us onward!*

The importance of this principle of self-questioning can hardly be over-estimated. Instead of making positive but vain assertions such as "I have a soul" or "I am a soul", it turns around and asks "Have I a soul?" or "Am I a soul?" *and then leaves the soul-part of one's being to supply the answer.* Whereas the former method is but intellectual dogmatizing, the latter humbles the intellect, silences its constant babbling and waits for the answer to come from the only part of our being truly competent to give it. This means that we no longer overvalue the intellect, but rather keep it in its rightful place. A spiritual quest can only end in success when it receives satisfaction in the spiritual region of one's being, and not merely in the intellectual. Thoughts will bring one along the road to the spiritual self, but they do not in themselves contain that self. If it were claimed that they did, then the accusations of critics that one might become the victim of auto-suggestive visions, would be correct. And truly, if the soul did not exist, if divinity were but an illusion and body the be-all and end-all of man, we could never obtain a genuine spiritual answer to our questions and we should have to remain satisfied with mere theorizings. Therefore, this method takes its stand upon the reality of the divine self of mankind. Because the Overself is indeed a reality, such a method can be confidently given to the world in the knowledge that those who will sincerely and patiently pursue it must one day obtain demonstrable results, demonstrable, that is to say, within their own experiences. If the Overself did not exist, or even granting its existence, if it were completely indifferent to the truthward aspirations of man and to his yearnings for a higher solace than material life alone can give him, then would this method be of no avail and no result. But on the contrary the Overself is the most revealing fundamental factor of our existence and it stands ever-ready to reveal itself, to give the supreme consolation of life to all those who will fulfil the requisite precedent conditions. That is why such self-investigation does not pass unheeded, but in due time the investigator who remains faithful to his quest is made aware of the divine self.

This principle, therefore, involves a complete turning of the mind from the attitude of positive affirmation to that of humble interrogation. Truth does not care to reveal herself to the intellectually arrogant, but she gives herself to those who have dropped to their knees in intellectual humility; and practice of this method must inevitably bring a man to such a humbleness of spirit. Not for nothing did Jesus utter those words about the Kingdom of Heaven being open only to those who became like little children. What he said there was a symbolical reference to the same condition of intellectual humility which is even more needed in our own epoch. Although we must first strive with sharpened intellect to pierce open the shell of the ego, we must nevertheless not hesitate to lay aside that instrument when we reach the point in our practices where we realize that it has now fulfilled itself. Such a readiness to "ask" for truth at the right stage in the spirit of a little child, after having exerted all one's intellectual powers, is not a sign of weakness. Could our proud age but understand this, it is rather a sign of spiritual strength. To acknowledge freely the limitations of the intellect when one has reached the far-thest boundary of that faculty is to invite the oncoming of something higher. This is the true fulfilment of yoga – to wield thought as a master and then discard it.

11

THE MYSTERY OF BREATH

Whoever has practised this process of self-enquiry for a sufficient time and has made appreciable progress in the art, must then learn how to manage his thoughts during his daily meditation-practice in a different manner. In the most elementary stages, he has been formulating and re-formulating an analysis of his inner structure. He has been intellectually dissecting himself by means of trained concentrated thought. But, with the passage of time, he should develop an attitude which intellectually at least can thoroughly comprehend that the soul or self is not limited to the body. When this attitude is reached he need not continue with dry detailed repetition of the analysis, and indeed may feel no further inclination to do so. Instead, his meditations may take a turn and, with swift generalizations, he may pass rapidly through the phases which formerly took him some considerable time.

What is he to do next? The Overself, however perceptible by intellectual cognition, still remains undiscoverable by experience, although he now understands where it is not, or rather where not to look for it.

Now he may enter a new and advanced phase of this

work, when by the adjuncts of breath-regulation, visual fixation and imaginative training, he is enabled to progress into this deeper realm. It is indeed a critical phase for it precedes the grand and glorious attainment of the Overself.

The time has come when this very function of thinking which has served a man so well and so usefully during the detailed dissections of himself must be suspended altogether *because it imprisons him in time!*

He should not do this, however, until there comes at last an inner sense which tells him that he is really ready for it; if he does it at the bidding of impatience for quick results, he will get nothing and end with disappointment. The intellectual quest must now be succeeded by an intuitional quest, but the point at which he will be ready to pass from one into the other must be determined with the greatest care. If he attempts this too early, his efforts will be frustrated and if he leaves it too late, he will lose valuable time and become overwhelmed by a sense of dreariness. Whilst nothing is to be forced, on the other hand, nothing is to be forgotten.

To attempt to suspend thought at too early a point upon this path is to rob one's human personality of the full enrichment which is its due. How to determine when this point has really been attained is not easy. One must be guided by a kind of inner sense; such a sixth sense does indeed begin to arise and make itself increasingly felt within a man after he has persisted in these mental quiet practices for some time. He cannot create it for himself; we may say only that it comes. But when it does manifest, he should trust himself to it unreservedly and let it lead him whithersoever it would have him go.

The greatest difficulty in this process is now to free the attention from the incessant flux of unwanted thoughts. It is only when one attempts to do so that one discovers how enslaved he is, how unable to keep away those tides of thought which constantly dash against the shores of our being. To bid them be still will seem at first the hardest thing in the world, yet this can and must be done by slow and steady effort.

To stand aside and watch one's thoughts for a time every day is to see how no sooner does one thought die than another at once rushes into the brain to take its place. This goes on with endless repetition. The wheels of the brain never cease to revolve until sleep at last supervenes and bestows a temporary respite.

To Eastern people this difficulty of arresting thought is not so formidable as it is to Westerners and they do not always realize that an Occidental must make a much greater effort to lift himself into the region of calm abstraction than they need to make. The help which the average European or American needs in this direction must be partly physical at least; he needs some indirect method *involving a physical act* to strengthen him in his task of mental self-discipline. Moreover, the Orientals are accustomed to resort to the presence and society of spiritual guides whose personal atmosphere spontaneously assists others to bring the thoughts under subjugation, whereas Occidentals can rarely find such guides in their own lands.

Help is close at hand, it lies in the regulation of the flow of breath. Pre-eminently for persons who are always active with inexorable and pressing affairs or who are strongly attached to the material world by desires and ambitions, this exercise is particularly suited to bring the mind under control.

Our Western savants have accumulated a store of knowledge which must impress every mind by its colossal proportions and yet there are still a few things which have escaped their discerning eyes – things, however, that are of the utmost importance to mankind. For instance, the breath holds a somewhat peculiar position. Its more immediate effects are clearly visible and physically registrable, but, the Eastern seers declare, there are remoter effects not so easily perceived. Thus we make our greatest exertions with *inheld* breath whereas we make our fussy minor ones with quick breaths. Again there is a special inter-relationship between breath and thought. These two possess a common ancestry, a related origin.

The Oriental seers did not leave these doctrines undemonstrated, but frequently proved their truth in their own persons. By disciplining and controlling the breath in various ways, they succeeded in producing the most extraordinary physical and mental results. The faqueers who, even in our own day, permit themselves to be buried alive in an airless chamber for one to forty days at a stretch illustrate one of these remarkable effects and show that life can continue within the body even when the function of breathing has been completely suspended. This well-authenticated fact should at least render us less over-hasty in scoffing at the ancient doctrines.

We may now proceed to prove the connection which exists between breath and thought in a simple manner. Take the case of the man who has become greatly excited with inordinate anger – watch his heavy breathing and one will perceive that it has become as flurried and flustered as are his thoughts and passions. His breath comes and goes in short, hurried gasps, and the more violent his behaviour the more violent is his breathing. Take, again, the case of a poet musing in reverie over some half-formed line of verse and one will perceive that, on the contrary, his breathing is placid, thin, calm and slow. Take next a man pondering over some abstruse mathematical problem. He automatically breathes more slowly and more gently. Man's life-current, like a tree, has put forth two branches: the one being mind and the other breath. Take further the extreme and abnormal case of the Oriental faqueer who has forcibly repressed his respiration and been buried alive for a time, and who later re-emerges into active existence.

His after-statement is that his mind has been blissfully unconsciousness, and that all thoughts disappeared with the
suspension of his breathing. Does not this last case alone show
that the function of thinking, *so far as the physical life is concerned,* is inter-related with the function of breathing, no less
than the other two cases show that a change in one frequently
brings about a corresponding change in the other?

When the writer had written the foregoing paragraph a
man appeared unexpectedly at the threshold of the bungalow,
perched on a lonely range of hills and overlooking unpeopled
forests and jungles, where he happened to be staying, and
desired to see him. The visitor turned out to be Sinha, a young
yogi of Mysore State, who successfully performs the identical,
just mentioned feat of being buried alive! It is in line with many
curious experiences of a similar order that the concentration of
the writer's mind upon a particular theme synchronizes with
events that just happen or are induced to happen. Young
Sinha illustrates in his person a perfect case of the power of
breath-suspension completely to blot out all consciousness, all
thinking, whilst bodily existence still continues; he himself tes-
tifies that breath and thought disappear simultaneously in his
own experience. "Seven years' practice of breathing exercises
brought me this power," he adds.

Take, finally, other cases of Egyptian faqueers who lac-
erate their bodies with ghastly yet almost bloodless wounds,
and who eat live scorpions and writhing snakes; of Indian yogis
who walk on red-hot stones and drink strong nitric acid; and
of Tibetan hermits who sit naked amid the Himalayan snows
yet feel no sense of cold. All these men, when questioned and
their confidences won, usually reveal that they have gained
control over the body through hard and long practice of secret
and difficult breathing exercises, whose results have altered the
frailty of the flesh and raised its powers of resistance to aston-

ishing degrees. *Through the same medium but by different and, fortunately, far easier exercises, it is possible to win control over the mind also.*

The vital force immanent in breath and the mental force which activates the brain, arise from a common source. That source is the One Life-Current which permeates the universe and, in each human being, becomes his Divine Self, his Overself. "Breath is the sign of life," is a phrase which possesses a deeper significance than its users commonly know.

As a result of this close interrelation, changes in breathing produce changes in mind, and vice versa.

§

One may now attempt to profit by these curious facts and to put them to practical use in the quest upon which one has embarked. The rhythms of breathing work in unison with the rhythms of our mental states; excitement induces an irregular and staccato series of breaths; quiet contemplation, on the contrary, automatically brings about a regular and smooth series. Because thought and breath are so intertwined, one has only by an act of will to pay conscious attention to, and regulate one's rate and mode of, breathing in order to produce the corresponding effect upon his thoughts. Hence, the stilling of the breath tends to still the thoughts. When, as in the following exercise, thinking and breathing are made to coalesce for such a high purpose, a state of steady calm will begin to arise within which true meditation becomes infinitely easier to the ever-active Western-mind.

One must take up, then, the following four-in-one exercise which is to be practised immediately after the intellectual analysis of the self and not before it.

There are three brief preliminaries to be noticed, however. The first requires a straightening of the spine in an easy, natural manner whilst one is seated. This is because bodily posture affects the breathing and right posture is an aid to breath-control. The Indian yogis of the "Body-Control" school are acquainted with no less than eighty-four different postures whose prime purpose is to bring about certain changes in the breathing, but such complicated and arduous practices are not required upon this path. Then the eyes must be closed and kept shut throughout the period of breathing practice. Finally, all stale air from the lungs is to be expelled by forcible exhalation repeated four times. This accomplished, the process of altering the usual rate of one's breathing must be attended to.

(1) *One should gradually diminish the speed of breathing little by little each week and for about five minutes once or twice daily until, roughly speaking, it has been lowered to about half its former rate; (2) at the end of each inhalation one should gently check the entire breath-activity, retain the air for two or three seconds, and then exhale the impure air again; (3) simultaneously the breathing is to be carefully rendered quiet, unstrained, gentle, placid and effortless in quality; (4) careful watch should be kept over the movement of the breath and all one's attention should be turned upon it.*

This exercise is given because it is infinitely simpler than any of those hoary traditional ones which the patient faqueers of the Orient have to practise, and because the writer believes that the modern man must achieve his spiritual effects with the utmost economy of means and the flattest trajectory of time. True, it will not produce such startling and such dramatic results, but then the modern man has far more need of the anodyne of mental tranquillity than he has of the ability to swallow a great gulp of H_2SO_4 without falling dead on the spot! Moreover, it is as safe as the others are dangerous.

Now it is important that the exercise be properly performed, despite its simplicity. It will be effective only if all the conditions are attentively fulfilled. These will therefore be explained more completely.

The number of respirations under normal conditions is between fourteen and twenty per minute and varies in different kinds of individuals. That is to say, the average man takes a complete breath for this number of times every sixty seconds. The breathing-in and breathing-out together count as one complete breath. This normal cycle is to be reduced. It should be brought down within a period that may vary from as low as one month to as much as six months according to the physical type of the individual, to a rate of about seven complete breaths per minute. Those who are naturally and normally slow breathers will not need to reduce the rate of their breathing so much as people whose breathing is quicker. In this matter of working down to the required rate all who practise this exercise must be guided by bodily instincts; they should go forward slowly and not go beyond any point where they feel strain or pain, suffocation or a sense of intolerable burden. Let them be warned how far they should decrease and slow down the breathing by the sense of comfort or discomfort in the lungs.

Thus if one normally inhales fifteen times a minute, the exercise may be first begun by lessening the frequency to a dozen times per minute for the first week, to ten for the second week and then down to seven breaths per minute by the end of a month. These figures are given only as a rough guide to suit some individuals; each must find his way for himself. A watch may be used to time the breath-cycles during the first few weeks of practice, but the habit of relying on external aid for this purpose is not good and should be discontinued as soon as possible, i.e. as soon as one is accustomed to gauge correctly if approximately the desired rhythm, which is about half the normal rate. One need not and ought not to adopt the same finicky precise attitude wherewith a cook times the boiling of an egg.

One should carry on this practice for about five minutes at a time – not more. If it is done in the morning, it may be repeated if desired in the evening.

One ought not to try to go ahead too fast; one ought to progress slowly and naturally in this particular sphere.

In all cases the diminution of the breath-rate should progress in such a way that no acute, abnormal discomfort is experienced. Naturally, in the beginning a slight giddiness or discomfort will inevitably be felt, because when one starts to use an organ of the body in an unaccustomed way, that part naturally resists for a time the unusual activity which is being imposed upon it. If actual pain, definite distress of a sense of suffocation or any other obviously abnormal symptom becomes noticeable, the exercise should be stopped at once and the student should revise carefully the method prescribed to see if he is doing it absolutely correctly, because these symptoms can appear only through misunderstanding of the method, or through organic disease of the heart or lungs. No breath exercise should ever be practised by people who suffer from such disease.

So long as the average person keeps to the minimum of seven complete breaths per minute during the brief period of exercise he need have no fear of any danger. The exercise is quite safe and indeed before the present writer first published it to the world in *The Secret Path*, he asked two friends who were physicians of long experience to examine carefully from every aspect and to give him the assurance, which he already possessed from his own viewpoint, that it could work no harm in any way, provided it were faithfully followed. They gave him this assurance.

When one can breathe like this without discomfort, and

after he has practised for a sufficient period of weeks or months to enable him to feel confident and competent to do so, the five-minute interval of breath-control should be increased. It may rise gradually to ten or even fifteen minutes as one progresses. A longer period than this ought not to be consciously practised by any European or American, without special guidance, because in that case safety of this exercise will disappear, nor is it necessary. It is possible to reduce the rate of breathing during this exercise even to less than the minimum of seven given above and this further reduction may have a correspondingly more powerful effect upon the mind; nevertheless only those who are highly advanced should undertake this, and then under the personal guidance of someone who is expert in these matters, or the danger-line will be crossed.

The second condition of this fourfold exercise requires the breath to be held *but this should not be attempted for longer than three seconds*. This interval which is experienced after the inspiration and before the expiration of the air is of peculiar importance in a physical sense. When the movement of the respiratory apparatus becomes still, the consciousness becomes still also. Indian yogis of a certain class make a special practice of prolonging this interval for several minutes, knowing that it is the neutral or junction point *where breath meets mind*. They have been traditionally taught that if they can hold the breath, they can hold the thoughts as a result. This is quite correct, but the conditions under which they are permitted to carry on this practice are extremely different from those in which the average Western man finds himself. Therefore whoever tries to imitate them and to restrain his breathing for abnormally long periods – even for two minutes – does so at his peril. The yogic exercises are to be done with safety only in solitude, when no interference or interruption of any kind can occur, when the practitioner is living a life of absolute sexual continence, and above all when he is under the watchful care of a *guru* (experienced teacher). Europeans and Americans who have been lured into these practices by the promises of obtaining unusual psychic or occult powers usually live to learn – and to repent. Abnormal breath-holding exercises are generally disastrous in result for them, for ill-health and mental unbalance may follow in their train. Such dangerous practices will never be recommended indiscriminately by the writer to an unwary public, and he earnestly places this warning on record because he has seen too many instances of the unfortunate plight of those who disobey it. Three seconds is the interval laid down in this system for the average man, and there is not the slightest danger in such a cessation of normal breathing. Indeed, when one has continued the practice in comfort and become fairly well familiar with it, one may prolong the interval and arrest the breathing for five seconds. But that is the maximum. None should foolishly endeavour to exceed this figure, because the effort is uncalled for and may carry the person into danger unknown.

The third condition is easy. One should avoid a jerky series of quick movements when inhaling, and aim rather at a steady, light and continuous action. The breathing should be deliberately turned into a slow and smooth flow. Audible panting should be avoided. One's effort should be to tranquillize and calm the respirative process. The air should flow with such gentleness that, as the Chinese mystics aptly describe it, a feather held beneath the nostrils will not be fluttered. Just as one has to relax the body completely in order to attain the physical posture for meditation, so one must relax breathing completely too. Thus the art of relaxation must be carried right through the body into the lungs. By dint of correct practice the respiration may become so mild that only a slight current of air moves like a fine invisible thread in and out of the nostrils.

The fourth and final condition of this process demands steady and fixed attention upon it, so that one thinks of nothing else. A continuous vigil is required for the few minutes of practice, an intent *mental* watch upon the incoming and outgoing breaths. The mind must be abstracted from all other activity and fastened upon the breath-movement alone; such willed watchfulness will eventually bring the latter under control and reduce it easily to the lower ebb and flow which is the goal. One must keep one's mind entirely upon it so that both become united. The exercise must not be performed in any indifferent manner, but with conscious concentration upon the flow of the breath: this is very important if one is to profit fully. All other thoughts should be blotted out and forgotten, and one's self immersed entirely in the respirational rhythm. The potency of the method will be proportionate to such concentration as one brings to bear upon it. If the attention gets broken or unnecessary pauses occur in the exercises, its power to alter the mental state will be reduced.

Whilst doing the breathing exercise one may become acutely aware of the beating of his heart, not as excited throbbing but as gentle pulsation. This is a natural consequence of the heightened attention being bestowed on the breathing, and need occasion no alarm.

Success may come almost from the first, or it may come only with time, but the practice is not hard to do. Some will take longer than others to achieve it because bodies, minds and lung capacities differ with individuals.

What will be the result of practising this exercise?

The mind will be brought into a condition closely harmonized with the breathing. Thoughts will spontaneously become fewer and fewer as breaths become fewer too. The entire process of thinking will slow down. A general impression of inner calm and serene equipoise will gradually make itself felt. The fluctuating and restless passions will become pacified and stilled. The intellect will be netted like a captive bird; as one gets proper possession of the breath-life so will the thought-life be correspondingly possessed too. The utter serenity of quiescent inhalation will be reflected in the quiescent mind. In the long moments when the breath is actually held, the intellect will be caught by reaction and its vigour in veiling reality become diminished.

This is the precise effect which is needed to carry one forward to the next stage along the path of spiritual development. Intellect has reached its limits and the moment has come when it must be prepared to cease its efforts. Analysis beyond this point would be unprofitable and indeed a handicap. One must be prepared now to summon and to intensify all one's faculty of vigilant attention and dive deeper into his being in quest of the Overself.

A man diving into the sea will not take up a train of connected thoughts about the sea, but forgetting all else will hold his breath and directly make the plunge. Similarly, when one prepares to dive into the region which borders the Overself one must not indulge any further in meditations about it but, forgetting everything else, control the breath to the point of holding it intermittently and then directly plunge inwards into ever deeper being.

The simplicity of this breathing practice must not deceive one into regarding it as unimportant. On the contrary the writer has heard impressive reports as to its remarkable efficacy from those who have faithfully followed it in conjunction with the intellectual analytic exercises. Some persons have obtained good results from the beginning whilst others have had to wait months. One cannot therefore predict in advance how soon really noticeable results will be obtained, because individuals differ so much in their pre-dispositions, but one may rest assured that persevering concentration in this direction cannot fail to bring the unruly mind to yield. On the other hand, where such breath-regulation is not consciously allied with a spiritual quest, it merely ends, in its extremest form, either in a trance of useless blankness or a sheer self-hypnosis that is nothing more than sleepy abstraction from our ordinary life of desire and activity.

It is conceivable that there are some highly-metaphysical or spiritually-minded types of people to whom such a breathing exercise makes no appeal and who even feel that it is unnecessary. Such people may omit it provided they can find sufficient inner strength within themselves to pass without undue difficulty, from the stage of intellectual analysis into the intuitional stage beyond. But the overwhelming majority of Western people will not be able to make the passage from one stage to the other, however, except with the utmost difficulty and it is for their benefit that this simple physical exercise has been devised. For, extraverted as they generally are, with minds constantly producing images of the external world, they cannot easily tear themselves away from mundane matters into a region of profound spiritual abstraction.

One may profit also by this exercise even outside the minutes of one's period of daily withdrawal. *If at any time during the day one is troubled by moods of undue melancholy or inordinate anger, of extreme irritability or ungovernable passion, of uncontrollable nervousness or oppressive fear, one need only practise this slow-rhythmed breathing wherever he may be and it should have an immediate and beneficial effect in pacifying the nerves and harmoniously readjusting his outlook.* The breathing can be dropped down to the long cycle of seven per minute so quietly and so inconspicuously that nobody else need know, and it can be done whether walking, standing, or sitting, whether in the busy street or the quiet home.

There is a further little practice which may be added to (or even incorporated with) the foregoing daily exercise, although it is not an essential part of the process. Since that quiet December night seven years ago when the writer first heard it explained by a learned yogi in his home near the river Ganges, the latter's thin face illumined by the flickering yellow light of a small lantern, he has taught it in turn to other seekers who have found it useful and helpful.

This consists of strongly *imagining and believing* whilst one is breathing that a current of divine being passes into one-self with the inhaled breath and that it passes out with the exhaled breath, only in order to return again. In this suggestive manner divinity is identified with the breath-energy itself. The yogi further explained that when one attains divine consciousness the spiritual essence of each breath rises upwards to the top of the head and *remains there*, thus conferring deathlessness to the mind, whereas whilst one remains actuated by personal egoism the breath's unseen essence passes away into the void and is lost.

12

THE MYSTERY OF THE EYE

When one has become sufficiently proficient in the breathing exercise to be able to practise it almost automatically and effortlessly, he may then occupy himself with a further exercise which can be added to it and done concurrently. This, too, is a physical adjunct to the intellectual work, and uses the body's most delicate sense organ – the eye. The new practice should not be undertaken before this stage has been reached, for in the hands of the unready a different result will be achieved, one which will not only be inferior but may also be harmful. Because of this likelihood of its misuse or premature use by the over-eager but unwise and unripe persons, the writer has not hitherto published this exercise. Nevertheless its value when used in proper hands and at the right time is much and it can therefore no longer be withheld from a description. which purports to be at all complete, of this particular spiritual path.

The next stage demands a deeper withdrawal of the mind, but the hold of the external world upon us is so hard that some kind of external and tangible object is often useful to focus our thoughts, preparatory to the plunge out of reasoned meditation into abstract contemplation, and particularly to fix the attention internally. A visual exercise has therefore been devised which serves excellently to achieve this result.

Nature has not set the eyes in a position higher in the physical body than those of the other specialized sense-channels for nothing. The function of sight occupies a place of supreme importance in our life as human beings. The world thereby stands revealed to us in all its comprehensive character. Yet not only by this noteworthy position may we gauge the importance which Nature places upon our instruments of vision, but also by their peculiar quality. No other sense-channel is so delicate in construction, so refined in substance, and so sensitive in function as is the eye. This alone should suffice to suggest to us that Nature intends it to play a subtler and less materialistic part in our physical lives than the other organs. So it is in fact, for the eye not only to reveal the external gross world to us, but it can also help to reveal the internal subtle world, for in the words of Edgar Allan Poe, the brilliant American story-writer and poet, "The eyes are the windows of the soul." Behind the lustrous surface of the eyes the discerning may read the general trends of thought and emotion of their possessor. Such is their reflective power. That which lies within the brain or the heart in unperceived secrecy may become involuntarily manifest through the eyes.

Through no other sense-channel may we obtain such a true understanding, and estimate of a man's character and mind as through his own eyes. Indeed, so striking is this fact that a keen observer and thinker, Buffon, the great French expert in natural history, wrote as far back as the eighteenth century:

"The images of our secret agitation are particularly painted in in the eyes. The eye appertains more to the soul than any other organ; seems affected by and to participate in all its motions. It explains them in all their force, in all their purity, as to infuse into other minds the fire, the activity, the very image with which themselves are inspired. The eye at once receives and reflects the intelligence of thought and the warmth of sensibility. It is the sense of the mind, the tongue of the understanding."

And the late Lord Leverhulme, the millionaire business magnate who built up the world's largest industrial organization of his day, once confessed that, "To applicants seeking employment my first attention is given to the eye." It is obvious, therefore, that the eye, this most marvellous and beautiful organ of the human body, with its moving lids and rolling pupils, possesses a unique relationship with the inner being of man by means of some affinity. Let us explore the nature of this relationship.

The anatomist traces the course of an important medium of communication between the eye and the brain which he names the optic nerve. The simple act of seeing involves much more than is apparent. It is based upon the action of light vibrating through the medium of the atmosphere, both upon the object which one sees as well as upon the eye itself. The impressions received from without are caused by the light waves propagated from external objects; they are focused on the retina and there photographed by means of chemical changes. These changes are associated with currents of nervous energy and transmitted along the optic nerves to the brain.

We have already seen that the brain, however much it may condition our thinking and limit our consciousness, is nevertheless not the true creator of either, inasmuch as it, in its own turn, is also a channel or organ for the subtler intangible force of the Overself. We now know, through analysis, that thinking is effective even outside the motions of material brain-molecules; and that the Overself, the true selfhood which lies at the core of our being, is a great deal more than a transient combination of atomic material particles. It is this inner force alone which works the bodily machinery, causes the leap-over of the photographic impression into consciousness and makes vision at all possible. Now we must remember that mind is a force which is as real as existence itself and as registrable, in its own way, as the invisible wave of electrical energy which is hidden within the material atom and constitutes its essential nature. Therefore the mind cannot help but project a wave of subtle energy along the optic nerves to the eyes every time we look outwards at our physical environment, every time we glance at any external object and every time we gaze at another person. These vibrations must partake of the nature, character and intensity of the mind whence they originate. When we realize this we may begin to understand why the human eye should be capable not only of registering so much of the human personality, but also of transmitting the latter's special qualities. It is not only a passive, but also an active organ.

The force which thus reaches the physical eye from the brain with the same lightning-like rapidity with which the photographic impressions of environment reach the brain-centres does not, however, take up its final lodgment there. It uses the eye merely as a gate and then passes onwards and outwards into the world. To express this briefly and scientifically: *there is a definite radiation from the human eye.*

Science itself has offered precise testimony to the existence of these rays which stream from the human eye unobserved by our normal senses. And an instance of this occurs in Raoul Montandon's work entitled, *Les Radiations Humaines:*

"The mechanical action of ocular radiations has been demonstrated by various experimenters. Mr. Jounet caused the needle of a zoomagnetometer to oscillate without the intervention of any other agent save that of the 'will' transmitted without contact through the medium of what one might call the magnetic gaze. 'I tried,' he said, 'to direct the swing of the needle in a certain direction, by lowering the hands and having only the eyes in front of the needle; I succeeded in making it oscillate in the desired direction.' He concluded from this that it is possible *for certain people,* by the action of the mind alone, to put into action a copper needle suspended in an earthenware receptacle which is maintained both closed and stationary. No doubt the same would apply to any other sufficiently mobile device. A kind of electroscope is also known by the aid of which it is possible to measure the energy emanating from the human gaze. The experimenter, by fixing his eyes on a sensitive ring (it should be noted that the ring must be of genuine metal, either gold (preferably), silver, platinum, etc.) suspended on a silk thread, would be able to provoke an oscillation varying according to the individual performing the experiment . . . which permits one to conclude that a field of magnetic vibration is indeed a reality."

Another interesting instrument was demonstrated by Dr. Charles Russ, M.R.C.S., at the Ophthalmological Congress at Oxford in 1921. It was an electrical and magnetic apparatus whose chief feature was a delicate solenoid made of fine copper wire and suspended within a metal box by a silk fibre. The solenoid was held steady by a magnet which naturally came to rest in the magnetic meridian. When a human eye looked through a slot in the observing window and maintained a steady gaze at the solenoid, the latter started in motion, which was usually away from the observing eye. If the gaze was transferred to the other end of the solenoid, the latter moved in a reverse direction to the motion first induced. The effect of the gaze took place selectively in the line of vision during other experiments also. Hence Dr. Russ concluded that there was a force accompanying the act of human vision.

The ancient Hindus found correspondencies between the various parts of the human body and the various elements of Nature. Thus they linked earth to arms and water to tongues, but fire, the king of Nature's energies, was harmonized with the eyes. Therefore they believed that the spiritual consciousness of a man comes to expression in the appearance of his eyes. So much importance is attached to the power of the eye in India, that by Hindu religious laws, if any non-Brahmin gazes fixedly at a utensil or at some food belonging to a Brahmin the latter is directed to wash the utensil immediately and to throw away the food untasted in order to remain unpolluted by the inferior magnetism which the outsider is believed to have introduced.

This radiant stream of invisible magnetism is sometimes felt by sensitive persons, as, for instance, in the commonplace incident of a man turning round in unconscious response to the fixity of someone's gaze directed upon his neck or shoulders from behind. Why should the convergence of the eyeballs upon a single point give this strange power? This question does not go deep enough because it does not see that it is the power *behind* the eyes, i.e. the mind, which is concentrated. Still more, however, is its existence evidenced by the emotions we experience when under the gaze of some person who possesses a strong inner life, whether it be of thought, soul, or passion. Our everyday existence in the domains of business, professional activity, social or domestic routine, furnishes us from time to time with positive illustrations of this truth.

Everyone has but to consult his own past experience to remember how many cases have come within his own personal orbit. From the humblest toiler to the highest ruler in the land, no one living is exempt from such experiences.

Women understand this truth instinctively. Where women of outstanding personality seek power over the opposite sex or wish to indulge in mere coquetry, they cultivate the kind of glance which they believe to be most effective for their purpose. History affords numerous instances of women who have conquered men by using the glance as one of the effective weapons in their armour; Salome conquered King Herod, and Cleopatra subjugated Marc Antony, in ancient times, just as Greta Garbo has conquered millions in popular cinema audiences during modern times.

Turning to a higher plane, we find in geniuses, saints, mystics and yogis a still more striking exemplification of the power inherent within the gaze.

The eye of the true yogi is unmistakable. The man who has held thoughts under mastery for long periods of time, who has turned the mind inward upon itself in fixed contemplation, betrays it by his eyes. The Hindu sacred legends tell us that the gods are steady and flickerless in their glances, fixed and motionless. Napoleon's eyes were of this sort – a fact which was noted by Heinrich Heine when he saw the greatest of modern emperors ride victoriously into Dusseldorf. Moreover, "His searching glance has something singular and inexplicable, which imposes even on our Directors; judge if it may not intimidate a woman," wrote Josephine de Beauharnais of the young General Bonaparte who wished to wed her. Napoleon himself said: "I have seldom drawn my sword; I won my battles with my eyes, not with my weapons." Goethe's eyes were likewise similar, flickerless in inward thought, even towards the end of his very long life.

Napoleon was greatly misunderstood by his contemporaries; he was a psychological mystery and an unconscious yogi, an instrument in the hands of high powers, as was also the Indian Emperor Akbar who achieved the most astonishing success in building up and retaining a vast empire as much by his powerful personality as by military means; Akbar also possessed a distinguished-looking pair of eyes. The Jesuit missionaries who visited his court described them as being "vibrant like the sea in sunshine".

The power of the glance, however, attains its undisputed demonstration and supreme apotheosis in the case of the hypnotist. Here we plainly behold the effectiveness and power of the eyes as a medium for superimposing the will and thought of one person upon another. Such demonstration, when once witnessed, is more convincing than a hundred arguments.

§

Finally there is the curious fact that in profound abstraction or self-hypnotism induced through the eyes one may not only influence others, but *oneself!* Writers particularly are sometimes accustomed to go off into reverie when they have been revolving some idea centred in the mind whilst *simultaneously staring* fixedly at some tangible object. In this connection, we must remember that, when analysing inspiration, the condition of reverie was found to be peculiarly favourable to the high attainment of genius because it brought the subconscious or Overmind into prominence.

Jacob Boehme, the seventeenth-century cobbler-mystic of the little German provincial town of Goerlitz, received some remarkable illuminations during his lifetime, whereby the inmost secrets of Nature and God were revealed to him. His first illumination came when he was twenty-five years old and began unexpectedly as he sat idly in his room one day. His eyes happened to see a burnished pewter dish upon which the sun shone so brilliantly that his gaze was prolonged involuntarily, so beautiful and splendid was the reflected radiance of the dish. He fell into a trance of ecstasy and his mind was withdrawn to an inner world. Here and in this manner the knowledge of divine things came to him. All living things in Nature seemed to be lit up from within, the sacred forces behind creation became visible, and the mysteries of the hidden foundations of the material world were explained. Hereafter he lived in great peace but kept silent, writing his visions down for remembrance in a book. He said nothing of this to anyone at first, but praised and thanked God in silence. Of this marvellous change that was wrought in him he said somewhere in one of his books that it was like a resurrection from the dead! This uneducated shoemaker – whose humility was such that he prefaced his writings with the statement: "I was as simple concerning the hidden mysteries as the meanest of all, but my visions of the wonders of God taught me, so that I must write of his wonders; though indeed my purpose is to write this for a memorandum for myself," – was led from one spiritual revelation to another after this initial entry into a higher realm through the power of the transfixed gaze, until the final illumination came to him and he could write:

> "The gate was opened to me so that in one quarter of an hour I saw and I knew more than if I had been many years at an university, at which I exceedingly admired and thereupon turned my praise to God for it. I knew and saw in myself the three worlds, namely the divine (angelical and paradisical) and the dark, and then the external and visible world (being a procreation or external birth from both the internal and spiritual worlds)."

Some people will shiver at the thought of passing into a trance as the means of obtaining a superior state and will regard it as a highly obnoxious condition to be avoided at all costs. This will be particularly the case in Europe and America where the only phenomena of this order usually noticed have been associated with either hypnotism or illness. They do not know that there are various forms and phases of trance and that some are as valuable and as attractive as others may be harmful and repulsive. The Orient understands these things better. For the genius or inspired man who enters into a reverie during his creative moments is simply entering the elementary form of the trance state. If he could forget his work for a while, but yet retain his abstracted condition and endeavour to deepen it, he would most probably pass into a complete trance – and one which would be extremely delightful.

The eye is the sense-channel which is most closely in touch with the mind. It is not merely a photographic instrument, a passive receiver, but also a powerfully active mental and soul-instrument of the human personality. With this acknowledgment of the intimate relation which subsists between the eye, the ego and the Overself, one is better prepared to appreciate the value of such a gazing exercise as is now about to be presented here.

Just as the breathing exercise is intended primarily as a physical help to the achievement of mental control by people of active temperament and busy life, and especially Western people, so the following physical exercise is intended for the same type. But it will not only help to achieve this end; it will lead to a yet more advanced one – that of entering the state of reverie, of touching the fringe of the trance condition.

This exercise is not new; it has been known and practised since long ago by Tibetan lamas, Indian yogis and Chinese soothsayers, whilst every high priest of Ancient Egypt was expected to become an adept in it.

One ought not to take up this exercise until one has practised the breathing exercises for a period sufficiently long to establish its effectiveness and, most important, when one can do it automatically and without self-consciousness. The length of this period cannot be prescribed because it varies with individual persons: it may be a matter of a few weeks or of several months. But it will suffice to say that the point at which one may take up this eye-exercise is indicated by a definite if partial success in stilling the thoughts as a result of the daily breath-regulation.

One begins by placing at a convenient position at eye-level either upon a wall, a shelf, a table or some other article of furniture, the photograph of a person whom one truly venerates. If possible, the surface of the picture should be glossy. It may be the photograph of a living spiritual teacher, a living saint or a living sage, because such an object will possess a peculiar power to aid in the achievement of mental quiet. The writer could say something more about other important applicants of this curious method, but in the interest of public ethics he is forced to refrain.

The existence of such a power and the ability of photographs to act as transmitting channels for its influence is known to and taught by the Muslim mystics of Persia and Africa as well as the yogis of India, but the Western mind is unlikely to credit the assertion; such help, if it exists, will be ascribed conveniently to 'autosuggestion'. Fortunately a chance perusal of a newspaper, *The New York American,* brought the writer unexpectedly scientific confirmation of his assertion. In an issue dated March 30, 1933, he found a report about a newly-invented instrument which is capable of determining from a photograph whether the person has died since the portrait was taken. The journal adds:

"It detects the movement of 'life waves' or 'Z waves' on a photographic plate, and the stillness of these waves after the death of the subject was reported to-day by E. S. Shrapnell-Smith, one of Britain's noted scientists. Shrapnell-Smith, an authority on chemistry, said. 'Life, like a radio station, emits a distinct type of wave. These human life waves are transmitted to and fixed in a photographic plate. While the subject of the photograph is alive, movement of the waves is lively. The moment the person dies, no matter how far distant from the photograph, the life waves cease to emanate from the plate. I am unable to reveal at present just what the instrument consists of. But it is based and depends on first, radiation; second, magnetism; third, static electricity, and fourth, current electricity. There is nothing psychic or mysterious about it. It is the result of a new application of the laws of science.'"

To this may be added what the inventor does not yet know, that these life-waves carry the spiritual characteristics of the subjects, the mental atmosphere and personal imprint which he habitually bears. And the atmosphere of a man who has attained mental quiet is most definitely helpful to our high purpose, apart from his ethically inspirational value.

If one know of no such person as sage, saint or spiritual guide, or if one cannot procure such a photograph, one may substitute a painted picture or even a carved image instead. If, further, one prefers to bestow veneration upon some saint, sage or spiritual teacher who lived in former centuries when the art of photography was unknown, these substitutes may likewise be used. And if, finally, one does not care to adopt this attitude of veneration towards any spiritual personage, whether of the present or of the past, he may place before him instead any of the following objects: (I) a photograph or a painted picture of some beautiful and impressive natural scene. This should, as far as possible, contain but a single simple outline as in the Japanese style: for instance, a solitary peak rather than an entire forest. (2) A single flower, fragrant if possible, resting in a simple vase or holder. (3) A precious stone whose brilliance or luminosity is enhanced by the contrast of its colour with the background against which it is placed. Therefore the colour of this background. which may be a piece of cloth or silk. should be carefully selected. As, however, the magnetic radiation from certain gems is inimical to the practice of meditation, the choice of stones should be restricted to any of the following: diamond, sapphire, crystal, pearl, topaz and especially the black stones such as onyx, black agate and jet.

Whatever object is chosen it should be small in size and placed below the level of the eyes and never above them. Moreover it should rest so that the light, whether from a window or from the sun, falls directly upon it. One should then seat oneself at a distance varying from one to four feet from the object, and begin gazing at it. In the case of the use of a sage's photograph, one should fix the gaze *between his eyebrows*.

The eyes should not be fully opened, for they ought to be looking a little downwards. It is undesirable to stare continuously unless there is a long view of a distant landscape.

Those who are practising out of doors may not only use any of the above-mentioned objects, but may even dispense with them and concentrate their gaze upon some point in the surrounding landscape, such as a single leaf on a nearby tree, the summit of a hill, or the petals of a flower upon the opposite bank of a river. The Tibetan anchorites who have advanced to the stage of preparing to induce trance, begin by fixing their eyes either on a small bright metal ball the size of a playing marble, or on a distant object.

The reader is hereby warned that both meditation and breathing exercises are best done with closed eyes, because physical distractions are thereby diminished, and that therefore the present exercise ought not to be begun if the foregoing preliminaries have never been practised. Whoever embarks upon it without such preparation will get no beneficial spiritual result and will either sink into sleep or mediumship, or merely waste his time. *It is not a method for beginners but for proficients.*

After settling down in the chosen way and composing one's thoughts, one should concentrate and direct one's gaze entirely upon the selected object and endeavour to keep it within the field of vision for a period of about five minutes to begin with and for seven minutes maximum when one is more advanced in this particular practice. *It is inadvisable to prolong the gaze beyond this maximum time-limit.*

The reader is warned that there is some risk of developing a slight astigmatism if the exercise is overdone. He should again read the last paragraph of Chapter 8.

The glance should be kept unwaveringly focused and the eyelids must remain unblinking as far as possible during the period of exercise, even to the point of letting the eyes water. This will not be easy at first, but if one perseveres one will eventually realize such a possibility. *The mind should not be diverted from the object selected any more than the gaze,* nevertheless one ought not to permit any discursive thoughts whatsoever to arise in connection with it. One should not think *about* the object, but merely perceive it with an uninterrupted fixity of attention that permits no speculations to begin, nor incursions into logical sequential thinking connected with it. One should continue to look at it without blinking without any wavering of eyelids so far as one can sustain the effort, yet without getting into a strained or tense condifion. The endeavour ought to be to perform this practice in a natural relaxed manner without letting the eyes flinch.

§

Fixation of sight leads to fixation of mind. It cultivates and achieves fixed attention, because the latter faculty follows the route dictated by an outside object. When a man's conscious being is thus wholly placed on one point, his inner resources – hitherto merely latent – begin to show themselves.

After some practice this fixation of sight should become familiar and a firm steady glance attained; the second and superior part of this exercise may then be attempted. *It consists in mentally withdrawing consciousness from the outside object into one's inner self, whilst still keeping the gaze firmly fixed upon it, and to the exclusion of everything else.*

The effect of a few minutes' practice of this kind, when performed at the stage for which it is prescribed, will be to induce an intense calm within oneself and more especially a forgetfulness of everything external. The bright and gloomy memories of one's personal life will be temporarily blotted out as one turns the mind inward and one's entire being will become fixed, one-pointed as it were. A kind of semi-trance will ensue *in which one must endeavour to remain perfectly awake, perfectly alert,* and yet indulge in no mental, emotional or physical movement whatsoever. Absolute stillness should envelop one's seated body and penetrate one's mind, and indeed the body will become almost as unmoving as a log of wood.

Attention thus being withdrawn from the object focused upon, one should then seek for no unusual experience, but patiently be content with simple self-absorption, the look remaining fixed without seeing. Indeed when, by repeated endeavour and experience, one has progressed sufficiently far with the mental analysis of the self, with the control of breath and finally with this fixation of the sight, there will come a time when no voluntary effort need be made to withdraw the focus of attention from the object, nor indeed can be made, for it will automatically disappear from one's mental field as the profound concentration induces a reverie-like state wherein the mind sinks deeply inwards and wherein the habitual outlines of the personal self become blurred of their own accord. To explain this condition further the writer ought to qualify the word "disappear", as it is used in the foregoing sentence, by saying that the disappearance is from the foreground into the background of attention. There is thus no total disappearance; it is like the case of an actor of genius who may play perfectly the part of Hamlet, for instance, and live intensely in every word he utters, in every gesture he makes, but yet somewhere in the background of his mind there is the realization of his own personal identity. In the same manner one may be looking at the photograph, for instance, but no longer does he perceive it except in a dim, vague and entirely indifferent manner. He has used it as a builder uses a scaffolding; the structure having been built, the scaffolding is then cast aside.

Only when this exercise is successfully performed does one experience during this condition of deep reverie an internal change of awareness. One no longer makes any effort whatever of any kind, one remains in an extremely quiescent condition; all the things which one has been striving to attain – whether knowledge of the self, mental or emotional control – disappear into the background of themselves. The physical object upon which one has been focusing the sight slips away from one's mental grasp of itself, as it were, in the profound fixity which is felt.

What has really happened is that the consciousness thus becomes intensely concentrated in the region of its unfamiliar centre, whilst its familiar periphery has been anæsthetized. With the latter's cessation as a functioning entity, the first faint revelation from one's true being begins to diffuse itself into the circle of awareness. At first this diffusion will be extremely faint and difficult to retain for more than a few moments; one must therefore learn by repeated practice extending through weeks and months, perhaps, to yield oneself completely to its first manifestations and not to resist them. In this way one will gradually prolong those seraphic periods when man, deserting the circumference of things, turning his consciousness towards the centre, finds the bliss of unified being.

This power of fixed but *abstracted* gazing is called "Trataka" by the Hindu yogis. It is easily acquired by people who will faithfully practise it in conjunction with the other prescribed conditions. But if it is incorrectly done, one will develop a sensation of drowsiness and a tendency to fall asleep. In every case this should be avoided by rising immediately and discontinuing the exercise as soon as one becomes aware of the fault. Once more a warning is necessary against the misuse of this exercise. If practised before there has been proper preparation by means of the mental self-analysis and spiritual aspiration, it may easily lead to mere self-hypnotism or mediumistic trance and the higher spiritual result will not then be obtained; what may be obtained might indeed be quite undesirable. People who have not achieved a measure of balance between their intellect and their emotions should especially give heed to this warning Those who are spiritually unripe, or who have failed to conform with the work and qualification demanded of them in previous chapters, undertake this exercise at some risk. They may induce a condition of psychic mediumship and attract the attention of undesirable invisible spirit-entities who dwell on the borderland of the spirit-world and who can fasten

themselves upon unprotected mediumistic people and hypnotic subjects.

Because this exercise renders the muscles of the eye
intense and contracted, immediately after one has risen and
finished the practice the effect should be counteracted by ceasing to prolong the stare, deliberately blinking the eyes several
times and then letting the eyelids slowly and gently droop
downwards for a while. Thus the muscles will be relaxed. And
to bring the consciousness more quickly back to the external
world, one should press with the forefingers upon the closed
eyes.

To those who are ripe and ready, however, this gazing
practice helps to bring fulfilment of their aspirations, because
it renders easier the merging of the little self in the Overself. It
links up their personal ego with That which is its holy source.
Not for nothing did the Master Jesus say, in the course of one
of his homely illustrations:

*"The light of the body is the eye: if therefore thine eye be
single, thy body shall be full of light."* (Matthew vi, 22).

Millions of people have read this saying, but few have
understood its profounder significance. To get at the latter we
need to arm ourselves with the lantern of a little knowledge.

First of all, if the reader will refer to statements appear-
ing in other works by the writer,[1] he will there learn that Light
is actually the first and finest manifestation of God, the
Supreme Creator, in our material world. The first command
of the Creator was: "Let there be Light!" Out of this primal
Light came all created forms, because it is really Life-Force,
and inherent in every atom of matter. Front-rank scientists are
now seriously considering that light-waves may constitute the
ultimate essence of all matter. Light is the nearest element to

---

[1] *A Search in Secret Egypt* and *A Hermit in the Himalayas*.

Divinity which *physically-embodied* man can contact. For this reason, almost every ancient people without exception, from the shrewd Egyptians in Africa to the simple Incas in distant America, based their religion upon homage to Light and worshipped it in its supreme expression, the Sun. Mystics who behold God face to face have to behold Him first as a transcendental universal light of terrific radiance. They perceive this sacred light everywhere around them during their high transfiguration. Christian apostles understood this truth also. Thus there is a sentence in Ephesians v, 9, which complements the previously quoted one from Jesus. It runs: *"The fruit of the Light is in all goodness and righteousness and truth."* The writer is well aware that the current version of the New Testament substitutes the word "Spirit" for "Light", but it is a fact that the earliest and most authoritative manuscripts of this scripture, notably the Sinaitic, Alexandrian and Vatican Codices, together with the Bezan Manuscript in its original form, agree in reading "photos" (light) instead of "pneumatos" (spirit).

Now the Greek word "haplous" which is rendered "single" in the saying of Jesus, means literally "simple", or "single" in the sense of not being complicated. The word has another usage in the sense of "natural". By piecing both meanings together and using a little insight, we arrive at an interpretation which enables us to expand this sentence into its full meaning; thus:

"The spiritual light of the body enters through the eye; if therefore the eye be turned away from the complicated multiplicity of the world, and the mind using that eye be withdrawn into its own natural being, thy whole body shall be full of spiritual light."

The last part of this sentence is interesting: "Thy whole body shall be full of light," is a statement of literal fact and not merely a poetical metaphor. Among those who have had the opportunity to meet a perfect God-tuned saint or a Sage fully conscious of the Overself, a few have reported that they have momentarily seen the latter's body, during some tense period of meditation or prayer, encircled and pervaded by a strange luminousness. The haloes and aureoles which medieval European artists painted around their portraits of saints constitute a fragmentary reminiscence of this psychical truth. Hence it is no exaggeration on the part of Jesus to assert that a man who has unified his vision and withdrawn his mind into its natural simple state free from thoughts and impressions, will be fully illumined spiritually and psychically. *This practice introduces the spiritual light-force into the physical body until the latter is so permeated as to radiate it outwards, too.*

The Eastern scriptures also refer to this matter. "Release is in the eye," announces the Chinese *Yin Fu King*, or "Book of the Secret Correspondences". In India there is a group of 108 ancient Sanskrit books which were written by the earliest sages and which are still regarded by Hindus as containing the mystic wisdom of their religion. These books are called "Upanishads", and for thousands of years until the advent of the inquisitive British scholars, were kept hidden by the Brahmins. In one of them, the "Madala Brahmana Upanishad", we may find this significant sentence:

"When the spiritual vision is internal while the physical eyes are seeing externally without winking, this is the great science which is concealed in all the Tantras (Secret Books of Power). When this is known one no longer remains under the limitations of matter. Its practice gives salvation."

Finally, it may he mentioned that among the Magi of Persia in olden times and the Sufi mystics of the same land today, as among a few higher yogi schools in India in our own time, there has existed a special rite wherein the adept or teacher initiates the aspirant, who is qualified, into the inner life of the Spirit merely by gazing deeply, intently and deliberately into his eyes for a few minutes. The aspirant feels thereafter that a veil has been torn aside and his progress is rendered easier. This evidences that the adepts find the eye to be the only physical organ delicate enough and sensitive enough to be used as a medium of transmission and communication for their spiritual power.

The gazing practice here is based upon the psychological makeup of man, We have really to get behind our thoughts, interiorize our attention to an unaccustomed degree, to become absorbed in our own selves, but in an entirely different kind of way. This exercise is a powerful help toward bitting and bridling the horse of the mind. It leads the outward-running ego to subdue itself and its tendency, but does it by smooth gentle means. No violent efforts need be made to batter down the recalcitrant intellect into submission, for the combined breath and sight control attains the same goal. We possess an incomparable legacy in the divine nature and lofty possibilities of man, but we need to bestir ourselves and put in our claim; when our mentality is collected, concentrated and stilled, we prove our title to this inheritance.

13

THE MYSTERY OF THE HEART

Whoever has trodden this strange interior path thus far is now ripe to receive the revelation which is about to be made, and which constitutes an answer to the oft-put question:

Where is this Overself of which you write so eulogistically?

Let him first consider certain analogies which hint at a mysterious relationship between the divine Overself and its fleshly tenement. Let him observe the spontaneous and automatic action of a man, and especially a man belonging to a primitive race, who wishes by means of a physical gesture to indicate *himself* in contra-distinction to others. The man will raise his right hand and point his index finger towards his chest, towards that portion of his chest wherein the heart is located.

The importance of this action to the inquisitive beholder is that it has been dictated to the conscious mind of the man by his subconscious self. It is highly significant as mute testimony on the part of Nature, operating through the profoundest instincts of the human creature, to the association of selfhood with the most important physical organ of his trunk, the heart.

Moreover, man not infrequently puts his hand to his *heart* and says, "*I* feel" or "*I* think." Thus, his very use of the terms and gestures dictated by common sense closely indicates the same truth.

Let him next remember that it is a common habit for people to give instinctive expression to such phrases as "the heart of a subject", or "to get at the heart of the matter", whenever they wish to signify the fundamental essence of anything, and that the fundamental essence of man is his selfhood. Let him further examine the anatomical position of the heart in relation to the rest of the body. It is placed at a point which is roughly midway between the top of the head and the bottom of the trunk; that is to say, if a circle be drawn around the extreme limits of the trunk, the centre of this circumference would approximately be the heart.

It is a commonplace truism that the most important position in any structure, organism or design is its centre. That is the vital core around which every other part is built. Therefore when the heart is found to be the central organ of the human body one has a right to expect that it is also the most important. And one is correct. No man can function as a living being in this physical world without a heart. Surgeons have done marvels in patching up the piteous broken human relics of the last war, actually grafting new bits of organs here and there or fitting artificial substitutes for bodily parts, but they cannot keep any man alive whose heart has become useless.

The first beat of the heart means life; its last beat means death. The medium which it uses to act upon the body is blood, that red fluid which combines with the breath to carry the life-principle, building up and maintaining the body in its endless circulation. Physiologically, one finds the heart to be the hardest worked of all the bodily organs. It pulsates more than one hundred thousand times every day. It drives from seven to eight tons of blood through the arteries from head to heel. This position is analogous to that of a king having his abode in a capital city and communicating with, commanding and controlling the whole kingdom through the medium of officials. The heart is the capital city, the *centre* of government, the officials represent the blood, and the kingdom is the body itself.

The king represents the real essential selfhood – the Overself!

Mankind's age-old symbolical reference to its "heart" when it wishes to speak of its soul or spirit, as well as its universal assumption that the profoundest human feelings arise within the "heart", also afford unconscious testimony to some mysterious connection between the divinity in man and his physical heart. What feeling, indeed, could be more profound than that which he experiences when he becomes aware of this divine presence? The experience of the spiritual explorer who reaches the heart's depths and discovers the Overself, is thus remotely echoed in the common speech and actions of the generality of mankind, when it refers to its own essence. Can we not credit the possibillty of unrealized forces existing within this organ?

"This is my soul in the inmost heart, smaller than a grain of rice, or of barley, or of mustard-seed, or of a millet, or of a grain of millet's kernel; this is my soul in the inmost heart, greater than the earth, greater than the atmosphere, greater than the heaven, greater than these worlds," is the quaint description given in *Chandogya Upanishad*, a mystic ancient Oriental treatise which was formerly kept secret. There have also been Western mystics who have made the same discovery. Thus Mother Julian of Norwich – who belongs to the group of medieval English saints – wrote in her account of personal spiritual experiences: "After this I saw God in a *Point*, that is to say, in mine understanding," (The word 'understanding' means here, in this somewhat obsolete English, what we mean today by the word 'consciousness'.)

Analysis has already brought to light the fact that the real selfhood of man is pure consciousness; that it transcends the entire machinery of the intellect, and that the whole series of thoughts which make up his mental life are ultimately rooted in the primal ego-thought, 'I'. We may now link up these results with the foregoing revelation. If the Overself is really simple consciousness by itself, the vital agent behind all mental activity, then the real seat of human consciousness is not in the brain but in the heart! Thoughts could not be born and reasoning could not continue without the existence of the light of consciousness to illuminate both. They are as dependent upon the background of self-consciousness as these words which are written are dependent on the white paper which forms their own background.

Thus the entire thought-movement receives its support and sanction from the creative force of the Overself. The ego-notion, being a conscious thought, albeit the first of thoughts, can have no other ultimate source than the real transcendent self, the Overseif.

There is, therefore, a subtle and secret movement always in progress between the heart and the head, between the Overself and the intellect. The former, being the ultimate origin of all the ramifications of the life-current and of the conscious being, is drawn upon by the ego and the intellect for the sustenance of their own existence. Without the Overself to feed them, both would perish and disappear.

This movement starts in the heart whenever, through ancestral race-habit, the sense-impression of external things sets attention in motion. The first consequence of this motion is the detachment of a minute fragment of transcendental vital force and greater consciousness. Like a sun separated from the blazing parent mass, this fragment begins a life of its own from that moment, resulting in the formation of the personal ego. This comparatively much-limited ego-sense then ascends *upwards* from the heart because the most delicate and sensitive organ with which it can come into communication is situated in the head. It is itself too fine, too spiritual in origin to contact the grossly material universe without some intermediary that partakes of the nature of both. In the brain, in the thinking mind, it finds such a suitable intermediary. Hence its upward passage to the brain.

Here the fragment of pure impersonal self-consciousness necessarily becomes narrowed down to personal thinking consciousness, and passes out through the various physical sense-organs, as through doorways, to associate with the external world, ultimately becoming drowned in the sea of external impression. By this time it has inevitably completely forgotten its place of origin – the Overself-atom in the heart.

Thus the ego loses itself utterly in the mental-physical life wherein it finally finds itself, and knows nothing of its divine origin and heart-birthplace. The brain becomes its home, an abode so familiar in time that the exile comes to imagine and believe that here is its primal home and the physical world its primal environment.

§

One should pay careful attention to the explanations in this chapter because they are based upon the invisible anatomy of the soul. If one begins so to order his thought-life as to bring it into harmony and not conflict with this anatomical structure, one can move forward along this path more successfully and more intelligently. To possess some notion of the direction and place to which one must advance, however remote the goal may seem, is extremely helpful.

This relationship between heart and brain, signifying the relationship between spirit and intellect, when understood throws light upon many a dark problem of psychology and religion. For one can now grasp a little better the process which, after ages of involution and evolution, has left man the spiritually blind creature that he is today.

If one pictures the Overself-atom as a bubbling spring whose waters are fed for ever by the Supreme Creator, then the triune stream of water which is sprayed upwards to the head is the life-current, the intelligence and the individuality. The last three appear in the personal ego, and they are to be found as elements running right through the great structure of the universe, as they are to be found in its microcosmic replica – man.

If one pictures them as emanations from the heart, travelling up and then outwards through the five sense-organs which open out to the physical world and bring them into relation with physical objects and creatures, they may be viewed as being caught and trapped by this process for so many ages in the history of man that the personal ego, which is their totality, now wrongly believes that it is entirely self-sufficing, independent and complete a creature.

This error, which has taken such a hold of the human race, reached its culmination in the nineteenth century when the scientific intellect proudly announced its abolition of all need of a spiritual soul in man.

The heart, the fount of life, was scorned, the head glorified, the soul forgotten.

Yet physiologically we perceive that the brain cannot function without the blood with which it is fed. This vital fluid comes to it from the heart. Therefore, even the physical brain is dependent upon the physical heart for its power to work at all. Thus, even in a purely material way, it can be shown that the intellect *ultimately* issues from the heart. Does not the heart, then, seem the most appropriate and symbolically correct place for the Overself to choose as its habitation? The incessant thought-flow in the head is backed by the consciousness from the heart. Intellect is merely a limited modification thrown up by the unlimited Overself What is the intellect but the total sum of all our thoughts? The time-gap between two thoughts – however infinitesimal and however unnoticed it must necessarily be – is the moment when the ego comes unconsciously into contact with the Overself, for at such a moment the intellect "picks up" in a lightning-like flash the light of consciousness necessary to continue its activity. That gap may be infinitely minute, yet it exists. Moreover, it may even be mathematically measurable in the ordinary man, for aught the writer knows. Without that interval, which occurs hundreds of times a day, the intellect could not function because the brain would fall into a blank stupor.

When the interval between two thoughts is prolonged there is created the *possibility* of entering, and remaining for a time, in the Overself state. This is the key to the internal work which has to be done upon this path when the advanced stage is reached. One thinks fewer and fewer thoughts during the period of daily mental quiet practice; the slowing of the breath-cycle and the fixing of the gaze bring this about.

The common notion that consciousness has its seat in the brain is but a relative truth. The brain is but the seat of *reflected* consciousness, a reflection which has been derived from the true centre – the heart. Intellectual light is but borrowed light, like that of the moon. Intellectual consciousness is secondary. Heart consciousness is primary, and is the sun which imparts its own light to the moon of intellect. But one ought to beware of the common error that by the heart-consciousness, mere emotion is meant. Nothing could be further from the real truth.

Just as, in the final philosophic analysis, the reality of the material world is only one's mental perception of it, so is the reality of the intellect no other than its secret source, its ultimate backing by the heart. The Infinite Being – source of all undying life and intelligence – specializes its entry into man through the heart, not the head.

Thus the personal ego has come into existence as a creature which derives all its power to exist, to understand and even to act entirely from the impersonal Overself, *but which unfortunately is nowadays unaware of this divine derivation.* It exists in its own belief which lives and moves by its own strength alone, but in this it is self-deceived. Without its secret link with its immortal essence, the Overself, it could not continue such existence for a single moment. The light of consciousness whereby it understands the material universe, thinks within the brain and acts within the body, is but the borrowed light lent to it by the everlasting Overself. The life which it maintains for a while within the physical flesh is but a mere trickle from the infinite and undying force of the Overself. So long as the ego keeps its attention perpetually turned outwards and is ever looking through the windows of the senses upon the material universe, so long will it persist in the delusion that this material universe, the body and itself constitute the totality of life.

This attenuated fragment – the ego-thought, the 'I'- dimmed down in the light of understanding like the dimmed headlamp of an automobile, has allied itself with the physical form in which it finds itself, and related itself with the physical world with which it is in contact, gazing ever outwards through the windows of the five senses like a hypnotized person. And yet, despite this immense reduction in its power, this vast limitation of its field of awareness, it still remains man's sole link with his Overself because its pedigree is divine and the ancestral line, however hidden, still exists.

If the ego-thought resides in the brain, it is nevertheless not completely isolated there. *There is a line of communication with the heart,* the line along which the Overself sends its life and light for the support of the ego. The latter, of itself, can do nothing for it depends upon this support. It has arisen out of the ageless Overself and remains its unwitting pensioner.

Therefore a route of return, a link with its birthplace, still exists. If it could be awakened from its exteriorization and induced to turn inwards and backwards, tracing its way to its own original seat, it would necessarily move towards the Overself. Once the latter were found, it would merely have to keep in constant communication with that holy source, to sip nectar with the gods and be happy. The true object of all genuine spiritual practices is therefore to persuade the personal mind to turn inwards away from the material universe and through such abstraction in meditation or prayer slowly to retrace its steps upon the path of descent to the heart. Then, and then only, when it has ceased its usurpation and withdrawn into its rightful place, and become dutifully resigned and obedient to the dutiless Overself, will it enable man to become clearly conscious of *what he really is*. This is the spiritual goal set before him by life, by God – and no other really exists! To achieve this liberation "We need the silence of the cow, the simplicity of the child, the egoless state of the utterly exhausted man, the still more egoless state of deep sleep," remarked Sri Vidyaranya, a sage still unknown to the West.

We have ascertained by analysis that this real self is entirely thought-free, emotion-free and body-free; that it subsists on the plane of pure matter-free consciousness; and that ratiocinative activity, processes of connected reasoning, really constitute a modification of its own divine nature. Hence when we reach the frontiers of the intellect and find we can proceed no farther, we have only to reverse the process of evolution, to shift the centre of conscious activity from the seat of the intellect to the seat of the Overself, in order to cross those frontiers and enlarge our horizon.

That means, in other words, that the current of consciousness ought to be shifted down from the brain to its primal seat, the heart!

With the mind rigidly concentrated and indrawn, keen and yet not anxious, the path proper now really begins. There should be a pressing inwards in anticipation of receiving a revelation. One has to pass through thinking into the unthinkable. Now that one has really entered upon the spiritual quest his condition may be likened to that of a deep-sea diver who seeks for precious pearls at the bed of the ocean. Only when the man has descended beneath the surface of the water does he really enter upon his pearl quest; his journey in a boat from shore to a point on the surface of the sea suitable for his descent, is but a preparation and corresponds to the intellectual analysings of the Overself-seeker. Then, too, the diver, with his faculties sharpened and concentrated, must go deep down into the waters, *his mind intent upon one thing alone,* upon obtaining possession of the pearl which lies at the bottom of the ocean. He is blind, deaf and dumb to everything else except the prized object of his search. Similarly, the spiritual seeker in this more advanced stage of his practice must be just as completely absorbed and just as intent on one thing alone – the breathless recognition of the Overself.

The parallel thus holds still further; the sea diver must keep his breath under perfect restraint during the time that he is in the deep salty waters; the spiritual seeker at this stage has also brought his breath-rhythm under control, although the kind of restraint needed by him is not so drastic as that needed by the pearl diver. The only thought which should ardently predominate is the thought of the Overself lying like a pearl in the deep ground of his being; all extraneous thoughts entering the mind at this stage would be like sea-water entering the nostrils or mouth of the pearl diver; they would distract him from his search and indeed spoil it.

We are now ready for the further and final exercise in this course. This is not to be attempted before the exercises involving the respiratory and visual organs have been practised over a period of time long enough to render them perfectly familiar and to enable them to be performed with absolute ease. Whoever tries the third method before he has properly ripened on this path will not obtain a successful result: his effort will necessarily be futile.

When the gazing exercise of the last chapter has been concluded successfully, the consciousness will have been withdrawn through the eyes from the external world into the head; at this point the following practice may be added.

One should offer up the personal self-will as a sacrifice to divinity. Then one should gently and gradually draw the conscious abstracted attention away from the head, introverting it still further but in a downward direction until it is brought and settled in the region of the Overself-atom.

The mental energy must be brought down and buried in the breast. At first there will be a tender melting feeling in the depths of the heart, a faint breath-like sacred presence that increasingly suffuses one. When it comes, it should not be ignored or its significance overlooked. Novices may underestimate its supreme but silent message. After sufficient trials and lengthy experience the consciousness will be found to settle by degrees of its own accord in a single point and to remain fixed there. This point will "catch" the attention in a soft grip, a sensation of captivity which will be relished as one of the most delightful imaginable.

It would be incorrect to say that there is no physical sensation accompanying this experience. *There is,* and yet it is one that transcends the material world! There is a very clear sensation of piercing the *spiracle* of the Overself. "True prayer," said the Prophet Muhammad, "is that which is performed with the heart *open.*" Simultaneously there is a contact with a world of serene inner being. But how can one describe this paradoxical point? The baffled pen must retreat.

To one's surprise it will be found that this process of 'turning' the consciousness will actually *deepen* it, rendering it still more completely withdrawn from the material world. The last reflexes of the outer world will vanish. That which was previously subjective – as, for example, a mental image – now entirely changes its relation, for it becomes objective to the inner self. In this new state even thinking appears as an invasion from *without.* One will have the relieved feeling that one is now really in contact with himself, that one is fathoming the heretofore incomprehensible background of his being.

The intellect will be caught and held in the heart; for many years of practice, possibly, a residue of thoughts may continue to exist side by side with this delightful sensation, but in the ultimate stage of development, which few people ever reach, all thoughts will cease.

During the latter stage of practice and sometimes when the heart has been found, one may experience a kind of warmth in its region; by some strange process of interior sight, he may even perceive a subtle fiery golden light glowing in the same spot. Sometimes this radiance may be as bright as the lightning flash. Medieval Roman Catholic painters have occasionally depicted the Virgin Mary and the Christ with a flaming heart. Religiously inspired artists not infrequently give forth that which is higher than their normal perception and knowledge. But such psychic sensations are no essential part of the process and are not to be valued as being more than its unimportant by-products.

In that sublime state one finds the fringe of the glowing centre of man's spirit, and then realizes how the heart is the true though hidden centre of all man's activities, of all his mental life and physical deeds. In this manner one is brought into initiatory experience of the Overself through a descent of consciousness from the brain, where it habitually resides, to the heart. Thus one dives deep into his own inner being, finding for reward the pearls of blissful harmony and eternal life.

What has happened is that the personal ego has prepared the right conditions for its severance from identification with the gross material body and for its return to its original seat. Everything is now ready for its final and supreme submission. Even this stage is immensely exalted and the flame of one's spiritual being now begins to burn brightly. The thoughts have been prevented from functioning outwards, and the mind must then perforce awaken in the heart.

The profoundest point in these practices which it is possible to describe here has been approached. Whoever has faithfully done what has hitherto been required of him, and who has continued until his efforts have met with some degree of success, has all along been preparing himself for this step which now awaits him. It is not necessarily the final *stage* through which he has to pass, but it is not possible to proceed further with an *external* description of spiritual states which now become so increasingly internal as to defy in their subtility and fineness the limited definitions of the intellect.

It might be said that the point now reached must be dealt with in terms of religion and indeed it will be difficult to avoid something of the kind, because there is a level where religious revelation and rational thought, artistic creation and scientific investigation, meet and unify, and the nearer one moves toward this level the more all must begin to converge and finally mingle.

The withdrawn consciousness should now occupy itself solely with itself, remote from the reports of exterior things and far from their recollections. It should press deeply inward, and let all thoughts lapse. It need no longer ask "What Am I?" in mere words, for the act of living deeply into the heart will now constitute the final formulation of that much-asked query. The ego is still making the effort, albeit it is an ego so transformed as to be unrecognizable in comparison with ordinary standards. In this spiritualized turning-in upon itself which it now attempts, the intellect must be wholly silenced, the breath restrained, the gaze steady but lowered, and the full force of attention brought down to the pinpoint within the heart.

Having brought oneself thus far, the most critical experience of all must now be faced. In a theoretical sense it is an easy step to take, but in actual practice it proves hard. For one must no longer say to oneself, "This is the next task which confronts me," but, rather, "I shall attempt nothing further. Whatever experience the soul needs must now come entirely of its own accord. I shall be merely a waiting, passive, and receptive agent. This personal life and this self-will are offered in surrender to the higher Power."

The ego must now vanish. Born in the human heart, it must return there *voluntarily* to die.

All that vast interior web of thought and feeling which has been spun around the first ego-thought, must no longer mirror itself in one's consciousness. One has to chance one's internal position and reach reconciliation with this unfamiliar Overself.

Here, the words of the Psalmist, "Be still and know that I

am God," must be taken in their literal fullness. There should henceforth be no purpose, no desire, no effort even for spiritual attainment.

One must "let go" of everything. It is only to the extent that one lets go of *all* that one has heretofore considered as oneself, that the real consciousness can possibly supervene. Suffice to ask, to wait and to listen, so that an invitation is sent sounding down the corridors of being for the unseen Overself to give its response.

Consciousness is now ready to free itself entirely from the ego with which it has heretofore identified itself. It will do so of its accord, if one permits, but any attempt to hasten the process by self-will defeats its own purpose and stultifies the "change-over".

The first-fruit of success will be a feeling that one is being torn asunder from one's mooring in life, a momentary loss of the sense of reality of the universe. It is like plunging into an abyss of infinity where the essence of one's existence threatens to pass away beyond recall. This curious condition mingles a momentary but powerful fear of death with a sense of being liberated. The two struggle with each other, seeking possession of one's soul, enacting a divine drama, which takes place within the centre of one's being. Absolute fearlessness, *a readiness to die,* is now called for. Such a burning purpose will, with time, turn all resistance to ash and dust. With practice, the day arrives when this struggle passes away and a premonition will come that the supreme change is rising to complete ascendency in the horoscope of one's mood. It should be met by an attitude of utter surrender. "Not mine, but Thy will be done," exactly reflects the required attitude. This involves even giving up all thought of being on a spiritual path, of seeking a spiritual goal. Formerly one was a worker for this or that stage of inner attainment; now one must become a vessel, self-emptied, which lies waiting for the divine influx to come when and how it will. There must be the fullest possible opening of oneself. There must not be the slightest reservation in any direction. One should rest, with breath subdued, like a darkening landscape hushed before the dying sun. One must wait patiently, perfectly patient, for a response to come out of the stillness. Instead of continuing to seek the Self by means of intellectual exertions, one stops and lets the Self seek him! It is only after this point is passed that the miraculous power of meditation leads one from the sublime stillness to the divine source whence the 'I' arises.

All these repetitions and reiterations of the need of dropping egoism in its subtlest and least-apparent forms – even that of effort – are necessary because of the crucial importance of this transformation from personality to impersonality. It corresponds to the stage when a pregnant mother, after nine months of trouble, anxiety, suffering and abnormal existence, arrives at the point of actually yielding the babe from her womb – a babe which might be born dead or alive, or which might be the innocent cause of its mother's death. The great care needed at childbirth is not greater than that which is needed now at the birth of the human being into the Overself. And with this the man is literally 'born again', and attains an unforgettable proof of his own divinity. His quest will *suddenly* end, and the soul, which seemed but a hazy abstraction heretofore, will become a living reality in his renewed existence.

§

Our meditations, it might be said, are movements from without to within because they tend to abstract our attention from the outer world into the self-centre of our being, but when we arrive near that centre we are then to make no further effort, but to remain still and to allow the Overself to emerge from the hidden depths and mystic profundities which we enclose, and *thus to move itself from within to without. For the Overself's 'without' is our 'within'.* The mental grasp of this principle is essential to a proper understanding of the work which is to be done in the spiritual practices. We start with self-investigation. We pass later into self-acquiescence and we arrive ultimately at self-rebirth.

This, then, is the final aim of all these spiritual practices, and of these mental endeavours that are for the most part so alien to our daily routine. We have sought to track down the ego, that which apparently constitutes selfhood, that which, so far as we know, is indeed our very life and then in the most paradoxical manner, when we have finally traced the ego to its lair and taken hold of it, we propose to sacrifice it, and entirely let go our hold. But we wish to lose it only to find the ever-shining Overself; we wish to fling it entirely into the sea of divinity, there to be absorbed and become perfectly conscious of the true source of its being. In the words of Jesus, "He that loseth his life shall find it."

It is indeed hard to wander sometimes with no light to guide us through the labyrinth of our inner being until the ego-root is discovered, but it is harder still to surrender it as a voluntary sacrifice upon the altar of devotion to the Overself. We have to play the same part that was played in the Biblical story by the Patriarch Abraham when he was bidden to sacrifice his son Isaac upon an altar to the Lord. The Lord demanded Isaac because *nothing else* was so dear to the Patriarch's heart, nothing else that was mortal was so beloved by him. And so we too must yield up as a voluntary offering to the Overself that which is dearest to us, the ego, the self as we normally know it. We must renounce the fundamental false-hood of outlook that makes the egoic standpoint the only possible standpoint in life.

After all, we cling to our desires and to the personal self only because we are seeking happiness, but the satisfaction of those desires is itself a shadowy reflection of the basic satisfaction which the Overself alone can bestow upon its votaries. In fact, the temporary happiness which we find when we obtain possession of the things or persons we seek after is a flicker – a spark only – from the fire of basic happiness of the spirit.

From the passing but perhaps intense satisfaction which we derive every time a want is fulfilled, we may gauge how sublime is that superior satisfaction which entry into the Overself condition gives us. For even the fleeting pleasures of earthly life provide a happiness which is itself like a crumb thrown from the feast. These pleasures, as it were, have extracted microscopic fragments of happiness for us out of the everlasting store whose repository is the Overself.

This is not merely a poetical statement but a hint of high psychological fact. *If the Overself were not the highest form of happiness possible to man, all his pleasures would yield him nothing, because the moment any pleasure reaches its highest is the moment when he suddenly lets go of the desire – it having been fulfilled – and of the ego which is the root of that desire, and in a flash involuntarily experiences the Overself.* During that instant he experiences the utmost pleasure which the fulfilment of that particular want could give him. He makes the cardinal error, however, of supposing that it is the satisfaction of his want which brings him the sense of pleasure: not so. What really happens is that for a moment he lets the desire fall away from him and feels the resultant satisfaction of intense peace. Attaining possession of the thing or the person desired, after perhaps years of longing, the desire naturally disappears when the goal has been attained; simultaneously its root, the ego, likewise vanishes. The man momentarily and miraculously enters the state of the Overself, perceives its earthless and fadeless beauty, but remains unaware of the real truth – that personality has been displaced. This can last but for a moment because so long as the ego rules man, so long will it present him with another desire for which he must seek fulfilment. Indeed, so swift is the psychological working of this divine introversion that he does not notice, indeed cannot notice, the completed transition from the gratified desire to the next which is yet to be gratified, and which may again cause him days, months or years of fresh longing.

The essential point which must be grasped here is that it is during a sudden flash of desirelessness, a lightning-like condition of ego-lessness which supervenes softly for an infinitesimal fraction of a second after sensual pleasure or gratified desire, that his highest happiness comes to him and irradiates his soul. The sensation of the disappearance of the personal self produces an extraordinary and unique liberation. At the moment when a desire is satisfied, there is an interval of absolute unburdening of the ego and the mind really withdraws to its secret source and experiences the bliss of the Overself.

Nature is for ever creative. When the fitful desires of the personal ego vanish, she supplies the permanent peace of the Overself as a divine equivalent. Hence the best place to seek for real satisfaction is not so much in gratifying shallow personal desires, which may indeed dwarf, degrade and shackle one, as in the profounder rapture of impersonal being.

What then must be the beatific condition of one who has reached this lofty condition permanently, who abides for ever untormented by longing and unafflicted by desires that await gratification? The answer is that the bliss which a pleasure-seeker experiences in its highest degree during the moment which supervenes upon full gratification becomes the bliss which is the eternal possession of the man who not momentarily, but permanently, is one with his exalted primary Overself.

It may even be revealed here that not only does the Overself-state supervene during a flash of desirelessness and egolessness derived from satisfied pleasure, but also at other unsuspected moments, such as those of sudden shock. Thus when one who is blithely going his way is *suddenly* and unexpectedly confronted by a situation of immense danger, as facing a wild beast in a jungle or being exposed to the outbreak of aerial bombardment, he experiences an extraordinary cessation of all his faculties. He quite literally seems to stand *still* in mind and body. His only participation in the event is as an impersonal spectator, not as a personal actor. But with the speed of lightning everything changes; he collects his faculties together, his instincts of self-preservation are let loose in a sudden uprush of fear and terror, his reason gets to work upon the situation and tries to find a way out of it, and finally his last state is infinitely worse than his first. Yet all-unknowingly during the first instant he experienced the divine stillness of being and let it fall away quite heedlessly. Another parallel occasion occurs during the infinitesimal interval between waking and sleeping, when the cares and desires of the personal life of the day have completely ebbed away, but before the utter unconsciousness of sleep has overpowered the mind.

What are all these mysterious moments but interruptions in the everflowing stream of egoistic thoughts? *If one could carefully watch for these intervals and consciously retain and prolong their mental condition, he could receive a transcendental realment and attain the highest state open to man.*

This point is extremely subtle and will require much examination of one's past experiences, much self-study before its revolutionary truth can be thoroughly understood. Almost all our modern Western psychologists have missed it, although they have analysed and re-analysed the human being in every conceivable way. Is it not, indeed, the supreme paradox of life that the culmination of man's highest self-development is achieved only in self-forgetfulness? Or, in the words of the Overself speaking through the person of Jesus: "Come unto Me all ye that labour and are heavy laden, and I will give you rest."

The ego-thought is like a string upon which our multitudinous sense-memories, interests, desires, fears, thoughts and feelings are threaded. And when one speaks of the surrender of the ego, it is not the surrender of one particular bead which is meant but rather of the entire string which holds together all the diverse beads and without which all would collapse. This is effected, and can only be effected by turning the mind inwards and by concentrating deeper and ever deeper within the heart until individual beads of thought and feeling no longer engage our consciousness, but only the single thought of self-existence. Then we discover that we are really angels fallen from the empyrean.

§

We need to make no outward gesture of world-renunciation, although destiny may command it to come, in order to arrive at this point of complete self-surrender. For it is not this subject and that person we are called upon to surrender, but the *personal sense* within us which keeps us enslaved to them. This ego-sense cannot be banished by any power of our own, just as a man cannot lift himself by his own shoe laces. Although, during the advanced phase the whole aim of our effort is to empty the mind of its thoughts and let the questionless Overself answer our question, we should not imagine, however, that we will be able to stop thinking by our own efforts. The thinking will only stop when a superior power exerts itself upon it. That power belongs to the Overself and thus what we really do is to invite, beseech and permit the Overself to touch the turbulent intellect into silence and quiet. What can be done is to prepare the way and to remove the obstructions to the advent of a Higher Power, which is none other than the Grace of the Overself. Grace is the gatekeeper at the shrine. It is this communication of Grace, this manifestation of an authority higher than our own which finally starts to extinguish our attachment to the ego and to give us the unimaginable peace of spiritual liberation. It is a far cry, perhaps, for most men to reach this point, but that need not deter one from making the attempt. "Many are called, but few are chosen," are the words of the Christian Teacher, yet the simple manifestation of interests in this path may well be a sign that one belongs to those fortunate few. And even if this high point is not attained, the *efforts will never be wasted*. Some degree of peace, some measure of inner enlightenment will surely be bestowed in return.

The operations of this power of Grace are mysterious. Our duty is to prepare the right conditions, the suitable atmosphere within which the Overself can vouchsafe its revelation, for we cannot predict the precise moment when that revelation will occur even after the conditions have been prepared.

The Grace is felt as a definite movement from the seeker's inner being, a movement which attempts to get hold of him and draw him deeper into himself. *It is experienced always as a manifestation within the region of the heart.*

It arises inside him with imperious power and takes hold of his feelings and thoughts in such a way that not only does he feel resistance to be useless, but he has no inclination whatever to resist, for it holds his consciousness as under a sorcerer's spell. It begins with a feeling of something melting within the heart. It continues by causing an upheaval of all his previous outlook upon life, during which pride, prejudice, rigidly-held ideas, desires and dislikes are all flung into a melting pot and disappear for a time. It ends in a more or less complete surrender of the ego to the divine ruler who has now appeared. This experience may be repeated frequently or it may not come again for a long time. If the former happens, then is the seeker fortunate indeed and his growth of illumination will be extremely rapid; striking transformations will then be brought about in his life, until he arrives at a revelation which is no less certain, precise and definite than it is sublime. Grace may descend for no longer than five minutes or it may persist for five hours. In the latter case again, he will be wonderfully fortunate and be greatly changed as a result. It is through such manifestations of a generously-bestowed Grace that the notable conversions in religious history, whether of the East or of the West, have occurred.

There are signs which foretell the coming of Grace. Principal amongst these is a strong yearning for spiritual light which grips the heart more and more, which torments a man frequently and which makes all else seem unsatisfying. Ordinary life seems to become dull, wooden, hollow, mechanical and oppressive by turns. The daily routine becomes phantom-like and aimless. When that intense aspiration becomes as a strong current in a man's emotional life, he may then begin to expect that its gratification is not far off. And the more powerful his yearning, the greater will be the manifestation of enkindled Grace.

Next among the prophetic heralds of the coming of Grace is the act of weeping, either at the absence of this spiritual light or at some word, event, person or picture which provokes one's remembrance of the existence of the Overself. Such weeping will not always be visible and external; it may take place silently in the secret chamber of the heart. When the tears, however, do make their appearance, one should not resist them, but yield to their poignant emotion, even to the point of shedding them frequently and constantly, so far as external conditions permit. *Such tears are valuable allies in the seeker's cause; they bear with them a mysterious influence which tends to dissolve those hard encrustations built up by the ego, which bar the gate to the entry of Grace.* By their gentle but powerful aid much is accomplished, sometimes as much as could be accomplished by the ordinary self-effort in meditation. Therefore let us welcome these visitors when they come and let us weep openly and unrestrainedly if solitude is available, or silently and invisibly if needs be, and thus permit our self-built handicaps to be washed away. Such yearning and such weeping to be effective must stir the seeker to the utmost depths of his being. Truly, the tears must emerge out of an inner compulsion. He alone who knows how to weep for the Highest, and how to refrain from weeping over worldly disappointments, is fit to know Truth.

Other signs may also manifest; the seeker may have a single clear and prophetic dream which he will be able to apprehend intuitively as a distinct message from his Overself. Such a dream will be extraordinarily vivid and unforgettable. Further, some change may come about in his worldly circumstances or even a complete crisis in his exterior affairs which will indicate that a time is at hand, or will shortly arrive, for moving into new environments with their corresponding new influences. In these and other ways, as well as by his own inner feeling, he may come to know that a period of spiritual light is approaching.

An important channel through which Grace may operate when, finally, it does come is that which connects it with some external human agency. Not infrequently the separation from, or death of, some person greatly loved brings this about, and as a consequence of the intense suffering that naturally results, the seeker's life may receive a completely new orientation wherein the Grace may come as a kind of compensation for that which has been lost. He will first, however, have to pass through all the phases of the agony of his loss and when at the end the Grace begins to touch him, he will gradually discover that he can bear the sorrow patiently. No longer is it a burden that crushes him, for he perceives how the withdrawal of that other person from his life bears with it a spiritual significance. The sacrifice which has been demanded of him may bring to birth within his soul, first a sense of resignation and then of self-surrender to the will of God which will finally bring him the compensation of inner peace. That very act of self-surrender will thus throw his burden on God and to a large extent free him from further suffering in this direction. Suffering in such an acute form may therefore be in its ultimate essence the herald of a compensatory serenity yet to come. We must not imagine from this, however, that Grace necessarily works always by hurting us where we can be most hurt. It may come indeed with no such dismal herald at all.

The other human form through which Grace may come to an aspirant initially is that of a sage or adept, or even a special disciple of such a one, who can be used generally as a convenient instrument to import it to others. But this presupposes some uncommon factors, and such men rarely cross one's path in this twentieth century, although self-styled adepts continue to delude others or themselves.

14

THE OVERSELF

What is the Overself?

Is it some kind of ghost-like person who is attached like a Siamese-twin to the mental hips of each individual? Is it a psychological appendage growing like an accretion upon the brain? Questions with these implications have actually been put to the writer, and the need for further definition now arises.

Before proceeding to answer this question the writer wishes to make it clear that he is here dealing with a matter that is really inexpressible, except to those whom life has prepared by a proper ripeness of experience, and therefore he fully realizes that the following words may well prove unsatisfactory to others. That cannot be helped. All words are but counters expressing thoughts, the product of the intellect. Here we are dealing with a region that transcends intellect. The only fit method of expressing that region is by *not-words*, that is, by profound *telepathic* silence. A book, being a collection of words, is an inferior method of communication, nevertheless it has its place if it will evoke moods and create an atmosphere and prepare mental conditions which make the true illumination possible.

Although the Overself is really a unit, intellectually it may be considered from different standpoints and thus one may find that it possesses different aspects. Be that as it may, it is essential, above all, to grasp the idea of its unitary nature. It is not composed of various layers or sections of our being but is indeed the central point, the innermost living core of a man himself.

First of all it might be said that the Overself is primarily man's essential being, the all-important residue which is left when he succeeds in banishing the thought of his identification with the physical body and the intellect. The emphasis placed upon the word 'thought' in this sentence must be noted. Scientists like Jeans and Eddington tell us that the universe is really an idea, but as the body is part of that universe we are entitled to regard it as an idea too. What an idea is, however, they cannot tell us. That is the next step ahead of them to learn, for by persistent enquiry and analysis ideas will one day be resolved into the Overself within which they are rooted.

The Overself is the creative force which gives birth to the personal ego, sustains it for a cosmic period, and then draws it back into itself again. This is the explanation of St. Paul's bold pantheistic phrase: "In Him we live and move and have our being." It is the invisible, intangible life-dispenser, supporting the existence of its creatures. Life distilled to the last drop – that is the Overself, too. We cannot bring a single thought to birth nor draw a single breath without its sustenance in the act. Even the minutest molecule of the stomach, the lungs and the face, is thus ultimately founded on the Invisible. It is the hub of a wheel in which all the spokes – body, intellect and feeling – ultimately converge.

Just as a single sun-ray cannot really be separated from the sun itself, so the Overself-atom in the body cannot be separated from its parent – God in the universe. When, in the previous chapter, it was said that the Overself resides in the heart, more could have been added to that statement. In fact, what has been explained so far has been but relatively true, has been told from a partial viewpoint, for the reader must be prepared by gradual stages for the final revelation now to be made.

That which exists within the human being as the Overself-centre, exists also outside him in the Universal Spirit, of which it is a fragment.

The position is paradoxical, because there is but *one* Overself, one universal divine self resting in all men. There is not a separate Overself attached to each individual, as it were. Monism is the ultimate truth. "I am in my Father, and ye in me, and I in you," announced the Overself through Jesus. There is but one Overself for all bodies, not a separate one for each individual. There are not millions of eternal Overselves, only millions of perishable individualities.

That which appears in one man as divine when the personal ego is subordinated, is precisely the same as that which appears in all other men. Just as any single sun-ray does not differ in kind or quality from the sun itself, so any Overself-atom, the God-ray, does not differ from the God-sun which sends it forth.

Thus the Overself is both a mathematical *hollow* point and simultaneously space enclosing a universe in one sacred alliance. This paradoxical statement is contrary to ordinary logic and common sense; it cannot be properly apprehended by the intellect; a mesh of words cannot capture its airy and elusive meaning; it can only be understood and grasped when reason has travelled to its farthest limit and then falls into abeyance in such a lofty presence.

The Overself is eternal. It has never been away from us at any moment. We, however, have been heedless of it.

Within its ether we live for ever.

"No man may see God and live," is what we are told in the Old Testament. The true meaning is that no personal ego may enter into the Overself state and continue its former limited personal existence. As soon as it comes to rest in the larger Self it melts away, wholly calmed, blent into its unity, acted upon instead of being the actor.

We do not 'see' the Overself; we apprehend it. Visions merely disclose its finest garments, its robes of dazzling light, albeit they are but robes.

We do not behold its beauty; our being dissolves into its breath and we *become* that which poet, painter, sculptor, musician seek but rarely find.

The Overself is the supreme reality, but its reality is too subtle, too exquisite, too rare, for audible expression. It is best savoured in long-drawn silences.

It is the ray of God in man, the immeasurable Infinite which pervades his measurable being, the true Spirit behind the human creature; that in him which is utterly free from the imprint of all passions, all desires and all frailties. It represents for him the summit of all genuine morality, the perfection of all real ethics, because it speaks to him of his oneness with all that *lives,* whether in the human or animal kingdom, *and hence inculcates the primary duty of universal compassion.* The Overself expresses nothing but itself. It does not express morality or virtue; these are man-made things. The Overself is independent of them; we create and re-create our morality from age to age, but the ethic of the Overself is eternal and absolute and unchanging. Yet all morality is ultimately derived from its glorious fount, and all virtue is finally imparted by its benignant touch. He who lives by its light is as superior in character to the good man as the good man is superior to the evil-doer.

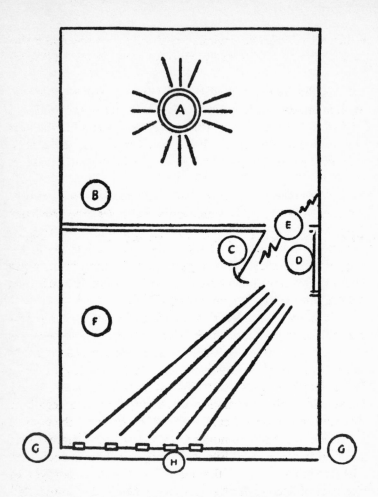

Finally the Overself is the feeling of 'I' deepened, made diviner, and ultimately changed into the transcendent element wherein that feeling takes its rise.

When one is attempting to understand the nature of something super-physical, it is often helpful to set the mind working upon a good analogy. While thus pondering, the mind is helped to evoke from within a sense of super-physical truths which might not be so easily grasped by reading the bald statement.

An analogy which will be particularly useful to those who wish to understand how the Overself is related to the mind and body and the interaction which goes on between all three, is that of a lamp set inside a house in a certain way. Like most analogies it is not perfect, and should not be pressed too far by critics.

The diagram on page 286 explains this arrangement. Here is a room (B) containing the lamp (A); between this room and the next there is a communicating door (C); a glass reflecting mirror (D) is affixed to a wall in such a way that it catches and reflects the light-rays from the lamp in the inner room and throws them across the outer room (F) and even beyond into an outer veranda (H).

The symbolism of this sketch is as follows: the lamp represents the Overself, the luminous fundamental consciousness of man. The inner chamber which contains the lamp is Eternity, the highest super-physical state, the region of true being which is universal, impersonal and in itself utterly remote from the commotion of our world; it is a region of absolute light and perfect stillness. If one imagines the door to be closed, there is then nothing but the Overself engrossed in itself or, in the poetical Biblical description, God brooding on His face in the waters of the deep. Thus the shut door typifies the state of deep dreamless slumber, wherein the central light of Overself awareness is least dimmed. *This means that in the condition of deep dreamless slumber, we are really nearest to the Overself;* everyone who has awakened from such slumber will remember the feeling of bliss and peace which hung over his awakening and which lingered on for a few moments as the subtle echo of that mysterious and beautiful condition. The cause is that the sense of personality has not yet been born. And if one imagines now that the force of a wind (E) arises and simultaneously blows the door open, this wind will represent the entry of the first factor to disturb the sublime harmony – time. The cosmic life-current has begun to set its forces in motion, according to predestined plan, and because the least movement produces succession, time appears simultaneously with the cessation of the deep slumber state revealing its inseparable ally, the personal ego, the primal thought 'I', the limited human mind. The latter is represented by the mirror.

With the opening of the door the reflecting surface of this mirror comes into operation. The light-rays of the lamp issue forth from the inner chamber, traverse the doorway, and strike the mirror. The divine consciousness of the Overself has come into contact with the human ego, with the intellect which so greatly diminishes the tremendous force that it now catches. A minute refraction passes outward into the second chamber. The latter stands for the dream-sleep state.

Thus the original spiritual consciousness undergoes a deep change; no longer is it a pure and pristine thing, but merely a shadowy *reflection* of the original luminosity; its first appearance in this transformed and weakened condition is therefore the dream-state. In the latter condition we begin to function as conscious-thinking individuals, as definite personalities. No longer is there the blissful unconsciousness of the deep sleep state, and the effect of this change is equally apparent upon awakening. We have then no sense of lingering serenity and of untainted joy which marks the exit from dreamless slumber. That peaceful consciousness has diminished to a pale semblance of its original self. The Overself – source of all enduring bliss – is no longer fitly represented, but rather misrepresented by the ego's activity. The ego is but the thought 'I' – root of the intellect. It is a reflector which, in the ordinary man, loses most of the light of divine consciousness, but which, in the sage, permits the radiance to pass perfectly.

Let us now follow further the onward passage of these symbolic light-rays; they move across the outer room and finally reach the five windows of that room typifying the bodily sense-organs. This means that self-consciousness has entered the physical body, and allied itself with it. Passing through these opened windows, they reach the open air of the veranda, which corresponds to the waking condition of everyday activity. We see then that this ultimate reflection ouside the room is the final state of a triply removed original luminosity. At each remove something of its brightness has been lost, so that the everyday condition of external wakefulness which we fondly believe to represent the maximum degree of human consciousness is really its lowest possible state.

The value of the prescribed spiritual practices may now be better appreciated, for it may be said that the habit of daily introspection eventually enables one to cultivate during moments of mental quiet a condition of reverie closely akin to dream. If the introspection is profound enough, the dream condition is perfectly reproduced. This is not to say that one has entered a region of mere phantasy. On the contrary, in this state one experiences oneself and one's thoughts to be at least as real as they seem during waking external existence. So clear and connected does this condition become with constant practice, that the vague and fitful dreams during sleep of the average person will bear no comparison. Only those who have experienced dreams of the highest degrees of vividness, wherein everything seemed to partake of the nature of the utmost reality, can appreciate the condition in which the meditator profoundly wrapped in his abstractions finds himself.

But this is only the first stage, although it may represent a result reached only after many years of effort. The next stage of advance along the path brings one during these practices to a blissful condition akin to that of deep dreamless slumber, but with this essential difference – one is fully aware and fully conscious of one's state. The importance of this difference is vital, one experiences all the bliss, all the lingering peace with which he emerges from profound dreamless slumber, but experiences it in full self-awareness throughout the period of practice. This is, of course, a very advanced stage along the path and may be reached only after years.

The third stage of the path is represented by the lamp itself. In this part one transcends the condition corresponding to deep sleep, and instead of sensing the beautiful presence of the Overself as a thing apart, in whose ray one basks, one becomes the light itself. There is then no longer any need to continue these practices for the goal has been reached and the light-ray has been retraced to its source; the narrow and little ego-self about which we make so much fuss and over whose petty fluctuations of emotion and thought we are so greatly moved, has merged into the one universal being.

This analogy is apt. The lamp is the source of light, heat and energy; similarly, the Overself is the source of the light of conscious understanding, the warmth of universal love and the energy of divine creativeness. The three stages through which the lamp's radiation passes, those of the inner chamber, the reflector and the outer chamber, accurately typify respectively nearness of profound slumber to the spirit, the borrowed nature of the intellect's power and the circumscribing effect of all our ordinary consciousness.

The question will be raised: "What is it that corresponds to the impulsion behind time's wind, which blew open the door?" The answer is that the force of evolution and involution which lie inherent yet latent within the deep slumber state that surrounds the Overself, set going an activity which works in a rhythmic manner throughout the universe. These forces, of course, are contained in a latent state within it and first manifest in the ego-mind. We can only say that within the great deeps of the cosmic being, these forces move and have moved through all eternity, expanding and returning like the systolic and diastolic action of the heart. How, when and why this action first began is beyond our immediate human purpose for it is as ancient as the universe itself.

The final stage is to return to normal, active, waking and working existence in the material world, whilst holding fast to the interior illumination which has been gained.

Thus the Overself, as the ray of God in man, is inescapable. Its ever-presence has been most eloquently voiced by the late Sir R. Venkata Ratnam, one of the heads of the Bramo Faith and one of India's rare God-immersed souls, whose devoted disciple, the Maharajah of Pithapuram, brought the present writer into memorable contact with him. Said this seer in one of his addresses:

"We forget, in the midst of man-made memories, that the central vitality is God Himself. He is not merely a distant driving power but the ever-present, immediate, inmost vitality. God is the plan and the purpose, the essential and enduring reality, behind this ever-unfolding scene called creation. Let us realize it as a literal fact that even now my tongue could not speak but for the direct working, nay the personal presence, of the Universal Witness in our souls through this seemingly trivial transaction. We misbelieve, we delude ourselves, when we talk of the laws of science and their compelling rule. All originate in, all emerge from, all converge towards, all terminate in the supreme God. The Lord in His sanctified Self is present in the inner soul, aye, seated in the very heart of every created being."

It may be asked why the Overself is located as an atom in the heart in the present book but is described in my later books as locationless? Is there not a glaring contradiction, an absurd position, here? The answer is that my earlier books deal with the practice of Yoga, not with the study of metaphysics. Yoga is a practical technique and for the sake of making this technique effective, the meditation on the heart centre has been prescribed since time immemorial in Asia. Hence the present chapter is correct in so far as it locates the Overself for the sake of providing a practical rule of meditation, and not for the sake of recording a sublime truth of metaphysics. It describes the Overself as attained by a process in time and space whereas metaphysics describes the Overself as it exists, timeless and spaceless, and therefore untouched by any process. The difference is a matter of standpoint. We must begin with the practical standpoint, that is the Yogic, supplement it with the theoretical, that is the metaphysical, but end with the philosophical, which includes and harmonizes both.

15

THE OVERSELF IN ACTION

The title of this chapter is less precise than suggestive, because the supernal Overself is always in action, always supporting and sustaining us, and never really dormant at any time. The present caption has been chosen because a wide ground must now be travelled in a few pages and it is the aptest.

A man who has followed this path for a sufficiently long period and has performed his spiritual practices with enough zeal will not have to wait until the full light of the Overself has appeared within him before he can experience some of its benefits. Various things will happen to show him he is on the right path and to give him growing confidence in its ultimate issue. Long before he is fortunate enough to enter the region of absolute divine light an inner change will become apparent to him. The benefits of even a partial illumination will appear in every department of his life.

Perhaps the first formidable effect is a gradual liberation of oneself from the tyranny of environment, whether of persons, places, happenings or things. One becomes inwardly detached from surrounding scenes and no longer largely at their mercy as before. What has happened is that the deliberate detachment which has been cultivated during the short periods of daily mental quiet, slowly spreads of its own accord like ripple over the whole of one's inner life. The questioning attitude which was first adopted towards the common notion of selfhood, reappears throughout the day and directs itself towards events and environments. No longer does one respond blindly to them, but, on the contrary, one reflects upon their true significance and real value. A sense of inner independence is thus felt which permits one to be influenced by externals only so far as he feels they are really for his good. In short, one is able to choose what impressions and what emotions shall flow into the mind and heart.

Such detachment does not render one unfit to carry on with the normal activities of everyday affairs, as will be shown a little later, nor does it render one inhuman. If to be human means that one must always be in an agitated, anxious, changing and desire-torn condition, then this satisfying serenity certainly lifts one out of the ranks of mankind; but why should we cling to such a low estimate of the proper possibilities of human nature?

A second effect will be to change one's attitude toward the value of life. One will increasingly shift one's interests from superficial to basic standards. He will tend to be less and less deluded by mere appearances; he will doubt whether the current and conventional standards of truth, happiness, morality and conduct are really acceptable. New and higher ideals will rise up on the mind's horizon. No longer content to accept mass-thinking on any subject, one will begin very definitely to think for himself. Within his own heart and mind he will discover unexpected resources which enable him to find pleasure and happiness where the world perceives them not.

Anyone who pursues these practices for a sufficient length of time will not be able to escape from the interference of a strange calm monitor, an inner voice which will arise inside himself in moments when the lack of self-control rises highest. When he is in the grip of undesirable emotions such as anger, hatred, jealousy and fear, this silent voice will come up out of the inner depths and rebuke him for his feelings. He will never be able to destroy its existence. Again and again, whenever he fails to exhibit proper self-control in his emotional life, it will manifest and endeavour to call him to regain his balance, for indeed it is an inevitable result of these practices that they should bring a man face to face with himself and always at appropriate moments.

In social life, he will remain silent when others argue futilely, never dispute with those who dispute for disputation's sake, and never try to persuade the unpersuadable. Nevertheless he will not fail to sow the seeds of truth on fertile ground.

When the meditator comes to the end of his meditation, moves hands and feet, passes out of his room or sequestered spot, and begins to take an active interest in the external world once more, the freshness of his spiritual revelation will quickly fade out and the vivid sense of an interior world will rapidly escape, like a spell which has lost its power. The more he attempts to analyse the sacred experience which has befallen him, the more he aids its disappearance. The paradox is that analysis helps to create it but, once won, it disappears with further analysis! For the novice, at any rate, the resumption of normal waking consciousness is not conducive to the retention of mystical states, although for the practised hand such retention slowly becomes possible and then habitual. Most people find it enough to live on the partial recollection of these hallowed experiences, whose dream-like remembrance will ever be a source of genuine solace and bright blessedness.

It is therefore of the highest importance to practise the

return from the inner centre without losing it. One must not only reach the stillness but he must hold on to it with one hand whilst gradually turning back to external life, for he ought not to become entirely lost in his surroundings again. This is a balancing feat he must learn – like that of riding a bicycle, where one has to look ahead yet keep on his seat. So he must learn to remain in the impersonal centre yet take an active part in the world's work and social life. It can be achieved by practice and habit.

It will be well to regress here to the case of the average Western man or woman who is caught up in the feverish activity of the modern epoch and who, because of the deep spiritual yearnings that are often secretly repressed, lives uneasily and unhappily through the inability to satisfy those yearnings amidst the gross materialism of his environment. He may feel the cramping effects of a position, a task, a vocation or a business which seems to bear no relation to his spiritual aspirations. He will sometimes despair under such circumstances of making any real progress until the conditions are changed. These cases exist numerously in all our large cities. What is the right path for such a person to take?

The writer counsels him to take up the spiritual practices with a determination the stronger because it has so much opposition to meet; such opposition should stimulate him to put forth the greater effort required to overcome it. Even if, during a day all too quickly filled by a long round of duties, he gives himself only twenty minutes or so for solitary spiritual retreat, he is sure, in time, to get the benefits therefrom. Such steady daily effort, pursued for years if need be, may seem unfruitful at first, but deep down in the subterranean corridors of his being, the call has silently gone forth and the ever-watchful, ever-waiting Overself will sooner or later give its response. Then, what was at first accomplished with difficulty and labour, will later be accomplished with the ease which comes from a practised mind.

Let such a person remember that what really matters most is not the length of time he devotes to his meditation, but rather its *quality*. Let his thinking during the practices be clear and one-pointed, and his concentration of attention be deep and steady. Let him sink his whole being in a decisive daily effort to forget his environment during this brief period of withdrawal, to obliterate all thought and memory of his everyday personal activities and to keep his attention unshakenly fixed upon the mental analysis or inner quest.

If, indeed, despite these hindrances of his situation, he sets about the performance of his daily practices with a zeal and a faith that refuse to be daunted, which recognize that a bad failure is always a good experience, it is far more probable that the circumstances which cramp him will themselves yield to the pressure of the spiritual forces which he has invoked. Outwardly he may continue his normal life as heretofore. When, however, such a change becomes imperatively necessary for further advance in spiritual life, the Overself working with destiny will assuredly so ordain matters that it will occur. And the disappearance of hindrances may reveal new and higher tasks for him, affording ampler scope and bringing to his heart a sense of intense satisfaction. Everything will thus work for the best. A man may actually find that the congenial work or even business opportunities which he has been seeking vainly, perhaps all his life, now come to him through the mysterious workings of the Overself almost without any effort on his part. Such a case illustrates the truth of the words: "Seek ye first the Kingdom of Heaven and all these things shall be added unto you."

This Secret Path is not alone a path of mind; it may, and should, easily become the forerunner of a path of outer achievement, the more dynamic because it is the more inspired. *Its object is not to withdraw men into monastic idleness but to help them work more wisely and more effectively in their own spheres of usefulness.*

In general it may be said that the man who has become sufficiently advanced upon this path will sooner or later build for himself an environment that is entirely congenial and will enter into a domain of worldly activity that will be pleasant to his higher outlook; such will be the external recoil to his inner mental creation.

There are exceptions to this general principle and they are constituted by those cases where men, as an act of deliberate self-surrender, enter fearlessly into uncongenial or even hostile environments as a voluntary service to others or at a diviner bidding. In a sense these men are really martyrs, but the surrender of their ego-will to the divine will of the Overself has removed the worst part of their martyrdom. They will expect no return for such service, they will ask for no tangible recompense or expressed gratitude.

We Westerners detest and distrust the philosophic conceptions which would appear to lead us away from the busy world into an 'unreal' cloudy realm. We believe and can only believe in creeds that sanctify the strenuous life. We are undoubtedly right. Yet a path is available which gives us the best of both worlds.

The concentrative power developed by a man during this daily practice will serve him equally well in the sphere of active existence. Whatever he undertakes will be marked by a more purposeful attention. For instance, his dealings with others will become more direct and fruitful to both sides and he will come far more quickly to the point in conversation. In short, a new element, a kind of higher practicality, will show itself in small matters as well as in the most important. He will always carry out with the utmost carefulness, devoted faithfulness and highest integrity whatever duty is entrusted to him by the combined forces of fate and the Overself.

Psychologically, the effects of right meditation practice will show themselves in a better quality of thinking, in greater depth of concentrative power, and in a general clarification of the mind. The principles underlying any subject or situation will be quickly grasped, when others are still studying the details.

A man who has made sufficient progress in these practices to obtain some degree of mental control, some closer feeling of the existence of the Overself, need not fear overmuch the materializing effect of continuous activity. He will illustrate repose in the midst of activity. Whilst his mind rests in a more or less abiding calm, his brain, hands and feet may indeed be busy with the active affairs of every day. Whilst his inner life flows gently and happily like a placid stream through English meadows, his external life may be undergoing violent storms. The value of such a balanced inner life in our unsettled age is beyond price. Such a man will demonstrate, however imperfectly, that the association of sublime inspiration with positive action is a perfectly possible combination. All days then become holy days. When the Overself thus goes into action, the meanest life is made sacred. The perfume of divinity is sprayed over the petty incidents of every day and glorifies them.

An extraordinary and indescribable inner peace will live within him. It will be his place of anchorage in a disorderly epoch when nothing else seems either secure or stable. He will thus move calmly on his road, his feet planted firmly at every step, where others rush wildly to and fro under the stress of twentieth-century convulsion. He will work with that spirit of gentle unhurriedness allied with exacting efficiency which is such a marked characteristic of the successful Japanese. The sublime serenity of the Overself seems remote indeed from the harsh rumble of New York's elevated railroad, from the ever-purring motor traffic of the Champs-Elysées, and from the teeming throng of London's Strand – nevertheless, even amid such environments, he will possess it!

Thus, living as close to the Divine Centre as he can, he may still be able to take his appropriate place in the world, no longer as its slave, but as Nature's co-operator. Whilst his inmost being dwells in a strange spirituality, he himself will be able to move in the very midst of stress and tumult, not blind to its existence or indifferent to its problems, but nevertheless inwardly poised and untroubled. Therefore he can cope more effectively with these problems. He has found that at the centre – whether of self or the universe – there dwells real safety and sanity.

All these effects will be brought about whether a man seeks them consciously or not, for he has introduced a new arbiter into all his enterprises.

The constant practice of these spiritual exercises will inevitably give one the right attitude, the right outlook, and then one need not fear to enter the arena where the world battles are fought, be they the bloodless battles of earning a livelihood or the sanguinary combats of actual war. Only novices, cowards or weaklings need take permanent flight from the struggle of existence to sheltered retreats and monastic life. For with control of mind all things become possible, but without this, man lives to little purpose. *This is inspired activity* and gives a spiritual aim, a lasting meaning, to what would otherwise be a purely ephemeral everyday existence. Such an inspired life represents true sanity. The Western world is really unbalanced, because it is for ever immersed in constant activity without interior compensation. If it would incorporate some kind of spiritual practice into its daily programme, it would not only save itself from the neurasthenic afflictions of the age, not only bring more peace, efficiency and understanding into the management of its affairs, but also achieve a higher life alongside of its working activities.

Thus man may fulfil the unseen and hidden purpose of his being. Then, indeed, as he moves about upon his daily activities, whether in the street and market-place, the home or the factory, *he will be able to say that he is moving about his Father's business.* The secular will have become the sacred.

We may learn the secret of taking the drudgery out of everyday existence by putting the divine into it. All things are symbols of the unseen God. Even work can be a prayer we utter. Every floor that is rightly swept is a pathway for the Lord. No work of ours is so worldly but in it we can show forth the qualities of God. We reveal ourselves by our work. The few who are filled with the spirit of God strive to show forth His perfection in perfectly done work; His wisdom in intelligent work; His power in energetic work. Our highest capacities can be revealed in this way; time can thus be turned to high account, and truths netted in heaven can be brought down to earth.

§

A man who depends on others for his help or happiness depends on reeds that may break; but a man who depends on the Overself will never be betrayed.

We may turn to brief consideration of the material help which the Overself renders when we ourselves seem helpless. There is really nothing beyond the scope of such assistance. Ill-health, organic disorders, lack of work, food, shelter, friends or funds, business perplexities, technical problems, distressing relationships – all these and more have been marvellously and divinely adjusted in the experience of various persons known to the writer. They were people who had learnt how to 'tune' in to the Overself, in however small degree, and to throw their burdens on its ampler shoulders. The powerful force of destiny had brought them these sorrows or difficulties, but the all-powerful force of the Overself delivered them in the end.

The economic problem, for example, seems to worry people nowadays as much as any other. Although one who is treading this path may continue to appreciate the value and necessity of money – second greatest power in the world as it is – he will experience less and less that overwhelming thirst for riches which so largely dominates the present age. For as he becomes increasingly aware of the Overself, as the mental steadiness and emotional equilibrium which the practice tends to create percolate increasingly into his everyday attitude, he will feel diminishing anxiety about his material welfare. Indeed, he will believe in the truth of the counsel of Jesus that the Father knows his needs and that he need not make friends with anxiety or despair; but this is not to say that he will degenerate and become apathetic or lazy; he will pay a keener attention to duty and do his work or attend to business more thoroughly and more carefully than ever before, because as already explained he will come to take an almost sacred view of duty.

The secret of all super-personal help is surrender. Not surrender to weakness, lethargy, laziness, hopelessness or short-sighted fatalism, but surrender of the personal power to the central power within oneself. Then, instead of pitting one's own limited faculties against the gloomier circumstances which are arrayed against him in the battles of life, he lets this central power get to work on his behalf. Where one fails, it succeeds; where one perceives only impassable brick walls of difficulty, it passes miraculously through. It will work for him and better than him, yet all that one has to do is to open one-self to its expression.

But before one can surrender one must first find the dwelling-place of this diviner power. Mere words cannot do it. The path here described takes one right into the centre of that dwelling-place. One has to work hard internally to reach this point, but once arrived one is not to labour, only to let oneself be laboured through. One must have the uncommon sense to say: "I shall interfere no longer. I shall cease this endless calculation of ways and means. I shall put down my load of cares and duties on the ground beside me. I see now what I, in my blindness, refused to see before, that the Overself which supports and carries me, can perform all calculations, manage all affairs, bear all bur-dens in a manner infinitely better than I could ever do, simply because it is itself infinite in power and wisdom."

There are times when prudence is but another word for error of judgment; and when a higher kind of prudence is called for, namely, trust in Providence. There are hours when calculation is seen to be but another name for miscalculation. For the personal mind is limited in outlook, dwarfed in depth beside the immeasurable intuition that arises unerringly from the Overself and, ignoring all distorting masks of men and cir-cumstances, points straight towards the right road. Our cares and anxieties are connected with the personal self, not with the exalted Overself. The elimination of this tyrannous condition depends on the return to the impersonal Overself. Our actions will then no longer be the outcome of mere personal whims, of the ambitions of greed and the desires of possession alone. We shall become clear channels of the Overself, useful instruments in its hands, and impersonal servitors of its divine will. We shall live henceforth without the strain of personal effort, with-out anxious forethought, knowing that our Father, the Overself, will make all the necessary effort and forethought on our behalf, itself working either through us or through others.

The way is open for all men to conquer the horrors of pain and the heart-breaks of poverty, the hardships of failure and the corrosiveness of anxiety, *if only they will conquer their minds.* No problem is too difficult for the Overself to tackle; it would not be the fortifying atom of almighty God within us if it were so feeble as that. No gloomy cloud of pessimism nor peace-destroying nightmare of fear need descend upon any man's life for ever and ever; *the blessed rays of the Overself are with him here and now,* ready to shine benignantly down upon his days as soon as he properly invokes them. The boasted strength of the personal self is really its weakness; true strength lies in that which dwells behind the personal self. We may draw on the infinite, if we will, and thus achieve the seemingly impossible. The powers of the body and the intellect can stretch thus far and no farther, but the powers of the Overself are illimitable.

The divinity which brought our souls into existence, as our mothers brought our bodies into existence, can support, sustain, heal, protect and guide us in precisely the same way that mothers support, sustain, protect and guide their own children. This is not a poetical simile; it is a statement of scientific reality, albeit the reference here is to the science of life. *And no less than every true mother loves her dear child and ever wishes to lead it to real happiness, does the divine Overself love its rebellious offspring, the personal self, and ever seek its true welfare by leading it along the path of repentance and return.* This is the whole message of practical religion, and to instil this truth into our shuttered minds God has sent His prophets among us and will continue to send them so long as we remain errant prodigals and have not the sense to say: "I will arise and go unto my Father."

The man who has attained for ever the full awareness of

the Overself needs neither guidance nor method from anyone else, for a higher power will give him both. But the man who is advancing and has already made some progress in mental quiet can profitably use a simple method of spiritual and material self-help which is always and instantly applicable to every imaginable set of adverse conditions. It will not give everyone everything which he desires, because other forces have something to say in the matter – the forces of destiny, universal evolution and That which created both, God! The personal self must needs fit itself into the cosmic framework which surrounds it, and not expect the framework to be altered to fit it. Nor does it really know what is best for it, what will bring it genuine happiness or true well-being. Suffering is not always to be shirked; sometimes it is a tutor as excellent as any to be found in the best university. We must look on the troubled side of life as spiritual education, and extract the lesson of wisdom from every misfortune. Therefore no method exists, despite the imaginative claims of certain schools, whereby unperfected man can dictate to God, can *always* avoid misfortune, ill-health, poverty, tragedy or oppression, and have all his demands satisfied. But a method does exist whereby he may verily make the "best" of circumstances and relate divine aid, not to his selfish demand but to his true need.

Before the actual exercise is given it will be well to reiterate that only the person who has already developed some degree of mind-strength through the practices of this secret path and mental quiet, can profit by it. We cannot build brick walls without mortar, and we cannot call up spiritual forces without having first prepared some kind of contact with them.

Whoever wishes to invoke the aid of the Overself whenever he is troubled, tried, tempted, hurt, depressed, anxious, worried, undecided or angry – in fact, whenever he is suffering or sinning in any form – should habituate himself to this additional practice. The method is as follows:

One should slow down the rhythm of breathing for two or three minutes and simultaneously question oneself:

"Whom does this trouble?" "Whom does this pain?" "Whom does this depress?" "Whom does this tempt?" or "Whom does this perplex?" – and so on according to the particular problem. Then a mental pause should be brought about and the thoughts kept calm, concentrated and fixed on the question. Everything else, whether external scenes or extraneous ideas, should be rigidly ignored and the mind introverted until it sinks as deeply into the inner self as the mental quiet practices have achieved. The entire exercise should not take more than a few minutes and should be done simply and naturally and undemonstratively.

This method is applicable to any kind of problem, which needs only to be brought into the sublime ever-presence of the Overself. Although the latter is quite competent to deal with whatsoever arises, one ought not to make the mistake of always looking for an immediate solution. Higher powers must take their own time, which is normally unpredictable. A striking result may flash forth within the hour or one may have to learn the lesson of quiet patience. These powers have not failed because they refuse to be turned on like a tap. Impatience breaks their charm and is always detrimental.

When a man has become habituated by long experience to this exercise he will marvel at its beautiful simplicity and effectiveness, as he relaxes and gently sinks inwards in silent submission of his personal ego. Trying can be very trying.

Whenever discord or disaster of any kind threaten one, this practice may be immediately begun. In this way the mental impression is intercepted and one refuses to identify himself with it. Half the mesmeric harm is thus swept away. The attitude of a vigilant *witness* is adopted, the disturbing impression quickly cut off, and everything undesirable neutralized as one invokes and realizes the Overself. The ordinary man who surrenders to negative thoughts courts and strengthens the very troubles he wishes to avoid.

Every hurt that threatens, every problem that arises, should be taken at once into the divine centre and contemplated from this newer angle. That is the right way to clarify, heal and enlighten oneself. In the midst of hard difficulties, heart-searing frustrations, crushing defeats or depressing perplexities, a man may yet obtain release by refusing to accept the imposition of conventional thoughts and conventional attitudes. And even when destiny is inexorable and refuses to unbend sufficiently to permit any problem to be solved materially, the latter can always be solved spiritually because it can be eradicated from the mind. Cosmic evolutionary purpose most come into conflict with personal happiness at some time or other, and when it cannot be deflected the practice of spiritual self-recollectedness will unharness the mind of its burden by introducing the radiant light and mystic power of the Overself. But such a method can work effectively only when one possesses the firm faith that the Overself is continuously available and its presence inseparable, when he rejects alertly the thoughts and moods which would drag him like a chained slave from its benign love and mysterious resources, and when he *immediately* displaces worrying, hurtful or degrading sensations by silent unshaken affirmation of his interior existence in the eternal.

Such is the amplitude of this exercise that it can be applied to help others indirectly and to a certain degree. If one has a beloved relative or friend who is in a difficult situation, after having performed the practice, one may picture the person in the mind's eye, and then raise him and his problem aloft to the white light of the Overself in silent blessing. Some illumination or protection will then surely wing its mysterious way through space to that other person.

In every case where a mental problem or material burden has been surrendered rightly to the Overself, a feeling of mental ease and a sense of emotional relief will manifest soon afterwards.

When this habit of swift reference to the Overself by questioning *who* is suffering, *who* is annoyed, and so on, has been fostered until it becomes instinctive, one will feel spiritually secure and materially confident. Although there are determinants of our destiny beyond the span of conscious intention and personal effort, most of us carry unnecessary loads of care. The Overself can bear the same burden far better. Let it – and let us accept its perennial invitation, its gentle guidance, and thus learn to meet life's varied situations with serene equanimity, knowing that its providential care can then never be absent.

Whoever faithfully follows this path will stand still at times with drawn breath when he perceives that a higher will than his own mysteriously intervenes in his affairs and always, in the highest sense, to his ultimate benefit. He will become an effective instrument in its divine hands. All events will become moves on a celestial chessboard. All things will conspire to work out for the best – bitter suffering no less than pleasant joys will provide accepted lessons in fortitude and wisdom. Even the harsh malice of his enemies will not be resented, for he will eventually learn life's last and loftiest secret – that every living creature bears the hidden tokens of divinity within its breast and is unconsciously striving amid its darkest sins for the deathless satisfaction, truth and power which exist in the Overself alone.

16

THE QUEST

During his Oriental researches the writer devoted some of his time in Egypt to silent interrogation of every corner of its proud colossus, the Great Pyramid. A peculiar and personal extra-physical experience came to him as he tried to wrest a few secrets from this cold architectural giant. This experience became alive with significant meaning, when he learnt later that an ancient tradition existed among the now-vanished priests of Memphis, which declared that the Pyramid was the sacred scene of initiations into Egypt's profoundest and grandest spiritual mysteries.

Among his explorations he traversed the upward shaft which leads to the famous King's and Queen's Chambers and carefully studied its structure by the light of a certain 'key' with which he had been provided. He also crept at night on hands and knees through the narrow downward passage, which cuts for hundreds of feet right through the rocky plateau on which the entire Pyramid stands, a passage which is barred and closed to modern travellers because of varied difficulties and dangers.

In a general way, he was constantly struck by the apt symbolism of these gloomy corridors. These material paths which lead from the entrance hole to inside chambers, fitly correspond with the spiritual paths which lead mankind from the state of gross ignorance to complete understanding of its true nature as being something divine. He could perceive that the interior of the Great Pyramid figures forth in stone the destined progress of every human being, whilst the whole building is a solemn symbol of human existence, bearing a silent message across the chasm of dead and vanished centuries.

The trembling neophyte of old had to pass through the Pyramid's craggy portal, and then feel his way through utter darkness along these passages by holding to the walls and planting each foot with the utmost care. His excited mind brought into existence unseen pits into which he might fall, but which in reality did not exist. Without courage he could not advance at all; without prudence he might advance only into the gravest danger. He possessed no other guide than an intuition, an interior impersonal voice which was always mysterious and often indistinguishable from his personal feelings.

At a further stage of his progress into the black tunnel-like passages, he had to encounter dangers which menaced his peace and sanity. For hostile psychic entities infested the place, malignant spirit-creatures prowled nightly around it. They might at any moment become visible to his heightened senses. Their opposition knew no bounds for they dwelt as guardians on that awful borderland which separates the other world from foolish intrusive men. If the neophyte fell a victim to his fears and to the effects of their natural enmity, his nervous tension would suddenly collapse and these effects might pursue him for years.

The struggles of every adventurous candidate, the writer reflected, typified also the struggles of every man who seeks to understand the purpose which pulsates through all Nature. He finds all life involved in impenetrable darkness, surrounded by thick clouds of mystery. He sees that we are born for not more than a few decades of uncertain and unsafe existence, and then all our ardent hopes, our besetting ambitions and strongest loves are extinguished like a snuffed candle by the clammy hand of death. He knows, if he thinks at all, that if this represents all there is to man, then it is clear that the hope of immortality is a delusion, the soul is a mere figment of imagination and religion or philosophy, mere dressed-up shows put on the stage by professionally-interested persons. Life does not explain itself easily. We are not born with the great secret hanging like a carved amulet around our necks.

Just as the neophyte in the Egyptian Mysteries had to grope his way up or down gloomy ascents or descents, so do we who are human have to grope our way through the darkness of unrevealed futurity, harassed by trials or pushed by temptations which convert existence into steep ascents or swift downward slopes. If any difference is to be noted, it is, perhaps, that the neophyte was not so content with his ignorance as are we. The restless quest of truth had brought him hither and dragged his stripped feet along these ancient stones, but which of us is willing to trouble himself for such an intangible reward as the second birth? The malign creatures which pursued him are types of the world's malignity and opposition, or at the very least, of misunderstanding, which those who seek to break away from conformity with materialistic standards must experience and suffer as the penalty for their rash unconventionality.

Whatever the pyramidal adventure taught him, the race of humanity will learn in any case during its progress from the womb to the tomb through the aeons of evolution. He condensed into a few hours or days lessons which need entire lifetimes for less adventurous men. Success taught him that each man bears a purpose beyond his own, higher than his own. When it brought him into the King's Chamber, it also brought him into the presence of those who were waiting and watching, themselves unseen, as the gods still wait and watch over mankind even now. And when, in the highest initiation, his consciousness entered the Overself-spiracle, the mystic chamber in the heart, he achieved in abbreviated and premature fashion what the whole human race must ultimately achieve. The world today sceptically regards such a universal spiritual awakening as impossible; the initiated wise confidently regard it as inevitable. Nature is patient, however.

To carry the allegory still farther, the Overself-atom lies hidden within the human body to the extent of less than a pinpoint in breadth, just as the King's Chamber lies hidden as a tiny space in the largest mass of worked masonry which this planet has borne for many thousands of years. The Overself is invisible to the naked eye of man, as the Pyramid's chief chamber is invisible amid the darkness of its interior. The Overself is the single secret whose solution most defies man, just as the corridors which lead to the chamber were once guarded by an entrance door which was cunningly made of stone as a part of the outer surface, with no sign whatever to announce its separate existence.

The ancient traditions of Egypt provided guides for those aspirants who were ready to be brought to this secret door, just as the spiritual tradition of the human race still provides guides for those who are ready to be brought to the Overself's threshold. Even the grave-like silence of the Great Pyramid's interior is fitly matched by the sepulchral stillness which surrounds the seeker's mind today when he steps upon this sacred threshold. Finally, there is the picturesque fact that there was demanded from the neophyte, as he crawled with bowed shoulders and bent knees under the swinging entrance door, a physical and mental humbleness which is still demanded in our own time. The priestless shrine of the Overself never opens its tiny tight-fitting door to the arrogant.

Thus the last quest which was set before the thoughtful Egyptian as the goal of living was none other than that which is set before the thoughtful twentieth-century man also. He had to recover full awareness of his real nature by ceasing to identify himself entirely with the physical body at first, and entirely with the personal ego later, as we have to recover this awareness today. We are empty when we could be full. We are like the young lion which was reared from cubhood among sheep, and which grew up to think itself a sheep, too. It lived and moved harmlessly among the flock until one day in the forest it heard for the first time the throaty roar of an older lion. The hidden nature of the animal suddenly awakened; it spontaneously roared back in answer and in that moment *knew itself* also to be nothing less than a lion.

The gospel of all men who have attained the divine region of para-personal being must come to intuitive auditors like the first-heard roar of that lion. It is a call that affects the mysterious depths of their hearts, and one which either troubles or delights them. For they can never be fully satisfied with the limitations, afflictions and ephemeralities of human existence. No one can honestly assert that he has found untainted happiness in the frail and fear-filled life of human personality, and even if he dared to do so the dreadful figure of death would still stand in his shadow to mock at all hopes for the future.

The divine beauty which lies buried within human nature exists already and has not to be created, so that the quest is not so much one of new attainment as of recovery. *Consciousness is our very nature;* the Overself is aware and alive, but because it is eternal it must also be impersonal. There is a sentence in the Hebrew Bible where the Lord answers Moses, saying: 'I AM

THAT I AM.' The importance of this statement is signified by the fact that it is written in capital letters throughout. The meaning is that the Absolute consciousness is the 'I AM' behind each individual existence, the very sense of being itself.

The divine atom is one and the same in all men, identical in Christ as it was in his hearers. It is indeed the Christ-self in each of us. When Jesus had passed away from this world, the most enlightened of his earlier followers thenceforward used and understood his name only in this universal sense.

The Christos was to them their own interior divinity – not a particular flesh-body which had been buried – and their work was to bring consciousness downward from the head until it was focused in the spiritual heart, where the kingdom of heaven was localized for all true Christians.

§

The man who follows this quest is like the ray which is returning to its source. When he follows the 'I AM' in him to its hidden root, when the intellectual process of his enquiry gradually develops into a subtler inner movement, he will sooner or later enter – intermittently at first – a condition of impersonal freedom and utter peace. When the mind's depth is plumbed he will arrive at a point where both the thinking intellect and personal self seem almost to become re-absorbed by the hidden element which created them. That element is none other than the Absolute Being, the One Overself, the Supreme Reality and Underlying Spirit which subsists eternally amid the births and deaths of mortal men and material worlds. This august revelation awaits him even at the beginning of his first fumbling steps on the quest.

Yet men fear such a path because they fear the loss of personality, which is to them life itself. The exact truth is that the personal ego is subordinated, turned into an agent for a higher power, and so long as the physical body lasts does not disappear. What then is there to fear? The individual existence is but a nutshell which, once broken, reveals the valuable kernel inside. Nuts are not to be treasured for their indelible shells but for their fruit. Those who are satisfied with the ego's limitations turn the long stretch of life itself into a delusion. They are working to one-thousandth part of their potential capacity, yet fear to travel a little farther. None are to blame, however, for the delusion is world-wide. They confuse personality with consciousness and do not know that because no one can ever escape from himself, the end of life cannot be mere death-like unconsciousness.

This doctrine is more ancient than the planet itself; yet, being always self-found by each man individually as the result of his own overwhelming spiritual illumination it comes to him as fresh in presentation as the latest words of the latest Western scientist. But man has ever feared it because he fears to yield up his personal ego, not knowing what will happen afterwards. He finds it hard to trust the higher powers. He has something to learn.

In the Biblical story of Abraham's sacrifice of his own-born, the bearded patriarch was about to carry his obedience to the point of stabbing the trembling body of his son when the Lord stayed his hand and told him that his son might live. Abraham's faithfulness had been tested in the severest manner possible; that was enough for the Lord, who did not really seek the life of Isaac but rather the love of Abraham. The latter had shown his willingness to put the divine before the personal; whereupon he was permitted to keep the personal for henceforth it would play a secondary and subordinate part in his life.

Whoever reaches the stage of this quest where meditation reduces all thoughts to the single thought *I*, and then bravely thrusts that very thought back into the seeming nothingness out of which it has arisen, will likewise be told by the Lord that he may have his ego and keep it unkilled. He may live out his personal life in the world, for it will not take more than its rightful place in his schemes of values, and he will understand that henceforth he is an agent, and nothing more.

Holiness, therefore, is simply harmony. It is to stop the incessant strivings of the self for this and that, to submit every hour and every year henceforth to the beautiful promptings of the Overself.

Yet we do not attain this blessed state until we have suffered, for such self-surrender is immensely difficult for human beings to make whilst they are yet human, and they do it only when they know that they *must*. They understand, then, that the higher power which has drawn them thus far will not permit them to stop; it will hunt them into trackless impersonal regions, as Francis Thompson has shown in his wonderful poem "The Hound of Heaven".

This condition of ego-mergence in the Overself was plainly described by the apostle Paul when he said: "I have been crucified with Christ, nevertheless I live; yet it is no longer I that live, but Christ living in me." This statement is clear when we understand that in his own mind Christ was not identified with the physical individuality of Jesus, *whom he had never met,* but with the Christos-spirit which exists within all men. The crucifixion to which he refers was in his own case and shall be in ours the crucifixion of the ego-sense, the immolation of separate individuality. His Christ is the hidden reality which is the substratum of every ego. Realizing his divine identity, the centre of his personal circle coincided with the centre of the universal circle, which is infinite.

Sacrifice can not be properly understood if it is restricted to external gestures only. It is primarily an inner *event*. It may or may not become an outward act, but that is not the most important part. Every man's destiny is different. If some lose all that is visible and valued when they lose their old allegiance to personality, others may have kingdoms placed in their hands when they take up a new allegiance to divinity. These events cannot be judged by appearances. Mysterious are the workings of the Overself.

Just as Abraham's suffering ceased when he led his relieved child away from the sacrificial altar, so the suffering which self-renunciation frequently inflicts disappears when the compensatory adjustment of the inner life is completed. The more intense the struggle has been, the greater will be the sense of peace which shall replace it. This feeling of inward relief is always a sign that the sacrifice has been a right one, and that the Overself has mitigated the hurt. All personal griefs become attenuated when they are brought into the light of the Absolute.

When a man has done what he can to understand these analyses and follow these practices with faithfulness and perseverance, he must then learn to wait patiently for the moment when his efforts shall ripen into real illumination. He may have his moods of depression, of a sense of failure, for it is difficult to attain anything worth while without relapses, but that is no reason for giving up the quest. He may be confident on one thing; that which is his due shall not be withheld from him in the end. There is an appropriate hour, a perfect moment for all events, all inner happenings. This is especially true of spiritual illumination or psychological upheaval. If it comes too early, we reject it; if it comes too late, we refuse it. It must come at the right hour, which means that it must come out of ourselves. When it does come, however, a marked change will occur, even if the gates of heaven are not opened for more than five minutes. Does not the man now know that the Overself really exists and is no mere figment of someone's imagination?

Is not its terrific intensity the supreme reality of realities? And in its blessed touch he finds final proof and indubitable evidence that the labour of his lonely meditations was not in vain, and that the divine powers are not wholly indifferent to man.

Those who mistrust this mysterious teaching sometimes allege that its deification of self is an attempt to equate God with the human personality, and to depose Deity in order to enshrine a part of His creation. This is a misunderstanding. Whoever enters into the experience of contacting the depths of his inmost being can emerge only with deeper reverence for God. He realizes his helplessness and dependence when he thinks of that Greater Being from whom he draws the very permit to exist. Instead of deifying the personal self, he has completely humiliated it. Self, in its ordinary sense, must indeed be cast away that God shall enter in. The New Testament story of the prodigal son is likewise the story of the prodigal ego-self. The father who has been deserted is none other than the Overself. However rebellious and wayward the ego becomes in its search of external satisfactions, it is born out of the loins of the Overself. The repentant prodigal in the story was suprised that his father did not greet his return with harsh words, but on the contrary, took him to his breast and kissed him. When the ego-self turns inward and travels along the homeward path of return to the Overself, the Overself's love has begun its conquest and is the real factor which is drawing the prodigal home. And when the two meet, which is the moment of initiation, there are no harsh words here, either, but tears of recognition and the warmth of affection. Here alone, in this repentant return and self-surrender, does man spell out the last letters of the word of his being.

Thus we arrive at the hoary and ancient truth which has been tongued by so many seers, that without this deeper inspired life of the spirit man must perish inwardly, or at best live an existence which is a dismal caricature of the sublimer one which is open to him. And even those who cannot understand the vast and deep reticence of the Overself, who cannot see the secret source whence they take their being, nor follow their lives in their winding courses beyond that mysterious moment which writes the fated physical end, even such may trust the words of those higher men who have been sent as teachers to our race and they may believe that there is a living divinity back of things.

§

Long before he actually penetrates to the hidden reality, the man who is engaged upon this quest will begin to feel a subtle inner attraction which makes him mentally abstracted at odd times. This is really the drawing towards his deeper self and expresses the centripetal power of the Overself. He does not need to wait until he has attained the goal before striking and tangible results of these practices are revealed. What the adept and the sage find there, all men may find to a lesser degree at earlier stages of the quest. The brief period of daily withdrawal, combined with persistent application of the method explained in the previous chapter, will gradually induce the personal ego to stand aside to some extent and permit higher powers to come into operation. Providential help and extraordinary guidance may begin to appear of their own accord. Without his lifting a foot or moving a finger, the true needs of a man who has begun to come into communion with the Overself may be supplied at his very doorstep and always at the psychological moment of necessity. This applies to his spiritual and mental needs no less than to material ones.

Does such a notion lay too heavy a burden upon our credulity? Why should not the Power which upholds the universe be able to uphold such a man, too? Its secret stream flows ceaselessly beneath the personal existence of every living creature. The physical body could not continue to function as an organism if the Overself were not present within every molecule of its flesh. For the Overself as Spirit is the source of life, a source that is infinite, and flows through all things and all beings. Its silent activity keeps the whole material universe in a state of constant procreation, which is the reason why there is no real death anywhere. It is an amazing yet universal paradox that the Overself, which is nowhere visible, is everywhere present. Scientifically speaking, matter is next to nothing and Space is reality. A distinguished scientist has lately pointed out that the porousness of the atom is such that if we eliminate all the unfilled space in a human body and gather the latter's protons and electrons into a single mass, the whole body would be reduced to a tiny speck which would need a magnifying lens to make it visible. So fundamental and so comprehensive is the Overself that it occupies all space.

This is not conjecture but ascertained knowledge, not theory but experience. It might have seemed nonsense to assert such things a century ago; it is almost rational to assert them today. Like ladies' hats, even philosophies fall out of favour. The old doctrines of mechanical materialism have met their fatal day. Time and truth have conspired to trip them up. Science knows now that there is no such thing as empty space, but rather a vast hidden universe of LIVING ENERGY which is the secret root of matter. In short, the Overself encompasses us all and lack of acquaintance must be laid to our own fault.

Moreover, the Overself is present throughout the three states of human life—waking, dreaming and deep slumber, otherwise we could never become aware of these states and existence in any of them would not be possible. From the Overself's standpoint there is no loss of awareness in the three states, the totality of which embraces the living and two of which embrace the "dead". The Overself is the Witness of all three, which are superimposed upon it but can never over-whelm it.

The recognition of its presence and power is, however, necessary before participation in its activity is possible. Application of the technique already described destroys all withering fears and reveals a higher element at work in our lives. This technique can be applied to all human problems because if there is a practical solution of them, the inner wis-dom will infallibly direct one to take the right practical measures, and if circumstances are so troubled that no visible way out is available for the time being, then strength will be given one to support them until they pass, to live mentally above them.

> "I have numerous proofs of the divine protection over me, especially during our Revolution, of which I was not with-out indications beforehand. . . . In a word, for me it is peace, and this is with me wheresoever I am. On the famous 10th of August, when I was shut up in Paris, traversing the streets all day amidst the great tumult, I had such signal proofs of what I tell you that I was humbled even to the dust. . . . My suspense, my privations, my tribulations alarm me not though they afflict me. *I am conscious in the midst of all this darksome anguish that a secret thread is attached to me for my preservation.*"

These words are remarkable. They were written in a private letter by Louis Claude de Saint-Martin, the eighteenth-century French sage. He had practised a method of mental quiet which made self-knowledge its aim. Many years later, when nearing the end of his life, he could still testify that: "My bodily and spiritual life has been too well cared for by

Providence for me to have anything but gratitude to render."

It is worth repeating again that the benefits of this method become apparent long before the goal is in sight. One is not writing here for would-be Christs and Krishnas, but rather for the many millions of people hemmed in by modern city life, cribbed within a materialistic existence of office, factory, shop and street. Nirvana is not easy to reach but many more might come closer to it and an attainment such as is pictured in these pages will be more than enough. Many more might find a satisfying degree of centrality, serenity, wisdom and power far above the average. Just as a lamp hung in a street on a dark night lights up a space far beyond itself, the light getting dimmer as it spreads farther, so the man who is approaching the Overself begins to reflect something of its qualities and powers long before he is likely to enter its full radiance.

Armed with this method one may thrust all weakening and harmful thoughts out of consciousness. One may challenge all crippling worries and achieve swift victories over depressing emotions. To meet the obligations of this technique is to derive its unique benefits. Disappointments can be dominated and one may learn to tap sources of higher strength, to exorcize half the phantoms of fear which haunt human life. Troubles are inescapable, but they may be taken captive and flung into imprisonment.

The silently-working mind is our link with the Overself, the creator of man's external life. Hence this method must be practised immediately a difficult situation arises or a disagreeable one confronts us. The normal suggestions produced should be refused and instead they should be mentally offset by turning towards the divine view of the situation. This view is obtainable by turning the mind inwards and questioning, as explained in the previous chapter.

One disentangles himself from such situations by ceasing to submit in mind, by disidentifying himself from them, and temporarily driving them out of the field of awareness, even if only for a few moments. When a man says to himself, "I am unhappy," he hangs chains around his mind. When, however, he meets the challenge of precisely similar circumstances by thinking insistently: "To whom has this unhappiness come?" he at once stands in objective relationship to his dark mood. Such definite questioning destroys these moods because it initiates a process which leads to the destruction of their very basis, which is self-identification with them. Although the quest begins as a mental process it will end, if faithfully followed, as a state of spontaneous spiritual being. The need of retiring inwards, however briefly, and awaiting the silent answer is real, for recognition of who the true self really is repels the false notion that the body's moods, the mind's moods, are one's own. In this way the most grievous sorrow may be kept at a psychological distance.

The true selfhood is never dismayed by the most awful circumstances. It confers authority over existence as soon as one changes his thinking from the purely personal standpoint and apprehends a higher view. Every man may see in the mirror the face of him who may be his best friend or worst enemy. For every man owns the title deeds of his mind and is alone responsible for the thoughts he generates. An affirmative state of mind can be acquired by habit, just as most people have acquired their negative states by foolish habits also.

The divine intelligence within man can deal with all his problems for it is wiser than he. When despair taps relentlessly at the doors of a man's heart, the time has arrived to hand over his affairs to the Overself. He may do this by redirecting his mind as quickly as possible inwards, and by keeping on with this redirection in the face of all opposition until he reaches the central core of quietness where mysterious help awaits him. He should become so absorbed in that quietness that the painful problem which was his starting-point, should be forgotten for a few moments or minutes, or even longer. Such forgetfulness always supervenes when the personal ego is captured and gripped by the Overself. *Even two seconds of it will suffice to bring remarkable results.*

To achieve this feat successfully not seldom demands that all sensory evidence to the contrary should be deserted, for the inner divinity must be approached with humble hope and confidence. Trial, trouble or temptation will fall away from the mind of their own accord, but the hour of external disappearance is timed by the permit of destiny. But one ought always to retire into the mental silence whenever one needs greater aid than either the intellect or external means can provide.

There is no field of human life wherein these truths are not practically applicable. Businesses fail, situations are lost, shares depreciate and illness depletes the body, but the inner protection arising from communion with the Overself will never fail a man, never depreciate and cannot be lost save by his wilful denial. Whether he wanders into the deserted plains of Central Asia or into the thronging metropolis of an American State, it will be an unfailing source of moral support and material provision, moving events and persons to his aid in a marvellous manner.

We must beware of self-deception, however. If the inner communion is not genuinely established then all talk of it becomes mere mental aviation, a cacophony of hollow words that lead only to delusion. These ideas are worth nothing if they are not workable or if they cannot produce effective results.

Passions that are otherwise ungovernable may be broken

by bringing the mind into at-one-ment with the Overself. Any passion or disturbing desire may be overcome and brought under control at the time it arises by completely stilling the mind. The process is swift in results, often instantaneous. As soon as one is aware that one is losing self-control, thought should be turned inward and held still, as still as can be. This act will simultaneously quieten the passion. The cause is simple but little known. All desires and passions have their real root not alone in the physical body, as we generally believe, but in the *mental habits* which the body's activities have created. They must be conquered in the mind and never will be conquered anywhere else. This is why physical asceticisms are often futile, and even lead to sensual reactions when the governing-wheel of will-power is removed.

This spontaneous stillness of mind should come easily enough to one who has faithfully practised this method, and he will be aware of a higher element rising simultaneously into consciousness with every personal desire.

The last words upon this method must be that whoever puts himself right automatically puts his whole life right. "Let us lay hold of the Beginning, and we shall make way with quickness through everything," was the earnest counsel of the High Priest of Amen-Ra in ancient Egypt. He meant nothing more than that which has been written here, that when one puts himself into tune with the Overself, which is the first fundamental of all things, one's individual existence thereafter receives higher support.

Destiny has something to say in all matters, for it is a working force as real as electricity. Nevertheless it works in harmony with the Overself, for the purpose of both is identical. Man must and will be redeemed.

He who knows when to submit to fate and when to resist it, is its true conqueror.

It is not always wise to dictate in advance the manner whereby any difficulty is to be solved, for the fruits of one's desire may be disappointing. The Overself knows, and knows best; why not trust it? So long as one does his duty, according to the light vouchsafed him, he may safely leave all questions of ways and means to the Overself. It alone knows how to harmonize one's needs with the fiats of destiny, and to reach solutions which are the best in the end.

"What will be, will be! It is the hand of Allah; let us not complain," murmurs the fatalistic Muhammadan in times of distress, turning his eyes toward the stars. But we Europeans and Americans are rebels, for we grasp unconsciously at the truth that the hand of Allah is none other than our own; we do not, however, grasp so readily the complementary truth so clearly enunciated by Jesus, that we shall reap what we have sown.

Without the principle of repeated re-embodiments, however, destiny becomes meaningless, Jesus's words become untrue, and all life a useless farce.

The practice of this method has nothing to do with magic. A mistake which most beginners make is to confuse the quest of the Overself with the quest of occult powers. The gulf between the two is not so apparent in the earlier stages but becomes extremely wide later on. The stately yet simple truth that man is essentially divine, as stately and yet as simple as the Doric columns of a Greek temple, can be learnt without wandering into the queer, complicated labyrinths of occultism. It is indeed a reprehensible notion which would have us dabble in weird and fantastic studies, in ghostly or ghastly experiments, or in roving among the sprites and goblins, for the sake of discovering what is fundamentally fine and beautiful in man. Those who do so begin by losing their spiritual path and sometimes end by losing their senses. Truth is never attested by thaumaturgy or miracle. It must stand or fall by its own work, its own sublime reasonableness and high efficacy.

Would-be occultists forget or do not know that the supreme power which supports all occult powers is the Overself's own power. All lesser forces take their rise therein. It is safer and saner to go direct to the source than to court the acquisition of fugitive faculties and dangerous gifts. Man easily loses his way in the twilit empire of occultism and has to retrace his route with some suffering. Nor are these super-normal powers less costly to gain than the higher fruits of Overself-finding.

Initiation into the Overself is often confused with psycho-sensational experiences. Such initiation is an inward and ineffable experience which no verbal clap-trap, no ceremonial theatricals and no occult miracle-mongering can confer. It is enormous and extraordinary, sacred and beautiful, and no gold can ever buy it. It alone ordains men to become true apostles and priests.

When studies of the psychic and occult are thus decried, this is not to say that they are without worth. They help to satisfy scientific curiosity and popular wonderment; they may even break the back of crude materialism. But they only deserve investigation by trained researchers; they certainly do not deserve our lives.

Jesus told the plain truth when he said that all these things would be added unto us if we seek the kingdom of heaven first. Whoever discovers the divine kingdom discovers also that extraordinary miracles begin to happen and that unexpected wonders mark themselves upon the calendar of his life. But in that case they come unsought, entirely of their own accord, direct from the Overself's mysterious and silent activity. He has not striven for them and thus they come rightly, easily, without harm to himself or others. Just as a fine flower is not conscious of the beauty it reveals or the fragrance it emanates, so a truly spiritual man is seldom *personally* conscious of the magic he works, any more than of the good he does or help he gives.

§

The equipoise derived from mental quiet cannot be over-priced. Hospitals could be made emptier, asylums could be less filled and countless homes become far happier if it were universally practised.

In these days of muddle, conflict and horror, the possession of a balanced mind, interior calm and mellow wisdom, of a sense of genuine values, will not prove to be without advantage. America, as a country palpitant with physical and mental activity, has more need of this quality of internal stillness than even Europe. Agitation, undue haste and over-anxiety vanish from the vocabulary of being when mental quiet is resorted to. It provides men with a fortifying philosophical outlook which makes them more efficient and not less.

The wise man turns all opposition into opportunity. The faults of those with whom he is thrown into inescapable contact become sharpening-stones for his own virtues. He meets their irritability with the sublime patience which wells up as soon as he switches attention to the inner self. He does not worsen matters by dwelling overmuch on negative critical thoughts. He lives his beliefs and converts principle into practice. He will not merely commend his friends and loved ones alone to the kindly care of the Overself, but also his enemies. He knows that we gain more than we lose by forgiving. Those who nourish hatreds are blind, and perceive not that they shall pay for their retention of ancient wrongs. Thus he becomes a secret envoy of the Overself to all whom he meets; within his mind there is a divine message to each of them, but unless they humbly claim it, the message remains unborn.

The potentialities of inspired action, of frictionless activity, are little known. We do not realize how immense an achievement is possible to the centralized man. Divinity and practicality are not necessarily incompatibles. The modern mystic can regard life as a participant, not merely as a percipient. He is not afraid to plunge into action. He knows that if he pays attention to thought, the actions will take care of themselves, and that whatever is conquered in mind is already conquered in deed and must bear right fruit as a tree bears apples. He does not need to deceive himself or others by adopting monkish asceticisms which belong to the needs of former epochs. The world is his monastery. Life is his spiritual teacher. Its experiences are the doctrines for his study.

Men plunged deeply in the world's affairs have found their way to the Overself. They hold an inward calm amid the turmoils of business. There is need at this critical hour in world history for more such spirit-illumined men who will harmonize the secular with the sacred, who can assimilate a subtle spirituality to their complex modern natures, and who will break through the chrysalis of public opinion to bespeak their inward light. There is need of men who seek the service of mankind as much as their own success. "Produce great personalities, and the rest follows," cried Walt Whitman.

Whoever becomes in himself the meeting-place of both worldly practicality and transcendental strength will find opportunities enough to serve. Apart from his chosen field of daily work, or fated sphere of daily business, he will always be sought out by those who stumble in despair or grope amid life's darkness for a ray of light. He will become a refuge, a centre of stable help. His words will never pass uselessly out into the void, on the contrary, unless a man speaks from that diviner life he succeeds only in stuttering. Whether written or spoken, his words will have a liberating effect on some, an inspiring one on others, but may stick painfully like barbed arrows in the minds of not a few. Each word becomes a living creative force, a magical medium of light and power, and will even travel the five continents to reach those persons likely to profit by it.

The starting-point of this quest is where we find ourselves and what we are. The finishing-point is the same. Religion, mysticism, art, science and philosophy are indirect paths only, for the issue of self-confronting cannot ultimately be evaded. Hence we can never bestir ourselves too early for the task. The work must ultimately succeed because the infinite is inherent within us as salt inheres in sea-water. The travail of dis-identification is not necessarily tedious but equally it is not a hobby for idle hours. No adventure is really so lofty. Nevertheless our brains are wilful and do not come to rest at our wish. The day-by-day discipline is needed to master them. The process given will turn the ordinary function of intellect to a higher use and transform it into an effective passage to the Overself. The everyday faculty of thinking will be taken up in the end by a deeper part of our being; it will be held motionless whilst we become aware of the wide free silence around us. This is possible because the life and work of intellect are ultimately derived from the Overself. Not that we shall be able to live without thoughts; we shall think so far as the business of living demands it, *but we shall be able to keep our inner experience of reality fully alive within those thoughts.* The result will necessarily be to give such thought-life unusual power and dominion, a significance quite other than that which belongs to ordinary uninspired thinking. Thus we may maintain a beautiful harmony between the life of the spirit and the life of the world, finding no contradiction between both.

No one who achieves this balanced life will become a

sentimental babbler, drifting on a sea of feeling and doing nothing of creative worth for himself or mankind. The ebb and flow of emotional ecstasy, the rise and fall of personal delights, are poor things beside the grand dignity of the Overself's unchanging peace. All religious ecstasies must pass, all psychic visions must vanish, but the Overself's stillness can remain for ever within a man because it is itself the Ever-Living.

§

Whoever experiences a single hour of such supramundane lucidity will become peacefully aware of the profound meaning behind the cryptic yet sublime expression which even now lingers on the mutilated face of Egypt's Sphinx. He will penetrate into the secret of the beatific smile which caresses the mute lips of Japan's gigantic Buddha-Image. He will understand, too, why a certain painting in a certain palace in Florence enthrals sensitive visitors to Italy into hushed awe.

He may then perceive that Truth is a goddess who sits on a high pedestal, well above the noisy throng. She is ready to receive all men, but all men are not ready to receive truth. The world must humble itself and court her, for she will not descend to court the world. Some who have been made recipients of her gracious favour, who have been admitted into her confidence and company, have perforce to act as humble messengers between her and the throng.

He may perceive, too, that this which has come into his life is not a thing but spirit, not living movement but living stillness. Words but ripple its surface and cover its truth. The silence of the Overself is a vital presence which is profounder than the profoundest speech. It reaches its finest eloquence, perhaps, among Himalayan mountains and Saharan deserts. It almost attains transparency in the face of the sage who understands that it is often better to travel to the Centre than to travel abroad.

Fools may learn nothing from wise men, but wise men learn much from fools. They learn that mankind universally mistakes wordship for worship.

The Silence will serve us better than the most eloquent sentences.

The man who has entered it for ever will engage in no sterile polemics nor invite others to winnow mere words; rather he will lead them to new thoughts and finer experiences. He will not strive to convert sceptics or convince the faint-hearted, for he now understands that every soul must climb the long ladder of spiritual growth, and that inescapable experience will teach it better than ever he can. The adept is infinitely patient and imposes his will on none.

Nevertheless, because he has realized the oneness of the Overself he has henceforth no other aim, can have no other aim, than the welfare of all beings. In his heart there will be no distinctions, yet the necessity of achieving his aim with the utmost economy of means and the minimum of effort confines his service to those who are ripe and ready for his help, who will not greet him with the resistance of scornful contempt or base ingratitude. Therefore he moves silently and quietly through the world, hiding his spiritually royal identity under the fleshly garb which destiny has given him, and pushing his disciples into public notice wherever a public task must be performed.

Such is this ancient quest which confronts mankind, this yearning of the fragmentary self for the fuller Overself. For this the tiny amœba struggled through immeasurable years to become two-legged man; for this the starry universe has endured its æon-long travail; and for this our poor earth spins through vast stretches of space.

Nature has set us the example of an immense, an incredible patience. We may fitly imitate her for a while. Even though our progress be doubtful or spasmodic, let us believe that this quest possesses an assured goal and a divine one. The light may shine for an elusive moment and then leave us bereft of sight. We may see with startling clarity for a brief minute and then become blind again. Through all this we ought not to forget that there is One who watches over our growing pains and adolescent maladies, One who is all-benevolent and aware of our glorious goal. The triumph of the evolutionary process will be nothing less than the triumph of Love, because we are all born out of the womb of the Supreme Mother whose love for us is not less than our love for ourselves.

And no matter even how tardily these truths may have come into our lives, they have never come too late. Jesus began his brief mission by placing into prominence the idea of repentance. The *New Testament,* repeating his opening words, uses the Greek word *metanoe* to convey this idea. The fullest significance of this word is really *to change one's thoughts.* This is our urgent need. Our minds have become estranged from their spiritual source. And a little period devoted daily to mental quiet will bring about this thought-changing.

Not to bring the world new religious illusions nor to teach it how to patter the litanies of worn-out superstitions nor even to animate its vain hopes of finding the solution of its practical problems by ignoring its spiritual ones, have these lines been penned. Mankind's material needs and mental distresses are inseparable from its spiritual outlook. The writer cannot state these truths in terms more definite than those which he has used. He who would comprehend them more adequately must endeavour to understand not only the words, but that which lies between and beneath them. His broken speech cannot express the barely communicable and ineffable transcendence which hovers impalpably around us all.

These thoughts are true ones or they are worthless. They can never grow stale as they can never be denied. They have held the world's best minds in pawn even since the dawn of time; they shall hold them yet when the last days of the planet are at hand. They may be forgotten for a while but they always achieve a new reincarnation. They are deathless and shall one day embrace the entire race. Truth may sit alone, neglected, but she is ultimately irresistible and mankind must one day yield itself to her compelling injunctions in silent subjection. The Absolute will re-interpret Itself anew to every age and every clime. The divine Silence will break its sacred reticence periodically by sending into flesh and form its endless message of Hope to man. Thus is "the Word made flesh" and those arise who remind us of what we may become.

Whoever holds these truths in exalted estimation shall not be betrayed.

Let us never fear, then, to submit to that higher power which has sovereign rule over all men's lives. Let us begin by learning the value of effortless effort. Let us learn how to be still, how to perceive our own soul by becoming one with it and thus sharing its loveliness, its benignity and its wisdom. Let each help in his humble individual way the coming of the kingdom of heaven on earth.

The final truth is that we are spiritual exiles. The inner world of the Overself is our true homeland and in its deserted shrines alone we can find silent and eternal solace for our hearts.

EPILOGUE

The darkest tragedy of our darkened epoch is the foolish belief that such thoughts as these are without use to a practical world.

On the contrary, it is from eternally true ideas that a man may derive genuine inspiration for more effective action, indomitable courage to face the worst problems, renewed hope to go forwards and onwards, even strength to endure patiently what must be endured – no less than a lofty incentive to work incessantly for the universal welfare as though it were his own. Locks are quickly unfastened, handles are gladly turned and doors swing readily open in many a home to admit the man who can bring into it the benignant blessing of the Overself.

Whoever studies and understands these vital ideas may learn so to live in the busy world as to call forces from a higher region to his aid. He will be no worse a member of society, but a far better one, if he converts truth into life, makes his mind at times as still as a mountain pool, and moves with a serene self-possession whose gentle current supports him through all difficulties.

Blinded men may say what they wish, but the Overself is our real redeemer and works its secret will in spite of ourselves.

Is it not wiser, then, to open ourselves voluntarily to its divine influence and thus avoid unnecessary sufferings which we bring upon ourselves through ignorance?

Many fear to entertain these thoughts because they fear that they will be led to sacrifice the world and all those pleasant things which mean so much in material life. Let them dismiss such hesitations for only the wild-eyed fanatic demands that they hang the heavy chains of unreasonable renunciations around themselves. With the mind brought under control, why should any fear the world?

The ability to handle life is simply the ability to handle one's own mind. We fail first in thought and only afterwards in action.

World tumult has fallen upon us and universal perplexity wrinkles our brows merely because we do not know that spiritual truth is neglected at our peril. Mankind drifts today like an unfortunate ship without captain, navigation chart or anchor – a wandering hulk which may strike half-seen rocks.

Yet the amazing Intelligence which planned the human anatomy and put the whiteness in a swan's feather still encircles this world and has not deserted its creation. We are not lost orphans.

Christ came from afar to our troubled planet. He was armed only with a message of higher ethics and a mission of spiritual healing. He brought hope to weary human hearts – not a sword with which to stab them. But peace is farther than ever from our pitiful star.

Did He fail, then?

They alone can answer who see the cosmic drama in its entirety and foresee its further acts. Meanwhile we hover at the spiked threshold of a new age. The youthful years of this earth have vanished beyond recall. An adolescent humanity must prepare to shoulder the intellectual and spiritual responsibilities of dawning maturity.

It is not every man's duty to guide nations and rule peoples. It is every man's duty, however, to guide his personal life and rule his turbulent mind, to win for himself what the State can never give him.

True comfort and unerring wisdom dwell in the diviner depths of the self alone. The practice of turning inwards whenever the need of them arises must sooner or later be begun by everybody. And that need is greater today than ever before.

None need fear to submit himself to the sublimer self, to make his ego the servant and not the sovereign. There is, there can be no real loss. That which supports the whole universe, will henceforth ardently support him also.

When men will give themselves ungrudgingly to the divine Overself – the divine Overself will give itself ungrudgingly to them.

> *To glorify the resplendent truth and serve the few who will heed it, this script is sent forth from the aged Orient to the younger West.*

INDEX